Undermining the Constitution

Author of:

*The Constitution of the United States:
Its Sources and Its Application*—
1922; revised in 1941.

*Losing Liberty Judicially:
Prohibitory and Kindred Laws Examined*—1928.

Undermining the Constitution

A HISTORY OF

LAWLESS GOVERNMENT

By Thomas James Norton

Member of the Bars of the Supreme Court of the United States, the United States Circuit Courts of Appeals for the 7th, 8th, and 9th Circuits, and the Supreme Courts of Illinois, Kansas, New Mexico, Arizona, and California.

New York · 1950
THE DEVIN-ADAIR COMPANY

Copyright, 1951, by the Devin-Adair Co.

All rights reserved. No part of this book may be quoted without permission in writing from the publisher.

MANUFACTURED IN THE UNITED STATES OF AMERICA

To the Memory of
My Sisters
SARA *and* KATHERINE

Contents

		Page
	PREFACE	xi
I	THE REPRESENTATIVE, OR REPUBLICAN, FORM OF GOVERNMENT, CAREFULLY CHOSEN BY THE CONSTITUTIONAL CONVENTION IN 1787 AGAINST DEMOCRACY OR DIRECT ACTION BY THE PEOPLE, WAS FIRST UNDERMINED BY THE STATES	3
II	LONG-CONTINUED ATTEMPTS BY CONGRESS TO INTIMIDATE THE SUPREME COURT, ACCOMPANIED BY HYPERCRITICAL WRITINGS OF POORLY INFORMED UNIVERSITY MEN AND OTHERS, LED UP TO THE ATTEMPT OF THE PRESIDENT AT COURT PACKING IN 1937	14
III	IN FAVOR TO POLITICIANS AND TO LABOR UNIONS, CONGRESS PURSUED ANOTHER METHOD OF ATTACK ON THE COORDINATE JUDICIAL DEPARTMENT	40
IV	THE SIXTEENTH OR INCOME-TAX AMENDMENT, HAVING OPERATED IN VIOLENCE TO AMERICAN PRINCIPLES RESPECTING PROPERTY AND JUSTICE, SHOULD BE REPEALED	51
V	FOLLOWING THE INCOME-TAX AMENDMENT IN 1913, THE NEXT VIOLENCE TO CONSTITUTIONAL PRINCIPLE WAS UNDERTAKEN IN 1916 BY A SOCIALIST-MINDED GROUP SEEKING TO BREAK DOWN THE TENTH AMENDMENT AND HAVE WASHINGTON ASSUME POLICE POWER IN THE STATES OVER PERSONS UNDER THE AGE OF 18 YEARS	83

CONTENTS

		Page
VI	THE LONG-PURSUED PURPOSE OF CONGRESS TO CROSS THE BARRIER OF THE TENTH AMENDMENT AND ENTER THE POLICE FIELD OF THE STATES, OFTEN CHECKED BY THE COURTS AND THE PEOPLE, WAS ACCOMPLISHED BY THE PACKERS AND STOCKYARDS ACT OF 1921	96
VII	THE RECONSTRUCTION FINANCE CORPORATION WAS CREATED BY CONGRESS WITHOUT AUTHORITY GRANTED TO IT BY THE CONSTITUTION, AND ITS OPERATIONS HAVE BEEN BEYOND THE SPHERE OF GOVERNMENT	102
VIII	WITHOUT A GRANT OF CAPACITY IN THE CONSTITUTION TO CREATE A CORPORATION, CONGRESS INCORPORATED IN MAY, 1933, THE TENNESSEE VALLEY AUTHORITY, WHICH MANUFACTURES, ON THE MONEY OF THE TAXPAYERS, ELECTRIC POWER FOR SALE IN COMPETITION WITH PRIVATE CAPITAL	110
IX	IN MAY, 1933, CONGRESS, BY THE AGRICULTURAL ADJUSTMENT ACT, UNLAWFULLY PERMITTED THE PRESIDENT TO REDUCE THE GOLD CONTENT OF THE STANDARD DOLLAR	133
X	FIVE MONTHS AFTER THE INCORPORATION OF TENNESSEE VALLEY AUTHORITY, IN 1933, TWO MEMBERS OF THE CABINET OF THE PRESIDENT, AND THE HEAD OF THE FEDERAL RELIEF ADMINISTRATION PROCURED A CHARTER IN DELAWARE FOR THE FEDERAL SURPLUS COMMODITIES CORPORATION, CAPITALIZED BY THE MONEY OF THE TAXPAYERS	150

CONTENTS

		Page
XI	THE NATIONAL LABOR RELATIONS ACT OF 1935 WAS A VICTORY FOR CAESARISM OVER THE STATES AFTER A CONTINUOUS BATTLE FOR TWO DECADES	161
XII	BY THE SOCIAL SECURITY ACT OF AUGUST, 1935, FOLLOWING THE NATIONAL LABOR RELATIONS ACT OF JUNE, THE REPRESENTATIVES OF THE PEOPLE IN CONGRESS STRIPPED THEIR STATES ALMOST ENTIRELY OF POLICE AUTHORITY	181
XIII	THE CONSERVATION OF SOIL IN FARMING STATES BY THE FEDERAL GOVERNMENT IS NOT AUTHORIZED BY THE CONSTITUTION	202
XIV	THE EXPANSION OF THE CONSTITUTION BEYOND ITS LETTER AND SPIRIT THROUGH JUDICIAL LEGISLATION BY THE SUPREME COURT OF THE UNITED STATES IS, BECAUSE INSIDIOUS, THE WORST THREAT TO LIBERTY AND PROPERTY	207
XV	THE COURSE OF PRESIDENTIAL ELECTIONS DURING THE LAST FORTY YEARS HAS MADE CLEAR THAT THE SAFETY OF THE REPUBLIC REQUIRES RETURN TO STRICT CONFORMITY WITH THE DIRECTIONS OF THE CONSTITUTION	254
XVI	IN CONCLUSION AND IN RETROSPECT	296
	TABLE OF CASES	301
	INDEX	323

Preface

The writing of this book was impelled (or compelled) by the very manifest indifference of the people of the United States to the constitutional doctrines of their country. This had been developing so rapidly that all ideas of constitutionalism seemed to have passed out of the American mind. That is, indefensible proposals and practices against the plainest limitations on power set in the Constitution provoked no objections even from the Bar. For two decades no great debate on a constitutional subject had been heard in either House of Congress.

The National Education Association, theoretically representing the teachers of the country, had for years been passing resolutions favoring whatever was before the public of un-American import, especially for getting the imperial Government at Washington, through "Federal aid," to take over the shaping in school of American ideas. Under the cloak of "academic freedom" men in the universities belittled those who wrote the Constitution and pronounced their work faulty and outmoded.

The schools, while neglecting to give thorough courses in our history, and especially in constitutional history or the history of Liberty, admitted objectionable textbooks and periodicals.

Laws enacted by States after the Civil War requiring the teaching of the Constitution in the schools became dead letters. Similar laws of more than forty States enacted after World War I became dead letters too. So the governmental chaos, as it appears to be, came not by chance. The Commission on Organization of the Executive Branch of Government reported in 1948 that in the President's Department there are 1,800 different administrative units, and that the proposals of the Commission would save the taxpayers "billions—not millions, but billions." Plain lawlessness in taxation and a brutal attitude toward the taxpayer were among the conditions that compelled the writing of this book.

The principles of our Government are not outmoded, as some say. They are as immutable as those of mathematics. The first of them, so well put by Jefferson, is that the man to whom power is given must be chained. The profound historians at Philadelphia who wrote the Constitution looked back over the centuries and drew that principle from the recurring tyrannies and unfailing breakdowns of governments. So, to prevent "the very definition of despotism," as they termed the union of powers in one hand or body, from coming to the New World, they separated the Legislative, the Executive, and the Judicial powers, and then, by the most careful specifications, limited the application of each class.

The States retained sovereignty in local affairs.

During the last three decades nearly every restraint upon the man in power has been broken. Worse than that, lawlessness provokes no reasoning objection.

In the Roman Republic there was an elaborate distribution of powers, but in time all were gathered into one hand. First the Republic and then the Empire fell. A historian tells us that "statesmen came to disregard all checks in the [Roman] Constitution in order to carry a point."

What John Adams praised as the "checks and balances" in our Government also will fail unless respect for them returns.

PREFACE xiii

My book [1] explaining 196 clauses of the Constitution, showing their origins, their uses, and their practical values in the development of American "life, liberty, and property," had been received by the people to over half a million copies, and it seemed my duty to prepare another volume to explain the causes and the consequences of departures from constitutional principle which had been in progress for many years.

As that is done by dealing with concrete cases, the presentation of governmental philosophy is made the easier to understand.

The reader is admonished to approach this subject not with hesitance or with the idea that it is difficult or abstruse, but with earnest expectation. For no novel ever had a theme as engrossing as the story of "life, liberty, and property," which is the Constitution of the United States.

Moreover, the reader is the ruler of this land, and it is therefore his duty to himself and his descendants to learn and ably and righteously to execute the law of our national being.

As the constitutional system of the United States was the first that man through all the centuries was able to formulate for the one purpose of controlling those in power, the American should know it as he knows the alphabet. Its study has been recommended to him by its adoption in Canada, Australia, Brazil, Argentina, and in other countries more or less fully. It is "the last hope of the world," Daniel Webster warned us.

Communism and other alienisms can be met and overcome, not by dollars or arms, but only by superior doc-

---

[1] *The Constitution of the United States: Its Sources and Its Application,* 1922; revised in 1941.

trines, as the teaching of the kindnesses of Christianity overcame the ideas, the brutalities, and the power of the Roman Empire.

By neglecting to indoctrinate each new generation with a knowledge of the superior philosophy of the American system of Government, we thereby left the people weakened to attack. Hence so many of them are taken with the false promises of Communism. And so many others want the Government at Washington to do things beyond its power and outside its jurisdiction.

As the provisions of the Constitution dealt with in this volume are quoted or stated, and as they are a very small portion of the Instrument, it has seemed best, in order to keep down the size and price of the book, to omit the Fundamental Law as an Appendix.

Also for brevity, titles of cases cited are omitted and only the volume and page of the report are given, enough for one desiring to look further.

A thorough Index at the end of the volume and a complete Table of Cases are commended to the careful study of the reader and the student.

THOMAS JAMES NORTON

New York City
September 27, 1950

Undermining
the Constitution

I

THE REPRESENTATIVE, OR REPUBLICAN, FORM OF GOVERNMENT, CAREFULLY CHOSEN BY THE CONSTITUTIONAL CONVENTION IN 1787 AGAINST DEMOCRACY OR DIRECT ACTION BY THE PEOPLE, WAS FIRST UNDERMINED BY THE STATES

IN 1893 SOUTH DAKOTA ADOPTED FROM SWITZERLAND THE Initiative and the Referendum, and from then until 1918 one or both of those plans, with the Recall, were taken on by 22 of the 48 States.

Three borrowings from Switzerland against our Constitution

By the Initiative the people can draft a law and put it to a vote; if the majority favor it the legislature is bound to pass it, even though opposed to it.

By the Referendum a bill passed by the legislature is referred to popular vote, and it may be approved or prevented from taking effect.

The Recall is used to unseat a holder of office who has become unsatisfactory, or to revoke a law.

Some States adopted the three expedients, some two of them, some only one. At first the belief spread rapidly.

The first attempt to recall judicial decisions

Colorado was the only State to apply (1912) the Recall to decisions by the courts, and that was held by the Supreme Court of the State to be in conflict with the Colorado constitution.

Theodore Roosevelt, displeased by the decisions of some courts, advocated the recall of decisions of the supreme courts of *States*. The prestige of the former President gave much impetus to the "movement." The American Bar Association appointed a committee to go to the country in refutation of the constitutionally destructive idea. In 1912 the committee reported the recall of decisions dead. Roosevelt afterward admitted that he had made a mistake.

Kansas limited the Recall (1914) to appointive officials.

The Initiative has never been extensively used, and for a long time not much has been heard of any of the "democratic" devices.

Large populations require representation, not "democracy"

Methods deemed useful to small populations in narrow areas, as in the cantons of Switzerland and the town meetings in New England, could not be accepted as serviceable or safe for large populations and extensive countries. Indeed, that point was discussed in the Constitutional Convention, and the conclusion was reached that for the United States as they then were, and as they would expand to be, only the representative or Republican system would do.

In 1893, when South Dakota led the way, the country

had undergone one of its severest panics. There had also been successive crop failures. The advocates of popular action contended that legislatures were not faithful to the people and that therefore the people should take over. However, the remedy was in the election of better legislators, not in a fundamental change in the form of government. And it is doubtful whether the most capable and honest legislators could have stilled the complaints arising from the panic and the failures of crops.

When people seek paternalism from their government

In all such times the disposition is to look around for a scapegoat, and the people usually feel that government should do something to correct conditions and relieve distress.

This inclination of the people in financial distress to look to the governments of the States to do something about it was the forerunner, as it were, of the wide calls for "Federal aid" of many kinds which were raised in the late 1920s and the early 1930s.

In 1920 the Supreme Court upheld (253 U. S. 233) the creation by a vote of the people of North Dakota of an Industrial Commission to take over and manage utilities, industries, and other business projects, some to be established by law. It was authorized to operate the Bank of North Dakota, the Home-Builders Association, flour mills, grain elevators, a fire insurance company, and other projects. It was empowered to issue bonds, and in 1937 it had floated such paper to the amount of $24,798,000 for rural credit.

From 1934 to 1940, in a time of peace, the National Government built up a deficit of $26,500,000,000, of which $21,500,000,000, or 80 per cent, according to the Governor of Virginia, resulted from "grants in aid" to States and individuals. Subsidies from the taxpayers of the country held up the price of wheat and corn to $3 a bushel as late as 1948. And like support to stockmen put the prices of their commodities so high that beefsteaks, roasts and lamb almost entirely disappeared from the table of the American.

Dependence on government brings unfortunate conditions

And yet the stockmen were unprepared with shelter and feed to care for their herds when the heavy snows and low temperatures came in the Winter of 1948-1949. The States were without organization to help. Governors and stockmen cried to Washington to come out and save them! Long dependence of the people and the States on miscalled "Federal money" had debilitated both.

The army was sent out. It kept the roads open and it fed and saved most of the herds.

Caesar, too, helped the people, but they lost their liberty to him.

The Constitutional Convention set up a thoroughly representative form of Government in each of the three Departments—the Legislative, the Executive, and the Judicial. The States, which wrote the Constitution by their representatives, provided in section 4 of Article IV particular protection for themselves:

Nation and States given representative government by Constitution

"The United States shall guarantee to every State in this Union a Republican [not democratic] form of government, and shall protect each of them against invasion."

They obliged the power over all, which they had set up for the common strength, to protect each in its Republican form, and to defend each physically.

Commenting on that provision for a *representative* form of government, Madison said in No. 43 of *The Federalist:*

"The only restriction imposed on them is that they shall not exchange Republican for anti-Republican [democratic] constitutions."

The choice by the Convention of the Republican or representative form over the popular or democratic government followed full and able discussions. In explaining what had been considered in this relation, Madison, the note taker of daily doings in the Convention, said in No. 10 of *The Federalist,* after pointing out the evils which factions had always done in democracies:

"The inference to which we are brought is that the *causes* of faction cannot be removed, and that relief is only to be sought in the means of controlling its *effects.*"

Why Convention rejected democracy or popular control

The turbulence and contention which had given short lives and violent deaths to democracies would be controlled by representative government:

"A Republic, by which I mean a government in which

the scheme of *representation* takes place, opens a different prospect, and promises the cure for which we are seeking."

By "the delegation of the government to a small number of citizens elected by the rest," Madison said, the public views are refined and enlarged "by passing them through the medium of a chosen body of citizens whose wisdom may best discern the true interest of their country, and whose patriotism and love of justice will be least likely to sacrifice it to temporary or partial considerations."

Accordingly:

"Under such a regulation it may well happen that the public voice, pronounced by the representatives of the people, will be more consonant to the public good than if pronounced by the people themselves, convened for the purpose."

The spread of a governmental evil

The Initiative, the Referendum, and the Recall led to other departures from the representative form of government. Officeholders or aspirants who hoped to advantage themselves brought out the direct primary. That primary suggested later the "Presidential preference" primary to seekers of the highest office, who believed that they could "swing" the crowd when the party might not be for them. In many instances the promoters of the "democratic" primary, which had been hailed as the voice of the people, failed of their expectations through them.

As the decayed apple in the barrel damages all the others, so the badness in principle of the Initiative, the Referendum, and the Recall spread after bringing the direct primary and the Presidential primary. In 1912 some members of the United States Senate, doubtless feeling that they would be more sure of holding their seats if they could appeal to the people from the hustings than if their return were to remain with critical legislatures, proposed an amendment to the Constitution, first suggested in 1869, for the direct election of senators by the people of the States instead of by the legislatures. It was ratified and became effective as the Seventeenth Amendment in 1913.

The great purpose in the Congress frustrated

Thus the two Houses of Congress became alike, whereas the Constitutional Convention designed a House of People and a House of States. The House elected by the States to represent *them* in the Congress of their Union was destroyed. Two Houses now represent the people and none stands for the States. Does that help to explain why the States have been passing out as the controlling forces in their Union? The extent of their diminution will be fully shown later in this book.

The proponents of the Amendment supported their advocacy by saying that money had been improperly used in some legislatures by backers of candidates for the House of States. But, as we have said with respect to the Initiative, the proper remedy for the people was in electing better legislators, not in unsettling the foundations of the Republic. Besides, candidates for the Senate, in the primary to get the nomination and then in the election contest against the nominee of the other party to get the office, have spent more money than was ever reported as used in a legislature.

A very capable and upright senator from California declined to seek a second term because the expense of the primary which nominated him and of the election campaign which put him in the Senate had been so great that he said the security of his family had been endangered. He was fairly well-to-do, but this "democracy" which had been introduced in the name of "reform" he could not carry.

Some capable men excluded from Senate

Had the Seventeenth Amendment not been put in the Constitution, the legislature of California might have kept him in the service of the State by reelecting him many terms. Thus, Senator Hoar of Massachusetts, an illustrious statesman without means, who did not want to go to the Senate, was chosen by his legislature during his absence from the country and kept there to the end of his life.

Senator Morrill of Vermont and others of those times gave all or most of their working years to their country in the House of States. They did not need to "campaign." That was fortunate, because they had no money.

A poor man who seeks a seat in the Senate now must have "backers," and he may therefore cease to be the owner of himself.

The cure which was sought in haste and some anger through the Initiative and the popular election of senators might have been reached by choosing better legislators. But when the American, after long indifference, arouses himself he is prone "to do the right thing the wrong way."

Lack of learning in Constitution dangerous

It is hard to believe that an educator provided the "slogan" for those two decades: "The cure for the evils of democracy is more democracy." We have it.

In No. 62 of *The Federalist* the faith in the House of States was expressed (italics inserted):

"It is recommended by the double advantage of favoring a *select* appointment, and of giving to the *State government such an agency* in the formation of the *Federal Government* as must secure the authority of the former, and may form a convenient link between the two systems."

Thus the States would be in Congress as well as the People.

Evil results from decline of Senate

None of the transgressions of constitutional boundaries of recent years could probably have been accomplished had the House of States not been broken down.

It is a fact to be noted that the Sixteenth Amendment, under which Congress has, without specific authority, been gathering the "graduated" income tax of Communism, became effective in February, 1913, and the Seventeenth Amendment, emasculating the House of States, became a part of the Constitution in May of that year. That imports very serious dissatisfaction of a people, unschooled in the principles of their Government, with the system designed by the Constitutional Convention, which contained, Bryce pointed out, "five men who belong to the history of the world," and many others "less known in Europe who must be mentioned with respect."

Warning of Washington against constitutional innovations

In his Farewell Address caution was given by Washington to resist "the spirit of innovation" upon the principles of the Constitution, "however specious the pretexts."

General and thorough education in constitutional philosophy is essential to our safety.

A final word from *The Federalist:*

"The necessity of a Senate is not less indicated by the propensity of all single and numerous assemblies to yield to the impulse of sudden and violent passions, and to be seduced by factious leaders into intemperate and pernicious resolutions. Examples on this subject might be cited without number; and from proceedings within the United States, as well as from the history of other nations."

The States in their House would be a check on sudden and ill-considered action by the House of the People.

In the day of the House of States the senators accepted seriously and discharged courageously the responsibility cast upon them by the Constitution in confirming or disapproving the appointments of the President. A confirmation then did not follow as a matter of course. In *Autobiography of Seventy Years* it is related by Senator Hoar that he went into the Supreme Court to hear Senator Daniel Webster make an argument in a case. Webster began by referring "very impressively" to the changes which had taken place in the Tribunal since he first appeared as counsel before it:

"Not one of the judges who were here then remains. It has been my duty to pass upon the question of the confirmation of every member of the Bench; and I may say that I treated your honors with entire impartiality, for I voted against every one of you."

The alterations in the American system of representative or Republican government here reviewed were as unnecessary as they were ineffectual for the purposes intended.

"Democracy" not suitable to representative system

A review of over half a century of tinkerings with constitutional representative government makes plain that "democracy" is unsuited to the United States.

The cases to be reviewed in the chapters following will serve to clarify the meaning in practice of the representative principle running everywhere through the Constitution. They will help also to an understanding of the structurally important—superior and sustaining—place of the States in the constitutional edifice.

Then it will be clear why, as President Cleveland said, "departure from the lines there laid down is failure."

II

LONG-CONTINUED ATTEMPTS BY CONGRESS TO INTIMIDATE THE SUPREME COURT, ACCOMPANIED BY HYPERCRITICAL WRITINGS OF POORLY INFORMED UNIVERSITY MEN AND OTHERS, LED UP TO THE ATTEMPT OF THE PRESIDENT AT COURT PACKING IN 1937

THE NEXT NOTABLE MOVE IN POINT OF TIME AGAINST THE constitutional structure of our Government was begun by Congress in the early 1900s.

For three decades before President Franklin D. Roosevelt attempted to set up a Supreme Court to suit his plans, Congress had been nagging the Judiciary from time to time with bills to "curb" it. Congress seemed to feel that it was an affront to its dignity and learning for the Supreme Court—when an American challenged a law as invalid because it would deprive him of property "for public use without just compensation," or for the reason that it otherwise disrespected constitutional boundaries set for his protection—to declare the act unconstitutional.

Lack of scholarship caused congressional attack on Judiciary

Members passing as constitutional scholars introduced bills to forbid that an act of Congress be held unconstitutional unless by a vote of 6 or 7 of the 9 justices, or by all of them. Fortunately, Congress had sound members enough to prevent the enactment of any bill of that kind into law. But the pendency of those bills from time to time and the discussion of them in Congress and in the Press operated to discredit the Judiciary in public estimation.

The proposition that an act of Congress should not be held invalid by (for illustration) a vote of 6 of the 9 justices of the Supreme Court means that the minority should decide the case. Our whole constitutional system operates by majority except in nine specified instances.

Majority decisions of courts constitutional

By the ancient rule of interpretation those specifications for more than a majority exclude in all other instances a higher vote. The Constitution having thus left the majority vote to the Supreme Court, it can be changed, not by Congress, but only by amendment.

"All provisions which require more than the majority of any body to its resolutions," wrote Hamilton in *The Federalist*, "have a direct tendency to embarrass the operations of the government, and an indirect one to subject the sense of the majority to that of the minority."

When Article III of the Constitution declared that "the judicial Power of the United States shall be vested in one Supreme Court," etc., it described the court of that day in England and in America, which decided cases by a vote of the majority; that court became the tribunal of the Constitution.

Men in schools aided in attack on Judiciary

While that exhibition of superficiality was in progress in the Congress, the professors in the universities, and in

16   *Undermining the Constitution*

many schools of law, wrote books in assault of the Supreme Court. Just what the sons and daughters of the supporters of the institutions of learning were exposed to in the way of contagion may be best understood from a few titles of the books which they published in the season of hysteria:

> *Our Despotic Courts*
> *Is the Supreme Court Too Supreme?*
> *Appeal from the Supreme Court*
> *Impeaching Laws of Congress*
> *Government by Judges*
> *Judicial Censorship of Legislation*
> *Big Business on the Bench*
> *Our Judicial Oligarchy*
> *Judicial Legislation*
> *Aggression of Federal Courts*
> *The Great Usurpation*

Those books showed the authors to be destitute of knowledge of constitutional history and principle. For example, *The Great Usurpation* asserted that the Supreme Court usurped power when it first held a challenged act of Congress invalid for conflict with a provision of the Constitution.

Hamilton made clear the function of constitutional courts

That the Court possessed the power was shown by Hamilton, a member of the Constitutional Convention, in No. 78 of *The Federalist,* written in 1788 and addressed "to the people of the State of New York," in answer to objections raised against the proposed new form of government in the convention having ratification before it:

"The interpretation of the laws is the proper and peculiar province of the courts. A Constitution is, in fact, and must be regarded by the judges, as a fundamental law. It therefore belongs to them to ascertain its meaning, as well as the meaning of any particular act proceeding from the legislative body. If there should happen to be an irreconcilable variance between the two, that which has the superior obligation and validity ought, of course, to be preferred; or, in other words, the Constitution ought to be preferred to the statute, the intention of the people to the intention of their agents."

Clear thinking and lucid writing, that.

Members of Constitutional Convention explained duty of courts

Before the Constitution took effect, Oliver Ellsworth of Connecticut, speaking in the ratifying convention of his State, explained the function of the courts in constitutional cases to be precisely what was later objected to by the author of *The Great Usurpation*. Ellsworth had been a member of the Constitutional Convention, and he should be taken as high authority:

"The Constitution defines the extent of the powers of the General Government. If the General Legislature [Congress] should at any time overleap their limits, the Judicial Department is a constitutional check. If the United States go beyond their powers, if they make a law which the Constitution does not authorize, it is void; and the judicial power, the national judges, who, to secure their impartiality, are to be made independent, will declare it to be void.

"On the other hand, if the States go beyond their limits, if they make a law which is a usurpation upon the Federal [National] Government, the law is void; and upright, independent judges will declare it to be so."

In the Ratifying Convention of Pennsylvania, James Wilson, who had been a delegate to the Convention which wrote the Constitution, who was the ablest lawyer in it and one of the most influential members, and who later became a justice of the Supreme Court, made a similar statement.

Foreign scholars saw importance of constitutional Judiciary

Bryce, Von Holst, and other foreign writers on our Government saw clearly our judicial principle.[1] Von Holst said that the Judiciary is the keystone of the American arch. Enemies of our liberty have been chipping at the keystone for a third of a century.

Moreover, in 1922, the leaders of organized labor, in concert with the critical spirit of Congress, sent a questionnaire to candidates for Congress asking whether they believed that five men on the Supreme Court "who had not been elected by the people, and who cannot be rejected by the people, should be permitted to nullify the will of the people as expressed by their representatives in Con-

---

[1] The Supreme Court of Canada, under the North America Act of the British Parliament of 1867, which followed our Constitution closely, passes on the constitutionality of an act of the Dominion Parliament and upon an act of the legislative body of the Province or State.

So, under the Constitution of Australia (1900), more closely following ours, the High Court, when the question is raised by a litigant, determines whether the law of the Commonwealth or the act of a State (not province in Australia) conforms to the Constitution.

gress and the Executive in the White House." That was the jargon of the books and current magazines.

Second, would they "work and vote for a constitutional amendment restricting the power of the Supreme Court to nullify acts of Congress?"

Third, would they vote for a clear-cut statute forbidding the issuing of injunctions in industrial (meaning labor) disputes?

Leaders of labor organizations supported attacks on Judiciary

On June 7, 1935, following the decision of the Supreme Court holding unconstitutional the National Industrial Recovery Act of Congress, a dispatch from Washington said that the President of the American Federation of Labor, "in a speech over an NBC network," voiced "organized labor's determination to fight for a constitutional amendment forbidding the Supreme Court to invalidate an act of Congress."

It has just been seen from Hamilton, a great lawyer who was in the Constitutional Convention, and from Oliver Ellsworth and James Wilson, also members of the Convention, that it is the Constitution, not the Court, that "invalidates" (a loose word of the unscholarly schoolmen) an act of Congress. The act is not invalidated by the Court, because it has no validity when not made "in pursuance" of the Constitution. "The Supreme Law of the Land," as defined by Article VI of the Constitution, consists of "this Constitution, and the laws of the United States [Acts of Congress] which shall be made *in pursuance* thereof," and treaties.

What makes an Act of Congress unconstitutional?

If Congress does not *pursue* the lines laid down for it in the Constitution, its legislation is a nullity. The Supreme Court does not "nullify" it, as so many law-school professors and others classed as educators have taught several generations of youth, to the great damage of the mind of the Republic.

On the provision of the Constitution just before quoted, Alexander Hamilton, in No. 33 of *The Federalist*, made this comment (italics his):

"It will not, I presume, have escaped observation that it *expressly* confines the supremacy to laws made *pursuant to the Constitution*."

Did the United States have no Constitution, the Nation would nevertheless possess all the powers essential to its existence—to raise an army and a navy; to appoint ambassadors; to make treaties; to issue money; to levy taxes, and to take other steps found necessary to its welfare as a Nation among nations.

But when a Constitution is written and adopted, it is for the purpose of preventing those inherent powers from being exercised at large and at will. The powers enumerated in the Constitution must be exerted as it directs.

It was said by the Supreme Court in 1936 (299 U. S. 304) that the United States has inherent powers of sovereignty *in foreign relations* external to the Constitution; and so it could forbid its citizens to ship arms to South American countries in conflict.

But it was unnecessary for the Court to drag in a dialectical proposition. The Commerce Clause, empowering

Congress "to regulate Commerce with foreign Nations," was authority enough to control the shipment of arms.

"Inherent power" in the President or the Congress over matters with which the States severally cannot deal has always been definitely rejected by the Supreme Court, it declared (298 U. S. 238) as late as 1936. In the foregoing case an opinion by Justice Story (1 Wheaton 304), written 120 years before, was quoted to show that the General Government "can claim no powers which are not granted to it by the Constitution; and the powers actually granted must be such as are expressly given, or given by necessary implication."

The Constitution modifying inherent powers

But when, for illustration, the inherent power to make war was brought under the Constitution and transferred from the King to the Parliament—or, so to say, given to Congress instead of the Executive—the intention was to restrict fundamentally international practices. The declaring of war and the raising of forces and money are with the Congress. The command of the forces is with the President. The treaty of peace is with the President and the Senate. The dangerous powers are well divided.

Is it in pursuance of the Constitution for the Government at Washington to refrain for years from proclaiming World War II ended in law when it was ended in fact in 1945? And to continue spending—carefully restricted by the Constitution to "the common defence and general welfare *of the United States*," not of any other nation or of the world at large—on nations which ceased to be our allies in 1945, and on nations which never were our allies?

Only powers of Congress respecting money

The Constitution gives power to Congress (1) "to coin money" and (2) "to borrow money on the credit of the United States"—but not to lend money, or to give it away, either at home or abroad. What is expressed in a Constitution is equivalent to a prohibition of what is not expressed. The powers over money mentioned are the only ones that the Constitutional Convention brought in from the world of inherent powers and *fixed* in the Fundamental Law.

Those specifications reject the theory of unlimited powers exercised by European monarchs in 1787. Not long before that, Louis XIV had kept Europe embroiled in wars by loans or grants of money to belligerent rulers. Did the Constitutional Convention, at least one member of which was born in his reign, intend to give that power to Congress? It did not say so. The power was therefore withheld by the people from their servants.

The United States is now, without authority—under a denial of authority—lending or granting money to Europe, and to the rest of the world. Postwar programs, 22 in number, for aiding foreign nations, in addition to the military aid program, have piled on top of the costs (330 billion) of War II $30,757,000,000, according to Senator Byrd of Virginia, speaking in September, 1949.

Thus, the limitations of the Constitution become what Madison gave warning of—"paper barriers."

What the Supreme Court really does

Nor does the Supreme Court "veto" an act of Congress when, in a case brought by an American claiming that his constitutional protection has been written off by the Legislative Department, the Court finds the complaint well founded and forbids the enforcement of the act.

This kind of constitutional illiteracy, which is chargeable against the schools, colleges, and universities, and is therefore all pervasive, exhibited itself in the Department of Justice of the United States when, after the failure of the President in 1937 to "pack" the Supreme Court, time was taken by the Attorney General to write a book defending the President's action, *The Struggle for Judicial Supremacy*.

The attempt to "pack" the Federal Courts

The three major acts of Congress for the "New Deal" of President Franklin D. Roosevelt having been held repugnant to the Constitution by the Supreme Court, the President determined to remake the Judiciary of the Constitution, with special reference to the Supreme Bench.

The purpose was clothed in the suavest language, but the robe had a stiletto under it. One of the leaders of the countrywide organization which was formed to urge Congress to resist the move gave it the name which "stuck"— a plan to "pack" the Supreme Court of the American people. That word soon became the sole designation of the President's scheme.

The National Industrial Recovery Act, to supervise and control industry, was held (295 U. S. 495) invalid in May, 1935.

The Agricultural Adjustment Act, for the support of agriculture, was held (297 U. S. 1) unconstitutional in January, 1936.

And the Bituminous Coal Act, to supervise that industry

and favor miners, was held (298 U. S. 238) to be in conflict with the Fundamental Law in May, 1936.

The "plan" kept secret from the people

It was in 1936 that President Roosevelt was elected the second time. But in the campaign of that year there was no whisper of the determination to "pack" the Supreme Court and the lower Federal courts. So, when the plan was revealed on February 5 following the November election, there was an instinctive outburst of protest. For the American *senses* his constitutional inheritance, even though his expensive schools have taught him next to nothing about it.

On February 5, 1937, the President sent a bland message to Congress, with a bill already drawn, providing that a new justice or judge be appointed by the President when an incumbent had reached the "retirement age" of 70 and failed to retire. A concurrent bill, which took effect on the first of the following month, gave to the justices of the Supreme Court the privilege of retiring at 70 on full pay, a privilege given to judges of the lower Federal courts in 1911. Of course, Congress could not fix a "retirement age," as the Constitution gives tenure "during good behavior."

The mathematics of the packing plan

At the time of the attempt at packing, there were on the Supreme Court 6 justices of the age of 70 or over who seemed content with their situations and their interesting work. To the 9 already sitting, the bill would permit the addition of 6 more. With those 6 and the two or three more known to be favorable to the "New Deal," the President would have a majority of the 15.

A HISTORY OF LAWLESS GOVERNMENT 25

In what public opinion called "a great state paper," the Judicial Committee of the Senate denounced the bill as an "utterly dangerous abandonment of constitutional principle," which "would subjugate the courts to the will of Congress and the President."

"It is a measure which should be so emphatically rejected," reported the Committee to the Senate, "that its parallel never again will be presented to the free representatives of the free people of America."

It had no chance of passage. Democrats as well as Republicans opposed it. But as the "New Deal" has held control for thirteen years since then, every justice of that time save one (who retired) has passed away, and all the justices of the Supreme Court are now appointees of Presidents Roosevelt and Truman. The majority of the Court have long been appointees of the "New Deal."

In 1933 President Roosevelt wrote *Looking Forward,* in which he said of somebody's suggestion for increasing the size of the courts that "such a so-called remedy [for congestion] merely aggravates the disease."

Department of Justice joined against Judiciary

Of course, there is no such thing as the "judicial supremacy" dealt with in the Attorney General's book *The Struggle for Judicial Supremacy.* It is the supremacy of the Constitution that the courts apply. The conception, expressed by many other book builders, that the Supreme Court has been in a "struggle" to raise itself over the Executive and the Congress would be dishonest were it not for the constitutional illiteracy from which it springs. The only "supremacy" involved is that of the Fundamental Law.

And when Congress, in taking for public use the property of a canal company, provided that nothing should be allowed to it in compensation for the franchise to collect tolls (without which none of the property would have had value to it), the Supreme Court was not promoting its own "supremacy" when it held the act of Congress void for withholding "just compensation" for property taken for "public use." It was simply observing the oaths of the justices and of the members of Congress "to support this Constitution."

Later the President appointed the Attorney General to the Supreme Court.

Law schools blamable for lack of learning on Constitution

Some years ago the American Bar Association made a survey of the law schools in 25 of the leading universities and found that only 8 of them made a knowledge of the Constitution a requisite to a degree. Hence, probably, the silence of the Bar while the alien idea of Communism and the alien idea of Socialism were introduced in government in violation of the Constitution.

Men and women who will be living in later generations through children and grandchildren and their descendants owe it to their blood, if they do not feel that they owe it now to their country, to take this subject of constitutional education to heart and change existing conditions.

And why should the President of the American Federation of Labor want an amendment to the Constitution which would leave Congress with imperial powers? For, notwithstanding the repeated complaints of labor leaders and their political lackeys that the Judiciary of the Constitution is prejudiced against labor, a long line of favorable decisions is found in the reports. Both State and Federal courts have upheld laws without number in the interest of workers. Forty years before a man of alien birth sponsored the National Labor Relations Act of Congress for "labor's gains," an act of Michigan was upheld requiring the employer to protect the employee from machinery and other perils.

Courts of Constitution never unfriendly to labor

In 1898 the Supreme Court of the United States (169 U. S. 366) upheld a law of the Territory of Utah limiting the hours in mines and smelters. That was 39 years before President Roosevelt undertook to set up a Supreme Court of his own, which would be partial to the laborers voting for him. Numberless laws limiting the length of the day for men, women, and children have been upheld by the courts through the years.

In 1908 the Supreme Court of the United States held (208 U. S. 412) valid—not in conflict with the National Constitution—a law of Oregon limiting the working hours of the day for women.

In 1913 the Supreme Court of the United States sustained (231 U. S. 320) an act of Illinois (which the Supreme Court of that State had upheld) limiting the age of the worker, a measure to protect youth.

In 1917 the Supreme Court of the United States sustained (243 U. S. 332) an act of Congress limiting the hours of railway trainmen.

In 1937 the minimum wage law of Washington of 1913 for women was sustained (300 U. S. 379) by the Supreme Court of the United States.

Judicial decision completely refuting charges of labor leaders

But the case affording the most striking refutation of the charge of labor leaders and the public officials was decided (281 U. S. 548) in May, 1930, by the Supreme Court of the United States. In disobedience to the often-expressed wishes of labor leaders that labor organizations do not seek redress in the courts of wrongs which they feel that they suffer (probably because that would prevent the leaders from taking the grievances to the White House or before committees of Congress), the Brotherhood of Railway and Steamship Clerks brought a suit in the United States District Court asking an injunction to prevent the Texas and New Orleans Railroad Company from intimidating the members of the Brotherhood and coercing them into an association of clerical employees of its own.

The trial court granted an injunction to the workers.

The railway company appealed to the United States Circuit Court of Appeals. That court of three judges sustained the trial court.

The railroad company went to the Supreme Court of the United States and again, and finally, the employees were held in right to an injunction. The employer was permanently enjoined from preventing employees from "freely designating their representatives by collective action" for dealing with the employer, as required by the Railway Labor Act of 1926, seven years before the Roosevelt regime.

The employer's act of contumacy

Notwithstanding that, the employer recognized its own association of clerical employees in the designation of representatives. In contempt proceedings brought by employees, the District Court of the United States required the defendant and its officers to disestablish its association of clerical employees and to reinstate the Brotherhood as the representative of clerical workers. Further, the employer was required to restore to service and privilege certain employees who had been discharged by it during the controversy.

What would the author of *Big Business on the Bench* say to that record?

Was not that a better way to try "a labor case" than to rush to Washington and be photographed with the President, and have a "hearing" for weeks or months before a Congressional Committee, with flashlight pictures without end and press conferences in large number?

Employees bargained collectively long before NLRA

From the foregoing it appears that "collective bargaining" by employees was secured to them by act of Congress 9 years before the alien National Labor Relations Act.

As a matter of historic fact, the locomotive engineers and firemen made a collective bargaining agreement with the Atchison, Topeka and Santa Fe Railroad Company in 1885, or 58 years before the "New Deal" took over the United States for party purposes. During the late '80s and early '90s the Shop Craft Unions were formed on that railroad. The Maintenance of Way employees, the Telegraphers, the Switchmen and the Clerks were organized at about the same time and dealt with their employer collectively.

Employees generally had collective bargaining

What has been said of the company mentioned is probably true of all the other important railroad companies in the United States.

Moreover, legislation favorable to the worker began about half a century before the National Labor Relations Act, which has been called "labor's Magna Carta." In 1886, the year before the Inter-state Commerce Act was passed, a bill for compulsory arbitration of railway disputes passed both Houses of Congress; but it was vetoed by President Cleveland because it provided fine and imprisonment for failure to obey the award, which was to be binding on both parties, without right to appeal and review. In 1888 a law for voluntary arbitration was enacted.

A look into the history of other large employers would doubtless show the rise of collective bargaining by labor organizations similar to its growth on the railroads.

Rights of workers and employers denied by NLRA

"Labor's gains" during the administration of Franklin D. Roosevelt were built on the closed shop, a denial of the liberty of man to work at will, and the denial of free speech to the employer, who was prevented from even discussing with his employees a subject raised by them.

Propagandism has been so stiff since 1933 that the multitudes have been led to believe that there never were any "labor's gains" before.

What this subject of employment needs is to be taken out of Government, in which it has no proper place. In view of the paramount interest of the public, which requires that production, transportation, communication and other essential services do not cease, and in view of the damages suffered by employer and employee from strikes, the legal obligations of one man or party to another present justiciable questions, which should be heard and decided by the courts of justice established by constitutions. There the "leader" will have no chance to parade and unfold his "philosophy" on compulsory membership, on the check-off, on the giving of no report even to the donors of moneys received, and on accounting to nobody for expenditures.

Courts could settle labor controversies nicely

In court the inquiry would be, not into "social science" or any other scrambled subject, nor into the right of any worker to join a union or stay out of it; the inquiry would bear on whether the property can pay what the employees demand and at the same time keep in condition to meet its obligations in service to the public now and in the future, while giving a reasonable return to those who furnish the money for the industry—in these times $5,000 or more to keep each employee in a place to work at a machine.

Those are the "rights" involved, not the miscalled "right to strike"—which cannot exist in any plant of any size, because a strike of any magnitude damages the public and individuals, and no person or group has a *right* to do damage.

"The condition of any particular business and of its owner must also come into question." Pius XII, 1931.

Of course, a worker may quit employment

The mere right of a worker to leave employment—if he is not under contract to stay with it—is not in point. To be sure, he may leave. Many may leave. But when he leaves, not for the sole purpose of severing the relation with the employer, but to do damage to the employer and the public, that may become, when done by many in concert, a conspiracy denounced by law. The Criminal Code of the United States (Title 18, sec. 51) provides:

"If two or more persons conspire to injure, oppress, threaten or intimidate any citizen in the free exercise and enjoyment of any right or privilege secured to him by the Constitution or laws of the United States, or because of his having so exercised the same, . . . they shall be fined not more than $5,000 and imprisoned not more than ten years, and shall, moreover, be thereafter ineligible to any office or place of honor, profit or trust created by the Constitution or laws of the United States."

That provision was enacted on March 4, 1909. It looks as though it would be highly useful to the Attorney General in time of a riotous strike.

Concerted quitting to bring the employer to his knees and cause him to pay more whether in justice he should, is contrary to the provision of the Criminal Code quoted. Even a purpose not in itself unlawful cannot be carried out by unlawful or criminal means, wrote Chief Justice Fuller (148 U. S. 197) in 1893.

All the liberties that the American enjoys and prizes, he must use with due respect to the rights and liberties of others. The rights of the employer and the rights of the public to continued production and peace have been disregarded too long.

Strikes in war were conspiracies

Most of the strikes during World War II were prima facie conspiracies against owners of property, against the interest of the public in unceasing production, against social order, and too often against the safety of persons. As they gave "aid and comfort" to our enemies in war, they fell within the definition of treason in the Constitution.

The National Director of the Bureau of Mines reported to the President in January, 1950, that for ten months of 1949, in comparison with the like time in the preceding year, the shipments of hot air furnaces burning solid fuels dropped 47 per cent. Does that indicate damage to innocent manufacturers from strikes of miners of coal?

It is of common knowledge that for several years the use of oils for fuel has been on the increase, owing in part to convenience in transportation and to easier firing, and perhaps to lower costs. But the figures shown and those following are too abrupt to mark only the long growth of a preference of oils for fuel. They indicate clearly that manufacturers and owners of large office buildings and others are in active construction of defenses against strikes of miners of coal.

During the time mentioned, sales at factory of mechanical coal stokers dropped 60 per cent. Did the conspiracy to stop mining of coal do damage there, and to an interest in no way involved in the dispute?

In 1947 coal produced 50 per cent of the heat content in the total energy used in the United States. In 1948 it produced 46.5 per cent, and in 1949 it fell to (estimated) 38.5 per cent. Other fuels rose in use correspondingly.

In the report of the Bureau of Mines there were other strongly probative facts showing damage to railroads, to the traveling and shipping public, and to the economy of the country in general.

Is destruction of property not preventable?

Are the owners of properties in coal to be destroyed in helplessness? Does the "Liberty under Law" which was chiseled on the front of the building of the Supreme Court at Washington mean anything substantial, or is it merely an expression of emotion?

To be sure, labor must organize and bargain collectively through its chosen agents. The notion that an individual worker can go to United States Steel or to General Motors, or to any other great employer, and make a contract of employment to his best advantage is in disregard of practices by the employer which made the union necessary. The union has been highly beneficial to both employer and employee, and it could be more so with better leadership on both sides.

It is a maxim of the law that there is no wrong without a remedy. The trouble has been that the Political Department of Government, instead of the Judicial, has been dealing with the subject. Only the courts can administer remedies for wrongs.

A dispatch from London through the United Press in October, 1949, said that the Government of England was considering the need of a court to adjudicate cases in the field of employment.

The Members of Congress and the members of the legislatures of the States (and many judges) who hasten, whenever the subject comes up, to declare for the *right* to strike do not look beyond the political aspects of the subject, of which it should have none. And the whole trouble is that by politicians the subject has been kept political whereas, because of the widely extended effect of strikes, the irreconcilable disputes are justiciable and are therefore for the courts.

A historic decision in point

When the American Railroad Union, an organization of trainmen, called a strike on several railroads hauling Pullman sleeping cars and announced that it would stop every railroad in the country if necessary, the Attorney General of the United States brought a suit for injunction under the Post Office Clause and the Commerce Clause to restrain the strikers from obstructing commerce and the mails. An injunction was granted and the trial court was upheld (158 U. S. 564) in May, 1895. There was no dissent from the opinion, by Justice Brewer, that "the strong arm of government may brush away all obstructions."

According to that decision, seizures from their owners by the Government of railroads, mines, and other properties in time of strikes (48 by President Roosevelt and 28 by President Truman), instead of protection of the owners and the public in the operation of the properties, were unlawful.[2] Those whose combinations or conspiracies interrupted commerce should have been brought to heel.

---

[2] Even in a time of war, property not in a zone of combat could not be seized for use by government. Where the courts are open in this country, rights of "life, liberty, and property" are adjudicated there. That was held (4 Wallace, 2) in a great case arising out of the Civil War. A citizen of Indiana, not in the military service, was tried (1864) by court-martial and sentenced to death. The accused should have been tried in a civil court, the tribunals of both Nation and State being open, and Indiana not being in the theater of war.

The courts were open to Presidents Roosevelt and Truman to stop strikes instead of seizing property illegally.

In November, 1946, when the President was put in a corner by a threat from the head of a union that the people would have no coal for the winter, the Department of Justice demonstrated that it is perfectly easy to stop that kind of performance.

Courts can determine fair pay to workers

Since 1906 the Interstate Commerce Commission has prescribed, after hearing both sides, reasonable rates for railroads. State commissions have long heard and decided controversies over rates of gas companies, electric light companies, street-car companies, telephone companies, and others; and their work has come to be fairly satisfactory to all.

The decisions of Federal and State commissions and of courts, in cases of disputes between labor and industry, would be quite satisfactory to the parties, including the public, if the President and the Senate and the governors would earnestly strive to appoint to such positions men of the highest legal learning and experience, instead of "lame ducks"—men put out of office by the people at the polls—or other political derelicts. The appointing powers have not been faithful to the public interest in this relation, which is the chief interest.

But no tribunal could do so badly as the mediation boards and other political devices have done in trying "labor" cases and maintaining confusion throughout the country.

Competent men can get justice done

The proposition that the appointment of competent men to judicial and quasi-judicial posts would cure most of our flagrant evils was demonstrated in late 1949 and January, 1950, by trials in two United States District Courts, in which the defendants were charged with acts of disloyalty. Judges on the Bench competent to conduct a trial correctly, competent United States Attorneys who knew how to prepare and present evidence, and competent and courageous men and women sitting as jurors, evoked the admiration of the people.

It can be done.

The service of the juries is specially emphasized, because for three or four decades advocates of the abolition of the trial jury have appeared in the schools and the Press insisting that the institution is "outmoded" and causes a "lag" in the administration of justice, to borrow the words of those jargonists.

But it is now clear that the jury never met the needs of social order better than it can meet them today. The jury is still "the country," the field of last resort. In the old pleading of the common law the defendant answered "that he is not guilty as in manner and form it hath been complained against him: And of this he puts himself upon the country." This right to put the decision to the country, to the Ultimate Power, the people, must never be parted with.

History gives us many cases in which "the country" refused to convict when directed to do so by a judge servile to the crown. "The country" in London repeatedly refused to convict, when ordered to do so by the judge, the founder of Pennsylvania of violation of the "law" in the exercise of his religious belief.

It is too bad—it is perilous—that we are not taught history. The Constitution was written by historians who worked to prevent in America the follies in governments past.

Controversies between employer and employee respecting compensation fair to both parties *and the public* must be taken out of the White House, out of Congress, and out of politics, and submitted to existing courts or to a special tribunal, which may become expert.

Attack of President on Supreme Court a result

The attempt of the President in 1937 to pack the Supreme Court was not a sudden outburst of alienism. It had been a long time in coming. The spadework, using one of the favorite expressions of the miners and sappers, had been done by many others.

As big a thing as the great American Republic could not have been put on the skids without years of steady work. Beginning with 1933, Socialism (control by government of production, distribution, and exchange), Fascism[3]

---

[3] The meaning of Fascism, a word much used in our country with evidently little understanding, may best be made clear by showing the corporations of government set up by Mussolini in Italy to take over all the activities of men.

The word Fascism indicates nothing respecting the operations of the government. It comes from "fasces," the name of the bundle of rods surrounding an axe and carried by the Roman lictor before the chief magistrate as a symbol of authority. Its being brought in by Mussolini was one more of those puerile attempts mentioned by Bryce to bring back somewhat of the Roman Empire. Mussolini set up 22 corporations. The first was the Corporation for Cereals, made up of designated numbers of employers and workers, and embracing growers, threshers, millers, bakers, commission and co-operative organizations. All the corporations were similarly divided. They were the Corporation for Fruits, Vegetables and Flowers; for Viticulture and Wine; for Sugar-beet and Sugar; for Edible Oil; for Livestock and Fisheries; for Timber; for Textiles; for Metals; for Chemical Trades; for Clothing Trades; for Printing, Publishing, and Paper; for Building Tools and Housing; for Water, Gas, and Electricity; for Mining and Quarrying; for Glassware; for Arts and Professions; for Inland Transportation; for Sea and Air Transportation; for Hotel Industry; for Credit and Insurance; for Entertainments.

(Socialism by corporations), and Communism (confiscation by government of private property through graduated taxes and by abolition of inheritance), all forbidden by the Constitution because in no way authorized, and in many ways condemned by implication, spread with the rapidity of a fire on the prairie.

But the seizure by them of the liberty and property of Americans began before 1933.

That defines Fascism. It is Socialism carried out by governmental corporations. It is at violence to our Constitution, but it has been coming for some years, and is now pretty well "dug in."

III

IN FAVOR TO POLITICIANS AND TO LABOR UNIONS, CONGRESS PURSUED ANOTHER METHOD OF ATTACK ON THE COORDINATE JUDICIAL DEPARTMENT

ANOTHER FORM OF ATTACK BY CONGRESS ON THE COURTS of the Constitution was in legislation directing them how to try cases.

In 1910 it passed an act forbidding the issue of an injunction against the operation of a law of a State except in a specified way.

In 1913 it passed a similar law forbidding the restraint by injunction of an order of the Interstate Commerce Commission except on conditions laid down.

And in 1932 Congress enacted the Norris-LaGuardia Act for denying injunctive relief to an employer, except under annoying conditions which might deny relief, where a labor question is involved.

Those invasions of the rights of litigants and the liberties of the American will be examined.

Constitutional Convention forbade Congressional dictation to courts

Prefatory to a discussion of the three intrusive acts of Congress mentioned, a quotation should be made from the record of the Constitutional Convention (*Formation of the Union*, p. 625) of August 27, 1787, only twenty-three days before the signing, when there was under consideration "the Judicial power":

"The following motion was *disagreed to,* to wit, to insert 'In all other cases before mentioned the Judicial power shall be exercised in such manner as the Legislature [The Congress] shall direct.' "

So the Constitutional Convention explicitly refused to authorize the Congress to "direct" the judicial power in any respect whatever. How Congress *has* lawlessly directed it, nevertheless, and how the courts have lawlessly submitted to the forbidden dictation, are to be seen.

The act of 1910 forbade the courts of the United States to grant an interlocutory injunction "restraining the enforcement . . . of any statute law of a State," or of any order made thereunder by a board, "upon the ground of the unconstitutionality" of such statute, "unless the application" be "heard and determined by three judges, of whom at least one shall be a justice of the Supreme Court or a Circuit Judge, and the other two may be circuit or district judges, and unless a majority of the said three judges shall concur in granting such application."

States objected to constitutional restraints

Some of the States had felt wounds in their dignity when a citizen who believed a tax law, for example, was intended to effect what President Coolidge later termed "legalized larceny," went into a court of the United States asking a restraining order upon the officers executing the law until there could be a full hearing on evidence. In addition to that, those were field days for the alien minded who omitted no opportunity to "go after" the Judiciary, which Von Holst rightly called the keystone of the American arch.

Of course, the Fourteenth Amendment forbids the State to "deprive any person of life, liberty or property without due process of law." That is, he must have a hearing when he asks it before his property is taken by taxation or otherwise. It was the constitutional intent that the legislature should not take property by fiat. And that was imbedded in the Constitution 46 years before the confiscation of private property was begun by Government through the "graduated" income taxes of Communism.

Article III, establishing the Judiciary, "extends" the "judicial power" to all cases arising under the Constitution, under the laws of the United States, under treaties; to cases affecting ambassadors, other public ministers, consuls; to controversies between two or more *States,* between a *State* and citizens of another *State,* between citizens of different *States,* between a *State* or the citizens thereof and foreign states, citizens or subjects.

Thus, ample provision was made for the States to use the courts of the Nation. But in the foregoing recital the States are ranked as litigants *on the level* with ambassadors, consuls, and *citizens.* No thought was entertained that a State as a litigant should be regarded as any higher than a man. Why should the creature, the State, be above the man, who created it?

Preference of State against Man not authorized

Since the Constitution left the State as a litigant on a level with the man, as it clearly did, where did Congress get the power to change that arrangement of the Constitution and put the State above the man? Only the people, by amendment, could make that change. Yet the courts submitted to the lawless dictation. The first judge appealed to under the meddling act should have refused to call two other judges, should have heard the application, granted or denied a restraining order or injunction, and let the losing party make a test of the law in the Supreme Court of the United States, which would then be in a position to sustain the Judiciary "in all its dignity and vigor," as President Cleveland sustained the Executive Department against encroachment by the Senate, and as Hamilton said in *The Federalist* that each Department would take pride in maintaining its prerogatives against one or both of the others.

Act of Congress interference with procedure

The act forbade that the application for a restraining order or injunction "be heard or determined before at least five days' notice of the hearing has been given to the Governor and to the Attorney General of the State, and such other persons as may be defendants in the suit." But if it should appear that irreparable loss or damage would result unless a temporary restraining order be granted, then one judge should give that relief.

As Article III set up the Supreme Court and then authorized Congress to "ordain and establish" such "inferior courts" as might be necessary, it was within the competence of the Legislative Department, probably, to establish a three-judge court. In 1891, to take from the Supreme Court part of its load, Congress established nine (now eleven) Circuit Courts of Appeals of three judges each. But to establish courts to meet the needs of the people is quite another thing from trying, or partially trying, cases in them.

"The judicial power of the United States" to try and adjudge cases, the Constitution put in "one Supreme Court and such inferior courts" as might be needed. That forever fixed judicial power until the people determine that it should be withdrawn from the courts and vested in the Congress or elsewhere.

No judicial power possessed by Congress

Congress may prescribe the *jurisdiction* of a court which it establishes (like the Court of Claims and the Court of Customs and Patent Appeals), but not the *power*. "The judicial power," says section 2 of Article III, "shall extend to all cases in law and equity." This power is poured into the courts by the people through their Constitution. Congress has no judicial power to confer.

Apparently emboldened by the success—or lack of opposition—which attended the act of 1910, Congress again dictated to the Judicial Department, in 1913, setting up a three-judge court and laying down with the fullest particularity the steps which the court would be permitted to take in injunction proceedings arising out of orders entered against citizens by the Interstate Commerce Commission.

Congress unduly magnified Interstate Commerce Commission

Again, why should the Interstate Commerce Commission, a bureau of Congress, have a court of three judges, when a court of one judge must meet the needs of the American, who created all that there is in and under government? This question is particularly pertinent in view of the fact that during the 63 years of the Commission no President has ever appointed to it a railroad man of standing in the field of transportation, finance or traffic, or a shipper of prominence, in the world of commerce. The body never has been what the President and the Senate should have made it—what the commerce of the country and those engaged in it were entitled to have to serve them. Then, why should its decisions be made so nearly immutable by restrictions on judicial procedure withholding from the American his liberty to seek justice?

Why put Interstate Commerce Commission above American?

As a specimen of the work of the Commission which the Congress was so desirous of making nearly immune to attack by aggrieved citizens, the reorganization of the Chicago, Milwaukee, St. Paul and Pacific Railroad Company will be stated.

Owing to the unemployment of 9,935,000 in the United States, there was a great shortage of production, which means that the railroads lacked freight tonnage and passenger travel, which means that many of them could not pay their way. In 1935, the Milwaukee Company filed a petition for reorganization with the Interstate Commerce Commission in pursuance of an act of Congress. Evidence was received in the year named and in 1936 and 1937. While the case was on trial the number of unemployed rose to 10,932,583, as reported by the American Federation of Labor.

The plan of reorganization approved by the Commission

wiped out all the preferred and common stock. On March 15, 1943, the Supreme Court of the United States upheld the finding of the Commission.

A year before that, in 1942, the net profits of the Milwaukee after interest and taxes were $12,174,831. In 1943 the net profits were $29,413,623.

Interstate Commerce Commission failed to see point

That shows that the railroad was in fit condition to handle traffic when the United States should be in condition to provide it. The United States needed reorganizing, not the railroads.

Shortly after the investments of the holders of preferred and common stock had been wiped out, the Company paid off a large volume of its old bonds. That is only one of many like cases of railroad reorganization in destruction of investments. The grossness of the injustice caused talk by members of Congress of impeachment.

It was decisions of that sort that Congress did not want the damaged American citizen to attack in court except under annoying difficulty and delay!

In 1932 Congress revamped a line of legislation respecting labor and told the Judicial Department of the Constitution just what it could do and what it could not do about the issuing of injunctions in cases affecting labor.

Norris-LaGuardia Act denial of justice

The minority report of the committee of Congress on the bill said that in practice it would amount to a denial of the rights of the employer. He was virtually outlawed. To be sure, that was the intention—that is what a powerful voting group demanded that Congress give it. And Congress responded to the demand, just as it bowed to the same group five years later and passed the National Labor Relations Act, to the appalling hurt of the States whose Congressmen enacted it.[1]

Those three acts of Congress were definitely lawless and against the liberty of the American. The courts were lawless when they submitted to the intimidations, and the organized Bar maintained a masterful inactivity while the undermining of constitutional government was in open progress.

Historic relief by injunction made clear

The "judicial power" which was poured into the courts by the Constitution was that inherent in the courts of England in 1787. It was brought to America by the colonists. What it was is plain.

Blackstone, whose lectures were taught in the College of William and Mary to Virginians who helped write the Constitution, told the youth at the University of Oxford a quarter of a century or more before 1787 just what were the inherent powers of a court of equity with respect to the restraining order, or the temporary injunction, and the permanent injunction:

"But if an injunction be wanted to stay waste, or other injuries of an equally urgent nature, then upon the filing of the bill [called application in the acts of Congress reviewed], and a proper case supported by *affidavits*, the

[1] The Norris-LaGuardia Injunction Bill of 1932 passed the Senate by a vote of 75 to 5. The House passed it by 363 to 13. The employers of the country whose equipment for production and transporation had won the first World War were all but friendless in the Government which had been saved.

court will grant an injunction immediately, to continue until the defendant has put in his answer, and till the court shall make some further order concerning it; and when the answer comes in, whether it shall then be dissolved or continued till the hearing of the case, is determined by the court upon argument, drawn from considering the answer and the affidavit together."—4 "Commentaries on the Laws of England," 443.

That language defined the power of a court of equity with respect to the injunction when the Constitution was written. Consequently that is what the Convention put into the Constitution when it provided:

"The judicial *power* shall extend to all cases in law and *equity*."

Congress powerless to defeat constitutional injunction

What a court of equity could do then it can do now. That is constitutional. Being constitutional, it can be taken out of the Constitution only by amendment. Congress can no more change or control the judicial power than it could wipe away the Bill of Rights. Indeed, this provision extending the judicial power to cases in equity is one of the many bills of right written in the body of the Constitution.

The court of equity established by the Constitution having had the power, as Blackstone shows, "to grant an injunction immediately," without notice, upon the filing of an application with affidavits proving that, if it be not granted without delay, irreparable damage will be sustained by the applicant, that power cannot be withdrawn or modified by Congress.

Rule of Supreme Court protected all

By Equity Rule 73 of the Supreme Court of the United States, governing the lower courts also, long in effect, meticulous care was taken to prescribe procedure in injunction cases—not alone in cases affecting the powerful group unconstitutionally favored by the Act of 1932, known as the Norris-LaGuardia Act, but in suits of *all* Americans.

The Rule directs (1) that no preliminary injunction issue without notice; (2) that no temporary restraining order be granted without notice unless it clearly appear from specific facts presented, *under oath*, that immediate and irreparable damage will otherwise result, and (3) that the temporary restraining order mentioned be brought to hearing "at the earliest possible time, and in no event later than 10 days."

That rule required *notice* to interested persons and parties—to States and to the Interstate Commerce Commission. It required the *oath* for the temporary restraining order, as described by Blackstone. It required speedy hearing. It gave to defendants complete protection, and the acts of Congress were as needless as they were invalid.

Judiciary in need of protection

On the Judiciary's being the weakest of the three Departments to defend itself, and on the need therefore of its receiving protection, Hamilton wrote in No. 78 of *The Federalist:*

"The Judiciary, from the nature of its functions, will always be the least dangerous to the political rights of the Constitution, because it will be least in capacity to annoy or injure them. The Executive not only dispenses the honors, but holds the sword of the community. The Legislature [Congress] not only commands the purse, but prescribes the rules by which the duties and rights of every citizen are to be regulated. The Judiciary, on the contrary, has no influence over either the sword or the purse; no direction either of the strength or of the wealth of the society; and can take no active resolution whatever. It may be truly said to have neither *force* nor *will*, but only judgment; and must ultimately depend upon the aid of the Executive arm even for the efficacy of its judgments. . . . It can never attack with success either of the other two; and all possible care is requisite to enable it to defend itself against their attacks."

But government by the educated is in prospect

In June, 1947, the Governor of Missouri signed a bill to require the teaching of the Constitution in all schools from the Seventh Grade up and in colleges and universities, and to forbid a degree of graduation to be given to any student until a rigid examination in the Constitution has been passed.

In the same month the dispatches reported that a similar step had been taken by the Legislature of California.

When the legislatures of all the other States follow those wise examples it will soon be impossible to draw from the population weak Congresses or Courts or Legislatures or Executives.

IV

THE SIXTEENTH OR INCOME-TAX AMENDMENT, HAVING OPERATED IN VIOLENCE TO AMERICAN PRINCIPLES RESPECTING PROPERTY AND JUSTICE, SHOULD BE REPEALED

As the panic of 1893 and the failures of crops which contributed to the insolvency of railroads and the closing of banks brought upon the theatre of government alien-minded philosophers advocating the imported Initiative, the Referendum, and the Recall as panaceas for whatever it was that was ailing them, so, after the panic of 1907, out came another group of politicians and "universitaires" and demanded an income tax to cure the sickness of the Nation.

For a time the panic of 1907 was worse than that of 1893, as in parts of the country the circulating medium disappeared and cities and various bodies issued "scrip" to be used as money.

Communistic beliefs from panic time in full effect

The platform of 1908 of the National Socialistic Party, speaking of that panic, demanded a "graduated" income tax and a graduated inheritance tax as a means of distributing wealth.[1]

It also called for nearly all of the "uplifts" brought into play a quarter of a century later and unctuously baptized as the "New Deal"—employment by the United States for the unemployed, help from the Federal Treasury for the needy, public improvements to provide work, nationalization of utilities and some industries, "development" of many fields not before thought to be within the competence of government, insurance for health, accident, old age, death, and other things insurable, and practically anything else that anybody wanted.

---

[1] Socialists have been charged with disagreement as to what they really stand for. From the platform of the National Socialist Party of 1908, following the very severe panic of the year before, a definition may be drawn. The writers of the platform betrayed a most comprehensive misunderstanding of the powers and obligations of our National Government. They called for:

1. Relief works through building schools and canals, by reforesting, by reclamation, and by extending all other public works;
2. Loans of money by the United States to States, municipalities, and for public works;
3. Ownership by the United States of railroads, telegraph and telephone lines, steamships, all land, and all industries;
4. Extension of the public domain to take over mines, quarries, oil wells, forests, and water power;
5. Extension of the graduated income tax and inheritance tax;
6. Abolition of the power of the Supreme Court to hold an act of Congress unconstitutional;
7. Creation of a Department of Health and a Department of Education;
8. Insurance against unemployment, illness, accident, invalidism, old age, and death;
9. Funds for the unemployed.

Some of those matters are within the police power of the States, but none lies within the jurisdiction of the Nation. The proposed taking over of property by taxation and by seizure is Communistic.

The reader should be profited by considering carefully how far we have already gone into that unconstitutionalism. How much of the "New Deal" and the "Fair Deal" comes from that—from the junk piles of futile expedients with which wretched governments have strewn the highway of history?

The fallacies of the "New Deal" were old even when Karl Marx demanded in 1848 "progressive," or graduated, income taxes—together with the abolition of the right to pass estates at death—to enable confiscation of private property and the rise thereby of the proletariat to political control. For they were employed by the several experimenters who tried to mitigate the conditions which brought on the French Revolution of 1789. And in the 300s the Roman Emperor Diocletian, in the interest of his soldiers, fixed maximum prices for provisions and other articles of commerce and set maximum rates of wages, with severe penalties for disregard of the edict. For the purposes of this regulation he issued a special copper coin of the value of one oyster. In 1950, the "New Deal" is operating in the United States without even that much for a standard of money.

After the close of the war in 1945 a new government in England undertook the acquisition of private property by what it termed "nationalization."

"New Deal" a very ancient failure

The "New Deal" is a very ancient subterfuge for statecraft.

Knowing the type very well, the historians who wrote the Constitution gave nothing that is in the "New Deal" any recognition whatever. Life, liberty, and property they left with men, to whom they belong, and for whom and by whom the Constitution was conceived for self-protection.

The "New Deal" is thoroughly unconstitutional.

Yet the persistence through the centuries of the idea that Government can do the business of man better than he can, which showed up in this land of liberty in 1933 with the effrontery of a Stuart king or a Bourbon, is a fact that must keep Americans on guard.

States deposed themselves from constitutional sovereignty

The Sixteenth Amendment to the Constitution of the United States wrought an unintelligent relinquishment by the States of the first power of governmental sovereignty—that of raising revenue for self-maintenance.

Hamilton failed to foresee that in time the States, instead of defending their sovereignty in local affairs, would, through their representatives in Congress, undermine themselves (*The Federalist*, No. 28):

"State governments will, in all possible contingencies, offer complete security against invasions of the public liberty by the National authority."

Plain income tax not objectionable

There is no objection to an income tax when legally laid—when not made confiscatory by graduation—but it should be levied by the States for use at home—not gathered by the Nation and then redistributed as doles or donatives toward the weakening of the States and the enlargement of the central power.

It should probably not be laid on the income of manufacture or production.

Since graduation was contrary to constitutional principle, it should have been foreseen by statesmen that the Income Tax Amendment as applied by Congress would work badly. It enabled the central Government, like an octopus, to thrust a tentacle into the revenue supply of each State and drain it, leaving the State partially helpless to perform its essential functions and making it a beggar at the Capital for a share of its own money.

Nation given worst form of power

It put in the hands of the National Government a power of money—in every hand the worst power there is—never seen in the world before, in comparison with which that employed by the Imperial City for the plunder of the Roman provinces was an evil of small consequence.

Money in excess at Washington has covered the country with a thoroughly disreputable organization of politics—the begging States having been to a degree forced to aid in carrying out, as baronies, the "objectives" of the superior authority from which they now hold their place on earth and to which they render most humble fealty.

Roosevelt totally lacking in knowledge of taxation

In the President's message to Congress and the country on April 27, 1942, the first and most important of his seven specifics for keeping the costs of living from "spiraling upward" and for winning the war was "to tax heavily, and in that process keep personal and corporate profits at a reasonable rate."

"Through tax processes," he said, excess profits can be kept down, and at the same time "further large sums" can be raised for the financing of the war.

The plain import of that language is that "tax processes" may be employed—as they certainly have been illegally for nearly three decades—for other purposes than the raising of necessary revenue for the support of strictly governmental functions.

When law was scientific, care was exercised to levy no more taxes than would meet the needs of government economically administered. President Coolidge said that taxation beyond that need is "legalized larceny." President Cleveland denounced almost as severely the taking by taxation of revenue not required.

Those two understood clearly the American meaning of the word "tax," as applied for upwards of 300 years. Neither to them nor to those before them was a tax a weapon. It was not an instrument for taking from those with possessions and bestowing, either directly or indirectly, upon those without.

President Roosevelt for the confiscation of Communism

The use of "tax processes" for transferring the property of the individual to the Government is the fundamental doctrine in the Communist Manifesto of 1848, promulgated by Karl Marx. By the "graduated" income tax, plus the abolition of the rights of inheritance, Marx would seize by government for the proletariat all private property.

"They [the proletariat] have nothing of their own to secure and fortify," wrote Marx; "their mission is to destroy all previous securities for, and insurance of, individual property."

The instrument to accomplish that destruction would be "a *heavy* progressive [graduated] income tax."

"The abolition of all rights of inheritance" would be

used by Marx and his followers toward putting an end to private property.

Karl Marx elucidates his idea

Communism, belief in which has been held by many in our Government, was made clear by Marx as follows:

"The distinguishing feature of Communism is not the abolition of property generally, but of the bourgeois [capitalistic] property. But modern bourgeois private property is the final and most complete expression of the system of producing and appropriating products that is based on class antagonisms, on the exploitation of the many by the few.

"In this sense the theory of Communism may be summed up in the single sentence: *Abolition of private property.*"

The "heavy progressive" taxes which he proposed would transfer property from the bourgeoisie to Government, and Government would be in the proletariat.

Marx again:

"The immediate aim of Communism is the same as that of all the other proletarian parties: formation of the proletariat into a class, overthrow of the bourgeois supremacy, and conquest of political power by the proletariat." [2]

---

[2] *Social and Political Doctrines of Contemporary Europe*, Oakeshaft, pp. 88 to 101.

Perhaps the best way to define Communism is to present an abstract of the Communist Manifesto of 1848:

1. Abolition of property in land, and application of all rents of land to public purposes;
2. A heavy progressive income tax;
3. Abolition of all rights of inheritance;

And men teaching and preaching that sedition have been permitted to run for the Presidency of the United States!

Communism the first "American way of life"

Communism was the first—and quickly rejected—American way of life. The Communism expounded by Lenin in *The Teachings of Karl Marx* had been the earliest experiment in America in living. It was tried in Virginia and in the Plymouth Colony in Massachusetts. It was a failure in both places, as it failed in several later attempts in the United States when supported by abundant funds and by men and women of the highest learning.

Lenin wrote that the worker receives under Communism "a certificate from society" for the amount of work done. He gets in return from the public warehouse "a corresponding quantity of products," after there has been deducted "that proportion of labor which goes to the public fund." In the main that is the method in Soviet Russia today, according to Gen. Walter Bedell Smith, former ambassador to that country, in *My Three Years in Moscow*.

---

4. Confiscation of property of all emigrants and rebels;

5. Centralization of credit in the hands of the state by means of a national bank with state capital and exclusive monopoly;

6. Centralization in the hands of the state of the means of communication and transport;

7. Extension of factories and instruments of production owned by the state; the bringing into cultivation of waste lands, and the improvement of the soil generally in accordance with a common plan;

8. Equal obligation of all to work. Establishment of industrial units, especially for agriculture;

9. Combination of agriculture with manufacturing industries, and gradual abolition of the distinction between town and country by a more equable distribution of the population;

10. Free education of all children in public schools, abolition of children's factory labor in its present form, and the combination of education with industrial production.

Governor Bradford on failure of Communism at Plymouth

In *A History of Plymouth Plantation, 1606 to 1646,* it is related by Governor Bradford (p. 147) that at first the land was tilled and other work done in common and that the product of toil went into general storage. From the warehouse those in charge of the colony made distribution according to service given. The undertaking failed from lack of incentive "even among the best settlers." After grave consideration by the officers of the colony a "parcell" of land was assigned to each family and the members of the family lived together. Immediately "corne" was much more widely planted.

"For the young men," wrote Bradford, "that were most able and fitte for labour and service did repine that they should spend time and streignth to worke for other men's wives and children without any recompence. The strong, or men of parts, had no more devission of victails and cloaths than he that was weake and not able to doe a quarter the other could. This was thought injustice."

Of course, it was unjust, an affront to reason, a burden at which human nature rebels.

Thus the communal life was rejected at the beginning for American private enterprise.

American spirit called "wealth" by Hamilton

That spirit of self-reliance was regarded by Alexander Hamilton (*The Federalist,* No. 11) as a considerable proportion of the capital which would build the United States:

"The unequalled spirit of enterprise which signalizes

the genius of American merchants and navigators, and which is in itself an inexhaustible mine of national wealth."

Government has been undermining that self-reliance until a critic has said that the people are more fearful of life than of death. And in 1949, so much had American spirit deteriorated (in places) that the Vice President could say in an address to an association of businessmen:

"As much as we wish for the good old simple days, the complexities of our lives have created an interdependence among all of our citizens. This has created a necessity for the guidance of the Government in the problems that beset our people."

Most of the worst "problems" have been created by men in Government who had never, before taking public office, exhibited any notable talent in the world of affairs. They have been incompetent "guides." Our constitutional system has been turned by them into a manufactory of problems and "emergencies."

Those problems cannot be solved by Communism.

"Graduated" tax of Communism never proposed by Congress

In 1909 President Taft, who succeeded to an empty treasury, asked Congress to propose an amendment to the Constitution authorizing an income—but not "graduated" —tax. Congress made the proposal and it became the Sixteenth Amendment in 1913, just before President Taft went out. By a tax on corporations he had filled the Treasury, thus demonstrating that the income tax was not needed.

The purpose of the proposed Amendment was to take out of the Constitution, as it would affect an income-tax law, the provision (section 2 of Article I) on which the Income Tax Act of 1894 foundered, namely:

"Direct taxes shall be apportioned among the several States which may be included within this Union, according to their respective numbers."

That is, according to population. The Supreme Court had held (157 U. S. 429) the taxes stated to be direct taxes, and that as they had not been apportioned by Congress among the several States, the act was unconstitutional. Hence, the Amendment:

"Congress shall have power to lay and collect taxes on incomes, from whatever source derived, *without apportionment* among the several States, and without regard to any census or enumeration."

Hamilton did not dream that the provision for uniformity in taxation which he was extolling would be stricken out (emphasis his):

"The abuse of this power of taxation seems to have been provided against with guarded circumspection. In addition to the precaution just mentioned, there is a provision that 'all duties, imposts and excises shall be UNIFORM throughout the United States.'"

Sixteenth Amendment gave Congress no power to tax

That did not give Congress the power to tax incomes. It had that power before. All the Amendment did was to remove the need for apportionment among the several States.

Especially it did not authorize Congress to take leave of the rule and practice of uniformity and equality of treatment which had always governed in every field of taxation and employ a method without rule, without reason, for the taking of money of the Americans for other purposes than the actual needs of government economically administered. It did not authorize Congress to confiscate the income of a man until it would not be what President Franklin D. Roosevelt called "too high." It did not empower Congress to drain the States of their resources and subject them to bureaucratic domination. Nor did it give authority to government to enter the fields of production, manufacture, agriculture, world saving and others, and to spend money for purposes not within the only area laid out in the Constitution, that is, "the common Defence and general Welfare of the United States."

Lawless government caused by money in excess

But those are among the many unconstitutional activities in which Government has been enabled to engage by use of the limitless funds gathered by the confiscatory income tax. Having mismanaged agriculture, manufacture, medicine, charity, and other nongovernmental activities at home, it took up direction of the affairs of the world by the worse than lavish use of money produced by the erroneous application of the Sixteenth Amendment.

For if what has been taking place in our land and other lands during the last third of a century had been intended by President Taft when he asked Congress to propose an amendment, he would have made specifications to that effect. He would have asked for a "graduated" tax.

"Graduated" tax not proposed by Congress

The Amendment proposed and ratified carried nothing on its face but the common tax levied on lands, buildings, livestock, machinery, and personal property from the beginning. The constitution of every State commands the legislature to make taxes uniform, or by valuation, or in proportion to value, or by some other method of "equality of treatment." All property of a class must be taxed at the same rate. If one man in a class has ten times as much property as another, he will pay ten times as much tax, the levy for both being on one rate. He cannot be made to pay twelve times as much by the use of a higher rate.

Without the clearest specifications in the Sixteenth Amendment for "graduated" rates, showing a purpose to bring about, by radical departure from American method, what we have witnessed with consternation, Congress had no power to pass the act of October 3, 1913, and subsequent income-tax laws levying graduated taxes.

People had shown no enthusiasm for income tax

As it took the Socialists and Communists fourteen years after the decision of the Supreme Court holding the tax act of 1894 unconstitutional to get the proposal to amend, and four years more to secure its ratification, it is reasonable to assume that had the proposal plainly called for the "graduated" or confiscatory tax of Communism, it never would have been ratified. Indeed, had the people dreamed that the money of the States would be drained away, leaving them mendicants at Washington, the proposal as it was would have been defeated.

Article V of the Bill of Rights forbids that "private property be taken for public use without just compensation." When the United States wants the land of an American as the site of a post office, or for any other purpose, it must bring a condemnation proceeding in the exercise of its eminent domain, when the need for taking the property will be proved and its value ascertained. That value the United States must pay.

Taxpayer entitled to benefit equivalent to tax

The law or doctrine of eminent domain applies in principle, and by sound authority, to property "taken for public use" by taxation, as it does to all other takings. The American whose money is thus taken by taxation must receive from government an equivalent value in return. That, he gets in protection to his "life, liberty, and property," for which purpose he established his constitutional system.

That principle was laid down as to taxation in a single, clear, short sentence by Judge Cooley in *Constitutional Limitations,* 2d edition, p. 495 (italics inserted):

"As all are alike protected, so all should share the burden, *in proportion to the interest secured.*"

A man with an income of $100,000 should pay ten times more in taxes than the one worth $10,000, because he has ten times as much value needing the protection of the government which he established. But he should not, at the caprice of the spirit of Communism, pay fifteen or twenty times as much. Nor does he so pay in any field of taxation except in that where taxes on incomes, and on estates passing at death, are levied.

"Graduated" tax not applied to other property

In every other field all men have paid *one* tax *rate,* which in itself is proof that the "graduated"—the arbitrary —tax rate is obnoxious to the "due process of law" (its fair play and procedural regularity) and to "the equal protection of the laws," which are the gist of all American constitutions.

As the statement of President Roosevelt was the most absolute assertion of an unlimited power in government to take property by taxation for other purposes than revenue, a belief which has for years been expressed in unscholarly seats of learning, in sections of the Press, and elsewhere, it is plain that at last we have "entered a boundless field of power," to use Jefferson's warning language, "no longer susceptible of any definition."

President Roosevelt for Marxist confiscation

In his radio address on September 7, 1942, President Roosevelt expressed this wholly unsound theory of the governmental power of taxation, which has been let pass without critical examination:

"Taxation is the only practical way of preventing the incomes and profits of individuals and corporations from getting too high. I have told the Congress once more that all net individual incomes, after payment of all taxes, should be limited effectively by *further taxation* to a maximum net income of $25,000 a year."

That idea of the President, that he or his Government could limit the income of an American, is one phase of a fatuous belief which the schools have made common, namely, that rights to property are conferred upon him by law. Whereas, the Declaration of Independence says that he set up this Government himself "to secure these rights" which come to him from the Creator, "among which are life, liberty and the pursuit of happiness," that pursuit including the acquisition of property. Necessarily his rights and property preceded the Government which he set up for the purpose of protecting them.

Tax must be for revenue, not punishment

In *Commentaries on the Constitution* (page 329), Justice Story of the Supreme Court wrote that a tax for neither of the purposes stated in the Constitution—"to pay the Debts and provide for the common Defence and general Welfare of the United States"—would be "an excess of legislative authority."

When members of Congress returned to Washington from their homes after the election in November, 1946, and undertook to draw a tax bill to meet the wishes of the country for a 20-per-cent reduction of the levies on incomes, they were astonished to find that it is the small incomes that are supporting the extravagances and illegal spendings of the Government, and that the cut indicated would leave the Treasury without sufficient funds. The big boys, who were to be "soaked" when the Sixteenth Amendment was proposed, by levies on vast properties hitherto untaxed, are paying comparatively little.

How the tax load was divided

Taxpayers receiving a net income under $2,500 (small money now), who numbered 35,625,683 persons, paid $4,693,000,000 in income taxes in 1946.

Those with net incomes from $2,500 to $5,000 (also small money), numbering 15,157,265 persons, paid $5,444,-000,000.

In the group from $5,000 to $10,000 net income there

A HISTORY OF LAWLESS GOVERNMENT

were only 1,314,457 taxpayers, and they contributed $1,509,000,000.

The group having from $10,000 to $25,000 numbered only 551,267, and they contributed in taxes $2,181,000,000.

There were only 143,725 taxpayers with incomes from $25,000 to $100,000 and they paid $2,673,000,000.

In the group with incomes above $100,000 there were only 9,599 taxpayers, who took a burden of $1,100,000,000.

Low incomes carry big load of government

The two low-income groups paid $10,000,000,000 and the four higher-income groups paid $7,000,000,000.

The foregoing figures are from the *United States News* of February 14, 1947, page 30, which commented that "in trying to give the big break to the little taxpayer, Congress runs up against those facts," and that "taxing the rich is not enough," although 86 per cent is taken from the income of those in "the highest income levels."

The report of the Secretary of the Treasury for 1946 shows receipts of more than 30 billion from "income taxes," but that amount includes "profit taxes" on transactions in business, as distinguished from wages, salaries, and other forms of personal income.

Who really got "soaked" when Congress passed a "graduated" income-tax bill which was not authorized by the Sixteenth Amendment of 1913, and which was therefore unconstitutional?[3]

---

[3] Whatever talk there may have been in the streets about "soaking the rich" by a graduated tax, or whatever may have been said by some in Congress on that point, the rule of interpretation is that the enactment must be taken at its face value. A radical change in the existing order—like the introduction of a form of taxation not used against any other kind of property—can be accepted only on a purpose most clearly

The very rich forsook the risks of industry and trade, forgot the troubles with employees over wages and working conditions, and retired to the velvet comforts of that most stupendous American business, the National Debt, largely tax exempt.

By beginning in time of peace (1913) the borrowing of money from the people of the country and securing, through the enticement of exemption from taxation, a high price in the market for its bonds issued therefor, Congress gathered away from taxable enterprises millions which rose to billions and are in 1950 headed for trillions—all cleared of the taxes which had before gone to the support of government.

Necessarily those not owning bonds had to take a larger load of taxes to compensate for the exemption.

How much will the depletion thus caused of this country's powers of production and transportation, which won both wars, imperil the future of the United States?

How much did the corroding debt of England, attended by widespread poverty, for 125 years before World War I contribute to the debilitation of industry resulting in its "nationalization"?

---

expressed. The amendment proposed by Congress and ratified by the legislatures did not use "graduated" to describe the tax. Therefore, a graduated tax was not proposed.

"Where the language of an enactment is clear," said the Supreme Court of the United States (278 U.S. 269) ". . . . the words employed are to be taken as the final expression of the meaning intended. And in such cases legislative history may not be used to support a construction that adds to or takes from the significance of the words employed."

That is to say, authority "to lay and collect taxes on incomes" was authority to lay taxes as they are laid on all other kinds of property—one rate on all property of the same kind, money in the case of incomes. In going beyond that, Congress violated the Constitution.

The talk about soaking the rich might have related to the fact that the big incomes (along with the little) never had paid any tax at all. It was quite proper to tax them—but only constitutionally.

Courts of States had denounced "graduated" tax

Before the Government at Washington entered upon this *coup d'état*, the supreme courts of several States had put legislatures right on the principles here under discussion.

In 1882 the Supreme Court of New Hampshire held a "graduated" tax on estates void for conflict with the command of the Constitution of the State, that taxes be "proportional and reasonable."

In 1889 the Supreme Court of Minnesota held likewise.

In 1894 the Supreme Court of Ohio said:

"The rate per cent must be the same on all estates. There can be no discrimination in favor of the rich or poor. All stand on an equality under the provisions of the Constitution, and it is this equality that is the pride and safeguard of us all."

In 1898 the Supreme Court of Missouri, eighteen years before the Supreme Court of the United States sanctioned the graduated or confiscatory tax, expressed (143 Mo. 287) the like view, saying that it was "without rhyme or reason."

The next year the Supreme Court of Pennsylvania held (191 Pa. 1) that classification of different amounts of money as different kinds of property, and therefore subject to different rates of tax, is a fallacy and "necessarily unjust, arbitrary and illegal."

In short, the graduated tax is Communistic.

Congress quickly repealed Civil War Income Tax

While in the income-tax laws of the Civil War there had been both graduations and exemptions, the levies were so light and the graduations so undiscriminative that the legislation could not be taken as a precedent to support what the people have been bearing since the Act of 1913 in violation of the Income Tax Amendment.

The Act of 1861 levied 5 per cent flat on incomes over $800.

The Act of 1862 levied 3 per cent on $600 to $10,000; 5 per cent above $10,000.

The Act of 1864 levied 5 per cent on $600 to $5,000; 7½ per cent on $5,000 to $10,000; 10 per cent on more than $10,000.

The Act of 1867 levied 5 per cent flat on more than $10,000.

The Act of 1870 levied 2½ per cent flat for 1870 and 1871, *"and no longer,"* quoting the words of the law.

Of the five levies, two were "graduated" and three were flat.

Congress recognized that such taxes could be justified only by the peril of war and through the exertion of the war powers, and it wiped them away as soon as it could. It never returned to nonuniform taxes until the doctrine of Communism had been taken up by our "intellectuals."

In 1864 Congress called for the prayers of the country "to implore Him as the Supreme Ruler of the world not to destroy us as a people, nor suffer us to be destroyed by the hostility or connivance of other nations"—referring to the unneutral conduct in our Civil War of England and France. In such circumstances of national alarm no American would question in a lawsuit the validity of taxes of whatsoever sort.

Income tax thus adjudged war measure

Congress itself, by repealing the Civil War taxes, declared in effect such levies to be unjustifiable in time of peace.

The most striking example of the fatuous condition of affairs in our country is in the call of States for an amendment to prevent their representatives in Congress from weakening them by the income tax and the estate tax of more than 25 per cent. Article V authorizes the States to apply to Congress "to call a Convention for proposing Amendments," and during 1949 many States made the application.

First, as a practical matter, the action is objectionable, because if Congress should get authority to take 25 per cent of incomes and estates, it will do so forever—whereas, our history for 130 years demonstrated that Congress can get along without either of those taxes.

Second, the needed amendment—if the States fear (as they may have reason to) that their representatives in Congress will not refrain from exhausting them by taxation —is one forbidding income and estate taxes by Congress except in time of war. As elsewhere shown herein, the Civil War income tax was promptly rejected by Congress as a tax justifiable in time of peace.

That definition of the tax should stand forever.

But the spectacle of citizens petitioning for protection from the men they elect to Congress! Can you believe it?

Exemptions as unconstitutional as graduation

And the exemptions granted in connection with the income tax and bonds, and in other relations, are just as obnoxious to the Constitution as is the graduation. The Supreme Courts of the States just cited condemned exemptions along with graduations.

During a housing and building shortage caused by World War I the legislature of New Jersey, to encourage construction, enacted a law exempting from taxation for five years all new structures. It was held (116 Atlantic 328) void for disregard of the command of the Constitution of the State for uniformity of taxation upon all.

Cooley, the great authority of his time, said in his work *Taxation* (2d ed., p. 215) that "it is difficult to conceive of a justifiable exemption law which would select single individuals or corporations, or single articles of property, and, taking them out of the class to which they belong, make them the subject of capricious legislative favor. . . . It would lack the semblance of legitimate legislation." [4]

Exemptions prime cause of French Revolution

When Louis XVI convoked (1789) the States General it appeared that the troubles of the country which resulted finally in the Revolution sprang from exempting government officials and the favored classes from taxation.

The Income Tax Law of 1894 exempted all incomes below $4,000. Although the law was held void for failing to "apportion" the burden among the States according to

[4] The constitutions of the States generally authorize the exemption from taxation of church property, of school property, of public property and buildings, and of other property not used for profit. Such properties are not in competition with those employed in providing a livelihood for men, who secure through taxes the protection of government in their endeavors. Further, by teaching and other work they give service to society equal to or above a yield in taxes. They are not really "properties" within the class for taxation.

A HISTORY OF LAWLESS GOVERNMENT

population, as directed by the Constitution, Justice Field took occasion to denounce the exemption of all incomes below $4,000. "The present assault upon capital is but the beginning," he wrote. "Unless the rule of the Constitution governs, a majority may fix the limitation at such a rate as will not include any of their number."

American officials like exemptions

Yet Congress, being ignorant of or indifferent to these fundamentals, has been tossing tax-free salaries to favored persons with unrestrained prodigality. In 1947 it so favored officers of the World Bank, making the $22,500 salary of the vice president equal to $38,000, the salary of the executive director of $17,500 equal to $26,000; and two employees of the State Department who had been working for $10,000 were given exempt salaries of $17,500, equal to $26,000. Frequently since then the dispatches from Washington have told of similar favors to those specially beloved.[5]

---

[5] Section 1 of Article II of the Constitution commands that the "compensation" of the President "shall neither be encreased nor diminished during the Period for which he shall have been elected." In January, 1949, just before the President entered upon the term for which he was elected in November, 1948, Congress increased his salary from $75,000 a year to $100,000.

In January, 1949, Congress granted to the President $50,000 a year to cover his expenses, which theretofore had been carried in the budget in support of the White House. This grant was made exempt from the income tax. If it was for expenses, it was not taxable as salary, and the exemption was superfluous. If it was in truth salary—for the usual report on expenses was waived—then it could not be legally exempted. And, more important still, it could not be enjoyed by a President before the next term, beginning in January, 1953.

It may interest the taxpayer to study those cards as played.

The whole White House force of 225 (53 under Roosevelt and 37 under Hoover) received increases from the taxpayers.

Colossal properties illegally exempted from taxation

In 1931, before the saving of mankind from want and fear by Government became known to Government as the first of its expanding duties, there were outstanding $22,536,000,000 of bonds wholly exempt from (1) the property tax, from (2) the normal tax, and from (3) the surtax of the United States, as shown by the Report of the Secretary of the Treasury for 1932, page 439.

That property, paying no taxes as property and not taxable on its income, was greater than the aggregate value of Class I railroads in the United States (95 per cent of mileage and 97 per cent of total earnings) as found by the Interstate Commerce Commission in 1945, namely, $19,571,000,000. The railroads paid over a billion in taxes that year.

Enormity of prejudice to overburdened taxpayers

What would the average man say if word were to be given out that Government (National and State) had determined to exempt the railroads from that burden and put the billion load on other taxpayers!

While at first the common man was to be very kindly treated under income-tax laws as Government would pro-

---

Special counsel was advanced	from $12,000 to $20,000 a year.
President's aide (labor)	from $15,000 to $20,000 a year.
3 secretaries, each	from $10,330 to $18,000 a year.
5 administrative assistants	from $10,330 to $15,000 a year.
10 Cabinet members	from $15,000 to $22,000 a year.

A number of lesser functionaries were favored with increases of pay, 900,000 classified workers receiving advances aggregating $130,000,000 yearly.

ceed with the new weapon to "soak the rich," it has come to pass that a person with an income of $600 a year (which takes in practically all wage earners) must report his earnings. Yet banks, many of them living largely on the Public (National and State) Debt, trust companies holding vast estates resting on exempt bonds, universities and other institutions with exempt bonds a considerable part of their endowments, are released from support of Government to the extent of their property in bonds and on the income of some of them.

Wrong should be righted by guilty States

The States, by proposal in Congress or by action of their legislatures under Article V, should amend the Constitution again by repealing the Sixteenth Amendment and resuming police jurisdiction of the wealth of their people, as they repealed the Eighteenth Amendment after becoming convinced that they had made a mistake in giving to the Nation a burden of police which it was not—and could not be—organized to carry.

Congress would then still have power to tax incomes, as it had before the Amendment, but it would be obliged to do so justly—for revenue only, not for the distribution of property, for leveling down possessions, for punitive purposes, or for stripping Americans for the help of Europeans who are antagonistic to our Government and our beliefs.

And it would be unable to bleed the States to financial helplessness, where the Supreme Court thought them to be when it gave sanction to the Social Security Law chiefly on that error. For if the representatives of the people of the States in Congress at that critical juncture had repealed the Income Tax Law, as they should have done, the States would have the money properly belonging to them and far more than enough to meet the needs of the people.

Washington preferred to treat the States as bankrupt, and execute a *coup d'état*. The police power thus exercised by Congress over the "health, safety, morals, education and general well-being of the people" was withheld from it by the Constitution and—for double security—denied to it by the Tenth Amendment. Its conduct was twice wrongful.

The States must return to the Constitution and resume control of their Union, their property, and their prerogatives.

The fallacious idea of the Supreme Court

The fallacy on which "graduated" (or what Karl Marx named "progressive") or discriminative—and therefore unconstitutional—taxes are based was expressed by the Supreme Court of the United States in 1898 in a case (170 U. S. 283) arising under a law of Illinois and involving *estate* or inheritance taxes.

Probably the success of that litigation for the tax gatherer induced Congress—which had failed with its Income Tax Law of 1894—to step in and enact (1898) a Federal *Estate* Tax Law with a "graduated" scale and thereby get some funds of a new sort. In 1900 that Act of Congress was upheld (178 U. S. 41) on the "principle" laid down in the case from Illinois, to be quoted presently.

Then came the Income Tax Amendment of 1913, which made no mention of "graduation." Congress immediately enacted, in October of that year, a "graduated" tax levy, which was upheld (240 U. S. 1) by the Supreme Court in 1916 on the "principle" of the two preceding decisions respecting *estates* passing at death.

Justice Brewer dissented from the doctrine established because "equality in right, equality in protection, and equality in burden is the thought which runs through the life of this Nation and its constitutional enactments from the Declaration of Independence to the present hour."

State Supreme Courts understood subject clearly

Before those decisions, half a dozen of the Supreme Courts of the States had held, as previously shown, graduation to be repugnant to protective clauses in all American constitutions, and especially to the clause commanding "equal protection." The Supreme Court of the United States made no reference to those decisions.

The "philosophy" enunciated by the Supreme Court in 1898 and repeated in 1900 and 1916 was in this language, practically a copy of the erroneous holding of the Supreme Court of Illinois:

"The right to take property by devise [will] or descent [by statute in absence of will] is the creature of the law, and not a natural right—a privilege, and, therefore, the authority which confers it may impose conditions upon it."

That is, the law may say to the transmitter or the taker (or to both as it has come to pass) that this property will not descend unless you accept a graduated scale of taxation on the "privilege" which a gracious government extends to you.

Some history on property rights

That is at once historically erroneous and contrary to the first fundamental of American Government, as stated by Justice Brewer. The Americans set up Government "to secure" (the Declaration of Independence says) preexisting rights to life, liberty, and the pursuit of happiness—the pursuit being largely the pursuit of property and the comforts and cultures which it brings. And as his Constitution twice puts property in the class with liberty and life, how can it be contended that law (which he writes himself) gives to him his property any more than it gives him his life?

In the earliest of English charters (1101) we find recognition by King Henry I of the preexisting right of a subject to dispose of property at death. By that charter, which Henry was compelled to sign as a condition of being crowned, he was restoring to the people rights which had been usurped by William the Conqueror (1066) and his son, William II. Section 7 of the charter reads:

"If any of my barons or feudal dependents shall fall sick, according as he shall give away his money, I concede that it shall be given. But if, prevented by unlikely chance of physical infirmities, he shall not give away his money or arrange to give it, his wife and children or relations and lawful heirs shall divide it up for the good of his soul as shall seem best to them."

Government not to take property at death

That is, in no circumstances could the King any longer take the property of a subject at his death. When an Englishman "arranged" to give away his money, that was a will (which need not have been in writing); when he failed to arrange, his property went by custom (now in the United States by his own Statute of Descent) to his widow and other heirs.

A HISTORY OF LAWLESS GOVERNMENT 79

Of that right, which did not come from the King of England (and does not come from Government or "law" in the United States), Blackstone wrote in 2 *Commentaries*, page 491:

"With us in England this power of bequeathing is coeval with the first rudiments of the law: for we have no trace or memorials of a time when it did not exist."

That is, the right to distribute property at death is a natural right. Feudalism in England denied it for a time. A recent English writer on the law says that the estate tax is a recrudescence of Feudalism.[6]

Hallam, the constitutional historian, tells us (*Middle Ages*, p. 445) that, in early England, man passed lands and other property at death by his own right, not by governmental permission, but by the custom of which he was, of course, the maker:

"The descent of lands before the Conquest [1066] was according to the custom of gavilkind, or equal partition among the children."

---

[6] On December 23, 1949, the Associated Press reported that a 9-million dollar oil company in Pennsylvania had sold its property to a larger company because "the higher and higher inheritance taxes, as well as income taxes, have meant that a business developed by an individual, or by a small group of individuals, cannot be passed on to a second generation."

William the Conquerer (1066), who rooted Feudalism in England, and his sons took the estate at death until stopped by the Charter of 1101.

So many properties in this country had been unable to marshal the cash to meet the estate tax levied upon the death of an owner or part owner that the practice became common to carry life insurance on the members and thereby with ready money prevent the destruction of the company.

In reporting to 1,000 employees the sale of the property first mentioned, the two men owning most of the stock said:

"In the event of the death of one of our principals, a sale of the company would be almost inevitable."

The history of tyrannical governments does not disclose many cases to beat that, of a common sort in our land of supposedly independent men.

Thus, the history of the law is that the English-speaking man does not get from government the "privilege" of transmitting property at death, or of taking it by bequest or inheritance upon the death of another.

Supreme Court decision rested on sand

The foundation of the decision of the Supreme Court of the United States upholding the "graduated"—capricious and confiscatory—tax of Communism was laid in sand.

From that developed the most cruel fleecing by taxation of a great people by the Government which they established to protect them and their property that the world has known.

From the money, almost beyond measurement, came the intoxication of Government with power.

The theory applied by the Supreme Court in the case of the "graduated" *inheritance* law of Illinois, namely, that as transmission of property is by permission of government, conditions can be added, should not have been employed to justify "graduated" taxes on *incomes*. For certainly the living man does not require permission of government to engage in income-yielding activities!

Historically and legally untenable as the first decision was, the last was worse.

Where are we "at" with this money?

Where have we been brought with the money yielded by the unconstitutional application of the Income Tax Amendment?

In 1949, the National Government spent $6 for every $5 collected. For 15 weeks of the fiscal year beginning July 1, expenditures were 12 billion and collections were 10 billion. That proportion for the full year would bring a deficit of more than 7 billion.

The Truman administration spends yearly	45	billion
The Roosevelt administration spent (including War)	31	"
The Hoover administration spent	3.8	"
The Coolidge Administration spent	3	"
The Harding administration spent	3.8	"
The Wilson administration spent (including War)	5.8	"
(Figures from Washington Bureau, Chicago Tribune)		

And at the close of the first session of the 81st Congress in October, 1949, it was announced that higher taxes would be levied at the next session!

Where the point of peril is

As remarked elsewhere in another relation, and as has been learned by the dwellers along the rivers of the country, it is the first trickle of the water over the levee that must be prevented. The Constitution is a levee to prevent power in Government from breaking into a boundless field "no longer susceptible of any definition."

It is the obligation of the schools, colleges, and universities to make the American competent to see what is coming before it strikes him down.

The Americans who founded the Republic had such education. In a speech in the House of Commons in 1775 defending them, Edmund Burke remarked on this, saying that "they *anticipate* the evil, and judge of the pressure of the grievance by the badness of the principle."

That is where latter-day education has failed the American.

V

FOLLOWING THE INCOME-TAX AMENDMENT IN 1913, THE NEXT VIOLENCE TO CONSTITUTIONAL PRINCIPLE WAS UNDERTAKEN IN 1916 BY A SOCIALIST-MINDED GROUP SEEKING TO BREAK DOWN THE TENTH AMENDMENT AND HAVE WASHINGTON ASSUME POLICE POWER IN THE STATES OVER PERSONS UNDER THE AGE OF 18 YEARS

As late as 1916, when the attempt at undermining the States by transgressing the Tenth Amendment was undertaken by a very formidable and persistent aggregation of forces, the assailants were three times hurled back in a battle which lasted twelve years. But the contest was close.

The Judiciary in defense of the Constitution

Congress passed two unconstitutional bills and the President, presumably advised by the Attorney General, signed them. Constitutional government, and the Tenth Amendment particularly, were saved by the Supreme Court.

Under the direction of the American translator of the writings of the patriarchs of Communism, Karl Marx and

Friedrich Engels, there was begun in 1916 an extraordinary attempt to break down the constitutional structure of the United States and thereby curtail the liberties of the American.

This woman pushed a bill through Congress which would forbid the moving in interstate commerce of manufactured articles into the making of which the work of persons under the age of 18 years had entered. The ostensible idea was to protect the young from oppression by ruthless employers and uncivilized fathers and mothers who were taking wages from the servitude of their children. From the strident propaganda that was organized and turned loose, a stranger just arriving on the planet would conclude that parenthood on the Earth was covetous wickedness itself.

Strategy of Communism in 1916

According to the "Woman Patriot," a paper then published in the City of Washington, the promoter of the Child Labor Law had boasted that in her legislative drives she never let appear on the front of the movement the real intent of the propagandists. That is the basic strategy of Communism. The Child Labor Act had no relation to child labor, because there was in objectionable volume no such thing. After the census of 1920 the Department of Labor made a boastful report to the effect that since the taking of the last decennial census so many laws of States had lengthened the months of school required; had set such severe conditions for a youth to qualify for work during vacation, had so completely forbidden work by minors in theatres and like places and prohibited working with dangerous machinery, that the so-called child-labor evil had been all but wiped out.

But even had the States been delinquent in the exercise of their police power to guard the health, education and welfare of childhood, that could not have conferred power on Congress to assume jurisdiction. It had no place in the field of the States. It has been shown from authorities that the States cannot abdicate their police powers and that Congress cannot take them over.

Had there been a child-labor evil—and there was none of magnitude—it was for the people at home to make their legislatures take police action.

But, as before said, the "ballyhoo" was so overwhelming and ceaseless that many good but uninformed people were taken off their feet, and they gave way to tears for the American child so victimized by his greedy and heartless parents.

No child-labor problem in 1916

There being no child-labor problem to solve, it is manifest that the undertaking was to remove the youth of the land away from the police control of the States—as the National Labor Relations Act, 19 years later, removed *all* workers—children and adults—of the country out of local jurisdiction—and transfer authority over them to the central Government at Washington. Making the central Government top-heavy would cause it in time to collapse of its own weight, and the collapse of the finest specimen of Government securing liberty and property has been the object of Communism for many years.

**Governor Roosevelt denounced
misuse of Commerce Clause**

The use of the Commerce Clause of the Constitution to bolster the act of Congress was one of those lawlessnesses which Governor Franklin D. Roosevelt of New York denounced in the strongest terms. And when he became President he broke all records in promoting this sort of legislative malpractice!

Why did men representing the people of the States in Congress vote for a bill by which the Nation would usurp power not granted to it by the Constitution, and the States would lose by abandonment powers inherent in them for the care and protection of youth?

Why did a President with an Attorney General to advise him sign such a bill? What is an Attorney General for?

Congress could not by its act gather to itself police power over "the health, morals, safety, education and general well-being of the people." Nor could the States surrender their local police sovereignty to Washington. That was decided (219 U. S. 270) in 1911 by the Supreme Court of the United States.

Of course, when an employer and a father both attacked the act as against liberty, the Supreme Court in 1918 held (247 U. S. 251) that, although it pretended to be a regulation of commerce between the States, it was in reality a seizure from the States of their police power, in violation of the Tenth Amendment, and therefore unconstitutional.

Did that stop the constitutional illiterates representing the States in the Congress in their push to degrade their commonwealths?

No.

Congress shifted from Commerce Clause to Taxing Clause

In 1919 Congress passed a Child Labor Tax Act and the President signed it, presumably with the approval of the Attorney General. By that enactment a destructive tax was placed on the product of child labor, so heavy that the manufacturer could not sell the goods in competition with other makers. The Commerce Clause having failed to support the other act, Congress resorted to the Taxing Clause.

But when a citizen affected by the legislation attacked it, the Supreme Court in 1922 held (259 U. S. 20) that as the tax imposed was intended to prevent the manufacture by youth, it would also put an end thereby to the revenue, for which reason it could not be treated as a revenue act. It was palpably another lawless attempt by Congress to take from under the police power of the States the supervision and protection of youth.[1]

Neither did that decision stop the constitutional illiterates of the States in Congress in their determination—or in the determination of the Communist-minded and unschooled sentimentalists who were lashing them—to weaken their commonwealths and enlarge the central Government.

The energy and fury behind this movement of Communism, supported by weeping women and educators, was frightening.

---

[1] This decision by Chief Justice Taft, that a pretended tax law which is not for revenue is unconstitutional and fraudulent, disposes of the preposterous proposition of President Franklin D. Roosevelt to Congress, namely, that taxes be made so heavy as to permit no income above $25,000 a year, and that all incomes be prevented from being "too high."
It also disposes of several poorly considered dicta of "progressive" judges, that taxes may be levied for regulatory and punitive purposes.

Members of Congress make third effort to degrade their States

Having failed twice in "dashing itself against the imprisoning walls of the Constitution," as Bryce described our legislative body, Congress proposed in 1924 an amendment to the Fundamental Law which would empower it to prohibit labor throughout the United States of persons under the age of 18 years.

It was immediately rejected by enough legislative bodies in the States to defeat it, but every time new legislatures were elected the promoters again urged adoption.

During the pendency of the proposal before the legislatures of the States, 20 of them repeatedly rejected it, in Massachusetts 8 times, in New York 7 times, in Texas and South Dakota 6 times, and in 3 other States 5 times.

In 23 instances attempts were made in Congress to modify the resolution so as to draw in some of its reckless implications, but they were voted down—sometimes howled down without a record vote.

When President Roosevelt took office he immediately urged legislatures to adopt it, which course was an illegal interference by the Executive with the functions of the States. It was also contrary to his declarations as Governor of New York. Some States acted as he requested; but when he telegraphed "my native State" to ratify the proposal, the legislature of New York promptly rejected it.

The rejection of the proposal by the legislatures shows that many Congressmen were as badly informed of the wishes of their constituents as they were on the Constitution.

Peril from uneducated public opinion

What insidious and unseen power could maintain for more than a dozen years that assault on the constitutional integrity of the United States? Why was there not force enough in public opinion to check Congress in its wayward course?

It may be that the defeat which Congress suffered in 1918 in the first decision of the Supreme Court respecting Child Labor was the cause of its classing in the Revenue Act of 1919 the compensation of the judges as income subject to taxation and thereby reducing their compensation, which the Constitution forbids.

The way to cure the weakness is by requiring the schools, colleges, and universities to make everyone graduating a sound constitutional scholar.

About forty of our States have laws requiring the teaching of the Constitution of the United States in public and private schools, but in not one State is our Great Charter thoroughly taught as a separate study to the youth who are to govern the land and hold the destinies of the Republic.

Could you believe this?

To show that references herein to constitutional illiteracy are not extravagant or unjust, it is mentioned that in March, 1947, a dispatch from Washington said that a member of the House of Representatives from the great State of Illinois and a member from the great State of Louisiana introduced bills making it a felony to try to bribe an athlete. There had recently been much in print about crookedness in baseball and other sports. The boy or girl leaving school before reaching High, as over 16 per cent of them do (while half of the 1,700,000 leave before the end of the second year), to govern the United States and direct its destiny, should know better than that. It is an indictment of schools, colleges, and universities that members of Congress should introduce such bills. Felonies fall within the police power of the States.

The man power of Congress has undergone change

Congress has no Sumner, no Conkling, no Cameron, no Hoar, no Ingalls, no duplicates of the many old worthies —chosen for the Senate by legislatures instead of popular vote—with experience in taking the President by the sleeve and showing him back to his place.

When the States take back their Union they should tolerate no more weak Congresses. It is discreditable to them as governmental entities and to their people entrusted with the present and the future of the Republic that there should have been Congresses deserving of the epithet of "rubber stamp."

General and thorough constitutional education only hope

They should require that every man and woman appearing to register as a voter present a card showing membership in One Great Union, a certificate from the County Superintendent of Schools that the bearer has passed a thorough examination in writing on both the History and the Constitution of the United States. The requirement of an examination in writing would disqualify, properly, the illiterates who control the great cities which drag down the States. The predicament of the State with an unclean city is likened in the memoirs of Senator Hoar of Massachusetts to the eagle in Tennyson, "caught by his talons in carrion and unable to rise and soar."

It would also repair the damage done by the delinquent States which frustrated the Australian ballot[2] and gave to the political bosses in the cities for the use of their illiterates the "straight ticket"—and too often the control of the Presidential election.

The rescue of the Union by the States and the preservation of it perpetually is that easy.

Spinsters worry about Maternity and Infancy

While the proponents of the Child Labor Acts and the proposed Child Labor Amendment drove their measures through Congress, like-minded groups "put over" in 1921 An Act for the Promotion of the Welfare and Hygiene of Maternity and Infancy, and for Other Purposes.

In a strong argument against the power of Congress to pass such a bill under the Constitution, Senator Reed of Missouri read the catalogue of the names of the women

---

[2] The Australian ballot groups the names of all the candidates for one office in one block, all the names of candidates for another office in another block, and so on. There can be no "straight ticket." If the voter is too illiterate to find the names of those for whom he would vote, that is to the advantage of the country.

Penalties are visited upon the citizens who do not vote unless they present valid excuses. The Australian Embassy said that in 1943 the vote in the Federal election was 96.3 per cent of the electors. All the States in Australia have compulsory voting laws.

In our election in 1948 only 47,500,000 persons voted, although, according to the Bureau of the Census, there were 95,000,000 eligible to vote.

Ohio adopted in 1949 a form of ballot to put an end to the "straight ticket." That looks like sunrise.

throughout the land leading the move toward centralism—and not one of them was married!

The law expired by limitation in 1929 after costing the taxpayers $11,000,000. The American Medical Association reported that not one new idea was developed by the expensive experiment. It is the only legislation of the socialistic sort from which Congress eventually backed away. A constitutional amendment may some day wipe out the others.

Had the Supreme Court accepted jurisdiction of two cases brought to test the validity of this Maternity Act, instead of questioning the right of the plaintiffs (262 U. S. 447), and had it shown for permanency, after the manner of John Marshall, the line between the power of the Nation and that of the States respecting such subjects, then A Bill to Alleviate the Hazards of Old Age, Unemployment, Illness, and Dependency, to Establish a Social Insurance Board in the Department of Labor, to Raise Revenue, and for Other Purposes, along with other kindred measures of the "New Deal," might never have been attempted.

A Judiciary without statesmanship to foresee the consequences to the Republic of a decision is not what the writers of the Constitution designed.

Where the States might have been constructively busy

While the representatives of the States in Congress were passing unconstitutional bills to deprive their commonwealths of police power over youth, maternity, and infancy, and proposing an amendment which the legislatures of the States rejected, many times by some of the States, the members of the legislatures were, seemingly, so occupied at home with building debt that they, also, were at fault regarding the constitutional position and the obligations of their States.

A notable illustration of this is in their failure to take hold of the matter of divorce, a subject of police which our "centralists" have for a long time been asking Washington to regulate. It has been before the public for a quarter of a century or more, and in January, 1950, it was discussed in a meeting of workers for improved social conditions. The Committee on Uniform State Laws of the American Bar Association, which framed bills on many subjects acceptable to all the legislatures for enactment, gave this problem up.

Of course, it is a subject for the States. Massachusetts long ago settled the question for itself, and all the other States need to do is to copy the statute of Massachusetts, which was upheld (188 U. S. 14) by the Supreme Court of the United States in 1903.

How Massachusetts laid down the law

The General Court (legislature) of Massachusetts declared that a decree of divorce granted to a citizen of that State by a court of another State would be valid in Massachusetts when the foreign court should have had jurisdiction of both parties; but that when an inhabitant of Massachusetts should go to another jurisdiction for a divorce for a cause arising in Massachusetts when both parties are domiciled there, or for a cause which would not authorize a divorce in Massachusetts, a decree in such a case would have no effect in that commonwealth.

The Supreme Court of the United States held that law not repugnant to the Full Faith and Credit Clause of the Constitution, requiring the judicial proceedings and public acts of one State to be given effect in all others. Massachusetts was not obliged to give credit to a decree to one of its citizens when obtained against its public policy.

Wherein the decree was void

An inhabitant of Massachusetts went to South Dakota and obtained a decree of divorce in a suit in which his wife did not appear. Because the court had no jurisdiction of her the decree was of no force against her in Massachusetts. The husband returned to Massachusetts and remarried. Upon his death his first wife brought proceedings to be adjudged his widowed spouse and to be entitled to administer his estate and take his property. She won.

A similar statute of North Carolina, requiring a spouse domiciled in that State and desiring a decree of divorce, to apply to a court of North Carolina, was upheld by the Supreme Court (325 U. S. 226) in 1945, respecting decrees granted in Nevada when the applicants were not in law domiciled there. The domicile is the place where a person resides and intends to stay. Marrying in Nevada immediately after receiving decrees, the two spouses returned to North Carolina. They were arrested on the charge of bigamous cohabitation, the former spouse of each being resident in the State.

Plain cure for laxity in divorces

So it would be a very simple undertaking for the legislatures of the States to copy the law of Massachusetts or that of North Carolina, both held constitutional.

That would bring down to earth the whole flock of

those "birds of passage," as one court described them, who are pictured day by day at the airports taking flight for Nevada, Florida, or Mexico to get quick releases from the first, second, third, or fourth bondage.

Neglect of this subject has been one of the most censurable delinquencies of the States.

VI

THE LONG-PURSUED PURPOSE OF CONGRESS TO CROSS THE BARRIER OF THE TENTH AMENDMENT AND ENTER THE POLICE FIELD OF THE STATES, OFTEN CHECKED BY THE COURTS AND THE PEOPLE, WAS ACCOMPLISHED BY THE PACKERS AND STOCKYARDS ACT OF 1921

IN ENACTING THE PACKERS AND STOCKYARDS ACT OF AUGUST 15, 1921, Congress did not move in obedience to powerful voting groups, as it did when it passed An Act for the Promotion of the Welfare and Hygiene of Maternity and Infancy, and for Other Purposes, and as it did in passing the bills on Child Labor.

It had no apparent reason for disregarding the Tenth Amendment and meddling in the duties of the States. There may have been complaints about the charges or services to the public of the stockyards at Chicago. If there had been dissatisfaction in that respect, the complaints should have been lodged with the commission of Illinois having authority. No default in the service of a corporation of a State could have given jurisdiction to Congress.

A belief of many dangerous to constitutionalism

While the opinion has often been expressed by persons otherwise well educated that if a State will not perform its duty, then let the Nation do it, the Constitution is not changeable that way: an amendment is necessary to a change. The idea, however, is startlingly prevalent. Multitudes believe that the National Government should take over more often than it has done.

Whatever the urge, Congress stepped into Illinois and took the control of the stockyards at Chicago away from the State. The sanction in 1922 by the Supreme Court (258 U. S. 495) of the action of Congress made the law effective as to stockyards on railroads in other States, and managing bureaus moved in.

The action by Congress was under the Commerce Clause of the Constitution, which empowers it "to regulate commerce among the several States." This clause and the General Welfare Clause are the two stand-bys for Congress when it finds the Tenth Amendment in its way.

Governor Roosevelt condemned congressional invasion of States

The Packers and Stockyards case was undoubtedly in the mind of Governor Franklin D. Roosevelt of New York when, in 1929, addressing a meeting of governors, he condemned unsparingly the "stretching" of the Commerce Clause by Congress to cover its intrusions into the States.

The stockyards at Chicago were being regulated by the State of Illinois. Livestock coming from other States was unloaded at the yards, fed and sheltered. Dealers in livestock had offices in or near the yards and made purchases there. Most of the animals received at the stockyards were taken by the large packing companies and manufactured into beef, pork, and other meats and foods. Those manufactured products were in part shipped out of Illinois to other States.

Someone in Congress or elsewhere conceived the idea that the transportation of freight was continuous, from the feeding lots where the livestock was fattened to the States in which the meats were consumed, and that therefore Illinois should have no control of such "interstate" commerce.

Stockyards Act superfluous as well as illegal

In the statement of facts preceding the opinion by Chief Justice Taft, it was said that "the act seeks to regulate the business of packers done in interstate commerce." But that could have been done without usurping the police power of the State of Illinois over a local industry. For the Sherman Anti-Trust Law had been enacted in 1891, thirty years before, to prevent or remove the conspiracies and combinations in restraint of trade and competition which were in this case charged against the packers.[1] The Chief Justice said that the Packers and Stockyards Act "forbids unfair, discriminatory and deceptive practices in such commerce"—precisely what the Sherman Law had long forbidden. Except that the Sherman Law was not an invasion of the State in disregard of the Tenth Amendment. The Packers and Stockyards Act was.

The Act made the Secretary of Agriculture a tribunal to

---

[1] The Sherman Law was supplemented in 1914 by the Clayton Act. In the same year the Federal Trade Commission Law was enacted to prevent "unfair methods in competition in interstate commerce."

In suits under the Sherman Law combinations like Standard Oil and Northern Securities were broken apart. But each of the leading parties charges the other with failure during its time in office to enforce the anti-trust laws. Senator Borah said in a speech to his colleagues that each party is enthusiastic for regulation of too-big business only in campaign time. It is a question whether the magnitude of many industrial and commercial organizations may affect people toward a belief in Socialism or Communism.

hear complaints of unfair and monopolistic practices and to make desist orders. That was unnecessary, for courts of equity had been giving such remedies under the Sherman Law.

Sherman Law had proved its complete adequacy

Indeed, as far back as 1905 a decree in a suit under the Sherman Law ordered (196 U.S. 375) the packers to desist from monopolistic practices in their trade in interstate commerce. And following the report of the Federal Trade Commission, and before the passage of the Packers and Stockyards Act, a bill was filed in a Federal Court of the District of Columbia to enjoin the Big Five packers from monopolistic practices in the purchase of livestock and the sale and distribution of meats. To a decree stopping the monopolistic practices complained of, the packers consented.

In 1912 these same packers had been indicted for monopolistic practices in violation of the Sherman Anti-Trust Law and upon trial were acquitted.

The Sherman Law also proved adequate to break up Standard Oil, Northern Securities, and many other powerful monopolies.

As has been shown, the courts had many times, under the Sherman Anti-Trust Law, made such combinations give up their controlling shares of stock and desist from the other practices complained of. There was no need for further legislation. The Interstate Commerce Commission had been, under the Commerce Clause, regulating transportation of commerce for more than a third of a century, and the Federal Trade Commission, under the Act of 1914, under the same clause, had for several years been making orders respecting fair practices in trade and commerce.

Long line of holdings submerged by Stockyards decisions

The decision in the Stockyards case was contrary to a long line of holdings by the Interstate Commerce Commission and the courts that interstate commerce begins upon the delivery of a shipment to a carrier consigned (addressed) to a point in another State, and that it ends upon delivery to the consignee. It was held, for illustration, in another case, that a shipment of property so delivered became taxable by the State where it was received. By many similar decisions the difference between interstate commerce and intrastate commerce had been clearly defined. By the definition so worked out the stockyards company in Chicago, chartered to provide for profit yardage, feed, and care for livestock, was no more engaged in interstate commerce subject to Congressional regulation than was a grocer in a nearby street receiving goods from another State. That the animals were later to go to other States in the form of foods did not make a through interstate shipment of the animals part of the way and the foods at another time the remainder of the distance.

Theory of decision of Supreme Court

The Supreme Court said that the Act treated all stockyards "as great national public utilities." But to call companies operating local yards for feeding and otherwise caring for livestock consigned to them and for facilitating local transactions between sellers and buyers, "great national public utilities," could not change the facts or confer jurisdiction on Congress to regulate their business to the ousting of the constitutional jurisdiction of the States.

However, the Supreme Court held (258 U. S. 495) otherwise, Justice McReynolds dissenting and Justice Day not sitting.

This decision is to be used later to support the extravagancies of the National Labor Relations Act as being, not what its title calls it, but a law regulating commerce among the States in accordance with the Commerce Clause of the Constitution!

Fond hope of Madison dashed

Madison fondly believed that the States would rise unanimously against any aggression by the National Government upon their local authority (*The Federalist*, No. 46):

"But ambitious encroachments of the Federal Government on the authority of the State governments would not excite the opposition of a single State or of a few States only. They would be signals of general alarm. Every government would espouse the common cause. A correspondence would be opened. Plans of resistance would be concerted. One spirit would animate and conduct the whole."

Those revolutionary worthies could not conceive of the pusillanimity of a century and a half thereafter! The representatives of the people of the States in Government have originated most of the invasions of the States.

VII

THE RECONSTRUCTION FINANCE CORPORATION WAS CREATED BY CONGRESS WITHOUT AUTHORITY GRANTED TO IT BY THE CONSTITUTION, AND ITS OPERATIONS HAVE BEEN BEYOND THE SPHERE OF GOVERNMENT

Following the packers and stockyards act of 1921, the next important venture of Congress was in creating (June 22, 1932) the Reconstruction Finance Corporation, after the panic of 1929.

It was fashioned after the War Finance Corporation of the Wilson administration. But the War Finance Corporation had been founded on the principle laid down in 1819 (4 Wheaton, 316) by Chief Justice Marshall with regard to a banking corporation. That is, to meet its own necessities —collecting taxes, transmitting money, issuing bonds—the United States can create a corporation. Maryland, which was taxing the issues of the United States Bank, contended that as neither *bank* nor *corporation* is mentioned in the Constitution, it was beyond the power of Congress to set up either.

Bank Act under Sweeping Clause sustained

The last clause in the grants of power to Congress authorizes it to make all laws which shall be "necessary and proper for carrying into execution the foregoing powers, and all other powers vested" in any department or officer of the Government. Under that language the Court held that it was for Congress to determine whether it needed the assistance of a bank in performing its governmental functions.

So it was for Congress during World War I to determine whether a War Finance Corporation was "necessary and proper" to the war effort under the war powers.[1]

Operations of Corporation not governmental

But the Reconstruction Finance Corporation does not in any sense come within the requirements stated. It was unconstitutionally created and it has pursued an unconstitutional course.

The first and most important activities of the Corporation were in reconstructing the financial status of banks, railroads, and other corporations threatened with collapse. Loans of the money of the taxpayers to banks, railroads and other big concerns ran into the billions. But thousands of individuals and businesses of small class had to suffer unaided the consequences of the panic. Whether that distinction or discrimination was warranted by a consideration of the relative importance to national stability of the

[1] The argument of counsel for Maryland against the constitutionality of the act creating the Bank of the United States was very learned. The question was discussed pro and con by able men long after the decision. In Jackson's administration a recharter was refused and the validity of the decision by Marshall rejected, Senator Benton of Missouri leading the opposition. In the light of the history of banking by the National Government, with its failures, with its inflations and deflations, and with its operating as the machine for manufacturing debt, one is justified in lamenting that it did not from the first do its fiscal business with bankers, restricting its activity in the field of finance closely to its granted power, "to coin money and regulate the value thereof."

applicants for loans is not known. It probably was, for money enough did not exist to "bail out" all that thus became involved in the catastrophe, for which the practices of many banks were much blamable.

A dispatch from Washington in April, 1949, said that the Committee on Organization of the Executive Branch of the Government, headed by ex-President Hoover, had asked Congress "to put the Government out of the money-lending business and eliminate 30 Federal agencies engaged in lending, including the Reconstruction Finance Corporation." Some months later another dispatch said that the proposal had been attacked by the Corporation as an "excursion into the controversial field of political economy." Of course, no bureau will "consent to death."

Reconstruction Finance Corporation departed from purpose

After the Corporation had enabled many forms of big money to recover their financial balance, it went out through the wide world scattering the savings of the people. Loans were made in South American countries and others for the construction of highways, railroads, and public utilities.

Under the National Defense Clause it lies in the judgment of Congress, the General Manager of the United States, as to whether the preservation of small nations friendly to us and favoring the governmental philosophy for which we stand, warrants the expenditure of American money for the protection of them from subjugation by Communism, the openly avowed and aggressive enemy of capitalism.

But the use of money for the uplift of lowly countries,

and for the other purposes mentioned, is without constitutional authority.

From time to time it was reported that a bank or a railroad or some other borrower had paid its loan, but there were many that never settled. In the report of the Corporation for 1948, the 17th year of operation, it is shown that $85,000,000 was held to meet "estimated losses in collection." If that estimate was calculated on the record of previous years, then its losses of the money of the taxpayers have been colossal.

The spender going stronger than ever

The United States News of October 7, 1949, reported from Washington that, instead of going out of action, as the Hoover Committee believed it should do, the Corporation disclosed that "its loans to business have reached an all-time high, and applications still are being received in increasing number." It reported, on October 21, loans to business—not to aid Government in its functioning—as $416,000,000 to 5,400 borrowers, with 1,200 new applications a month.

"The trend is sharply upward," says the report, because the commercial banks are becoming "choosey." That is, they are backing out of the field which they should have fought from the beginning to hold, and leaving it to the unconstitutional occupancy of Government.

The Associated Press reported on November 9, 1949, that Senator Fulbright of Arkansas, chairman of a subcommittee of the Senate on Banking, investigating policies of the Reconstruction Finance Corporation, said in a conference with the applicant for a loan of $44,000,000 that such a transaction would not be "in accord with RFC objectives." To newsmen after the conference he said that he did not think it "proper to hand out public money to private industry." He named three companies which had borrowed of the Reconstruction Finance Corporation and "now are being run by the Government."

That is what the corporation of Fascism is for—to take over private business.

Another press report said that the applicant had already borrowed from the Corporation $197,000,000.

In May, 1950, the Associated Press reported from Houston, Texas, that Jesse Jones, who had for many years managed the Reconstruction Finance Corporation, said in his newspaper:

"If you have any old loans that you would like to get rid of, you may sell them to the RFC—that is, if they are big enough and not sound enough."

And in the next month a corporation to which RFC had loaned $37,500,000 defaulted, was put in receivership by a Federal court in Columbus, Ohio, and at the receiver's sale the RFC made a bid of $6,000,000 more of the money of the taxpayers to get control of the assets of the borrower.

At the same time a committee of the Senate was looking into the loan record of the RFC, basing its action on reports of lendings "to new ventures speculative in character." It is for banks, not government, to lend money. Every youth coming out of school, and every graduate from the assembly lines of the universities, must be made to comprehend that the grant of power to Congress by the Constitution "to lay and collect taxes . . . to pay the Debts and provide for the common Defence and general Welfare of the United States" does not authorize (1) the creation of a corporation or (2) the lending of the money of the taxpayer.

Government out of bounds will not return

Thus, when Government has once fixed its foot in the door, it does not withdraw. That is a fact to cause grief in the mind of the constitutionalist. But greater grief comes from beholding the complete lack of understanding in the man of business of what is being done to him and to his country! The Government at Washington, having multiplied by bureaus the number of its feet until it is a centipede, now has a foot in the door of many commercial and industrial concerns; of agriculture, of banking, of building, of housing, of relief, of the schools, and of many other interests not within its constitutional field.

Will their ignorance entitle men of business to pardon for having contributed to the wreck of the Republic?

The 80th Congress, after lopping off some of the activities of the Reconstruction Finance Corporation, continued it "to aid in financing agriculture, commerce, and industry" —which are not of any constitutional concern of the National Government.

How one Bank grew to thousands

It has been a long progress—or descent—from that first bank for the needs of Government to all sorts of commercial banks in competition with citizens in the banking fields—to 7,000 National Banks, to the Farm Loan Banks, the Home Loan Banks, the twelve Federal Reserve Banks, the Export-Import Bank, the World Bank, and others.

From what has been shown, it is clear that the Reconstruction Finance Corporation has not been engaged in helping to carry "into execution the foregoing powers" of the Government, as the bank was held to be doing in the case decided by Marshall.

As statesmen and scholars and citizens long ago ceased to question whether any act of Government is "in pursuance" of the Constitution, the validity of the Act of 1932 creating this Corporation never was tested.

Irrigation by money of the taxpayers

In 1946 Federal aid was poured out in a flood to States and individuals; 50 million for milk and luncheons to schools; over 10 million for vocational rehabilitation; 57 million for soil conservation (the cover of aid to agriculture); 20 million for cooperative agricultural extension; over 10 million for general public health; over 9 million to control venereal diseases; and 5 million to control tuberculosis.

Those subjects are under the police power of the States, no part of which they yielded to the National Government, as they gave over coinage, treaty making, and some other nonlocal subjects by section 10 of Article I. As elsewhere shown by authority, the police power cannot be abdicated by the States nor usurped by the Nation. In the instances just before given, the course taken by Washington was usurpation and therefore unconstitutional.

Following the Reconstruction Finance Corporation came the Tennessee Valley Authority, the first step in "the electrification of America," a string of loan banks and credit corporations, and many other corporations having not the remotest relation to the constitutional functioning of the Government of the United States.

How invalid legislation infects the courts

"For the purposes of this case," said Justice Stone, writing the decision of the Supreme Court (306 U. S. 466) on a question whether the salaries of employees of the Home Owners Loan Corporation were taxable by the State of New York, "we may *assume* [italics inserted] that the creation of the Home Owners Loan Corporation was a constitutional exercise of the powers of the Federal Government." A text writer has already taken that decision as settling the proposition that all those corporations were constitutionally set up!

In creating the Home Owners Loan Corporation, Congress declared that it "shall be an instrumentality of the United States." But it could not be made so by a declaration if its functions were not to be governmental, as the functions of the banking corporation were in the case arising in Maryland. Congress gets power, not from its own declarations, but from the Constitution only. Nor can its proclamation of an "emergency," like that in the National Labor Relations Act, endow it with power not specified in the Constitution.

This brief account of the origin and works of the Reconstruction Finance Corporation shows the great danger of any break in the levee of the Constitution. The flood will go beyond control. The damage to taxpayers and the Republic by that Corporation is beyond estimate.

VIII

WITHOUT A GRANT OF CAPACITY IN THE CONSTITUTION TO CREATE A CORPORATION, CONGRESS INCORPORATED IN MAY, 1933, THE TENNESSEE VALLEY AUTHORITY, WHICH MANUFACTURES, ON THE MONEY OF THE TAXPAYERS, ELECTRIC POWER FOR SALE IN COMPETITION WITH PRIVATE CAPITAL

It might be argued that, under the coefficient or Sweeping Clause of the Constitution, quoted in the preceding chapter, as applied by the Supreme Court respecting a banking corporation for the needs of the Government, Congress could create a corporation deemed "necessary and proper" to aid its lawful activity in the control of floods of an interstate river and the promotion of navigation thereon.

But it certainly has no authority to create a corporation for the manufacture and sale of electric power in competition with private industry.

Making electric power not for
United States Government

That was conceded by counsel for the United States before the Supreme Court in the case to be examined, and was pointed out by Chief Justice Hughes.

A HISTORY OF LAWLESS GOVERNMENT 111

However, the Tennessee Valley Authority is manufacturing and selling electric power in large volume, and many persons and newspapers passing as among the thinking classes are charmed with the results.

Of course, the schools, colleges, and universities left those classes without understanding of what is more important than any valley made lovely with other people's money, namely, that "departure from the lines there laid down," as President Cleveland said of the Constitution, "is failure."

People easily misled by easy getting

Thus, what seems to some a great success in the development of a valley may be in reality a failure in government, tending to destroy free enterprise, property rights, and the liberty which the Constitution was designed to protect and promote.

There has been great rejoicing in the Northwest also and among Socialists throughout the country over the construction by the Government of the Bonneville and the Grand Coulee dams in the Columbia River, about 400 miles apart. But the question raised regarding the achievements in the Tennessee Valley presents itself as to those projects: can "departure from the lines" laid down in the Constitution be compensated for by all such developments imaginable?

As valleys from the Atlantic to the Pacific, and the wide plains between, have been developed without breach of the Constitution, why should disregard of the limitations which it prescribes be advocated and practiced now? In the development of the United States, unprecedented in the activities of men, prosperity in each valley and each region has been achieved by the brains, labor, and money of the dwellers. The residents of no area have thought of asking the people of the rest of the country to provide the money for bringing development to their locality!

Development of valleys not function of Government

Neither did the people of the Tennessee Valley ask for this project. The idea originated in the minds of Socialists, Fascists, and political adventurers far away. The idea was not so much to develop this particular valley, industrially, as it was to "grab off" this promising location as a means of demonstrating in the United States the beauty and utility of an alien belief at variance with our constitutional system. And, as before said, many who should know better think the demonstration has been a charmer.

It is the money of the people in all the States that paid for and is continuing to support "the wonderful works" in Tennessee. The doings are unfair as well as unconstitutional.

The propagandizing activity of the Tennessee Valley Authority in carrying the beauties of this Socialism and Fascism to the public has been so persistent (and expensive) as to draw criticism in Congress. It has had its effect on many.

Did General Eisenhower speak of power projects of T.V.A.?

It may be that those unconstitutional power projects were in the mind of General Dwight D. Eisenhower when, as President of Columbia University, he spoke on February 10, 1949, to a group of students about "a creeping paralysis of thought" which leads to dictatorship. Addressing 130 leaders of students in preparatory and high schools, the General, who had opportunity to learn all about the way things go in Washington, said:

"There is a kind of dictatorship which can come about through a creeping paralysis of thought, readiness to accept paternalistic measures of Government, and along with those paternalistic measures coming a surrender of our own responsibilities and, therefore, a surrender of our own thought over our own lives and our own right to exercise our vote indicating the policies of our country."

Revelations respecting extraordinary growth of bureaus

General Eisenhower may have had in mind too the report of the Committee on Organization of the Executive Branch of the Government, headed by former President Hoover, that "billions—not millions—but billions" could be saved by reshaping and reducing the 1,800 bureaus running at large and employing 2,200,000 civilian workers, increased from 580,000 twenty years ago. The pay of those employees increased from $1,000,000,000 to $6,500,000,000 a year. They, with the voting members of their families, can control the election of the President.

On May 13, 1933, Congress created the Tennessee Valley Authority as a body corporate "for the purpose of maintaining and operating the properties now owned by the United States in the vicinity of Muscle Shoals, Alabama, in the interest of national defense and for agricultural and industrial development, and to improve navigation in the Tennessee River and to control the destructive flood waters in the Tennessee River and Mississippi River Basins."

Agricultural and industrial development by Congress not authorized

What clause of the Constitution authorizes Congress to concern itself with "agricultural and industrial development"? None. That part of the Act is lawless.

By implication, the Commerce Clause empowers Congress "to improve navigation" of waters carrying interstate commerce and to control "destructive floods" in such streams.

But it receives from the Constitution no authority respecting "agricultural and industrial development." Then, why were those words employed by the nonelected persons who drafted the Act? Were they ignorant of the Constitution, or contemptuous of it?

"The properties now owned by the United States in the vicinity of Muscle Shoals" referred to the Wilson Dam, which was begun in 1917 and completed in 1926 under authority of the National Defense Act of June 31, 1916, which empowered the President to have investigation made as to "the best, cheapest and most available means for the production of nitrates and other products for munitions of war." That provided also for the designation of exclusive sites upon navigable or nonnavigable rivers or the public lands for carrying out the purposes of the Act; and it authorized the President "to construct, maintain, and operate" on any such sites "dams, locks, improvements to navigation, power houses and other plants and equipment . . . for the generation of electrical or other power and for the production of nitrates or other products needed for munitions of war *and useful in the manufacture of fertilizers and other useful products.*" (The foregoing italics are inserted.)

The National Defense Act of 1916 was passed in expectation of the war which we declared on Germany ten months later.

But why did the draftsmen of that act bring in with "munitions" of war "the manufacture of fertilizers and other useful products"?

Fascist corporation planned before election of 1932

That the Act creating the Tennessee Valley Authority, which is long enough to fill ten columns of a newspaper, and which is of almost infinite and very difficult detail, could have been put through Congress two months after inauguration, means that it had been worked out long before the election of November, 1932. It had been kept in the dark from the writers of the platform and it never was revealed from the stump to the people. Alien-minded persons outside Government had probably prepared the Fascist creature for the incoming group.

In 1946 the Tennessee Valley Authority, besides producing electric power, was engaged in the manufacture of agricultural implements, of fertilizer for agriculture, and of the instruments of sanitation. It was engaged in mineral development, in providing means of recreation, in the care and promotion of wild life, in demonstrations, in farm management assistance, and in many other activities. On these, it lost for the year the money of the taxpayers to the amount of $3,600,000.

Heavy losses to taxpayers maintaining T.V.A.

Its losses on the manufacture of power and all other activities amount to $8,041,000 for the year 1946. From its beginning in 1934 it has cost the taxpayers almost $100,000,000. These figures are from an analysis of the financial statements of the corporation by the Edison Electric Institute—a trade association representing about 75 per cent of the private electric light and power industry.

An analysis of the records of Tennessee Valley Authority for the United States Chamber of Commerce was made by C. J. Green, formerly accountant for the Federal Power Commission, and given to the Press in October, 1948. He found that from May, 1933, to June, 1946, funds of the Treasury—of the taxpayers—invested in all Tennessee Valley Authority activities totaled $742,386,524. From that he subtracted $74,525,261 in Treasury investments not connected with river power, and added $44,394,436 for power investments "omitted" by Tennessee Valley Authority in its accounting system, arriving at a net power investment of public funds of $712,255,699.

T.V.A. has advantages over private investors

He found that if Tennessee Valley Authority had paid taxes on the basis on which private power companies paid, it would have returned to governments $155,237,363 for their support.

Had Tennessee Valley Authority been obliged to pay interest on the funds which the Treasury provided from the pockets of the taxpayers, the money would have cost it $78,309,109.

How can private investors in electric power companies compete with a set-up like that?

And yet many commentators and propagandists have severely condemned the "selfish" and "anti-social" spirit of private investors who have complained of and offered opposition to such competition from the corporations of Fascism! Thus, we have almost reached in our Republic the equivalent of lese majesty. It may be with us tomorrow.

Congress apparently tiring of no returns

The Appropriations Committee of the House of Representatives has proposed that the Tennessee Valley Authority be required to repay within forty years the funds of the Treasury establishing and enlarging it.

But how can that be done unless the Authority has income? And how can it derive income from dams and reservoirs merely controlling floods?

"Flood control" is the disguise in which the Fascists wrapped themselves when they "put across" within two months after inauguration in 1933 a complicated bill of more than 10,000 words which must have been in preparation long before the election in November. The constitutional enemy from Europe was waiting to come in.

President Roosevelt's argumentation for Fascism

When the Government's entry into this business was under discussion, President Roosevelt argued that it was necessary to provide a "yardstick" for the prices which the manufacturers of electricity should charge the public, the contention being that those prices were then out of all reason.

Still, if that were true—and it was not, for the States had power to prescribe and regulate rates and were doing so —that was none of the business of the United States.

As private power companies pay Federal, State, and local taxes, it was determined that the Authority (probably to appear "fair") should not be entirely tax free, so it and its distributors contributed as a donative about 4.5 per cent of their combined gross power income to State and local treasuries. The Georgia Power, a competitor, contributed 5.5 per cent of its gross intake to State and local taxes.

Private investors support government

But the Authority paid (1946) no Federal taxes, while the Georgia Power paid 17.5 per cent of its gross to the United States. To Federal, State, and local taxation combined, the private owner thus paid 23 per cent of its gross income, while the Authority paid 4.5 per cent of the gross of itself and its distributors.

That is a mathematical demonstration of the purpose of the Government of the United States to drive private power companies out of business and become to that extent a corporative state of Fascism. In a dissenting opinion in the case arising out of this Tennessee Valley activity on the part of the native aliens in Washington, Justice McReynolds showed from the record that the purpose was to drive private investors out.

Competition by government destructive to private investors

And in March, 1947, a press dispatch from Boston said that the President of the Puget Sound Power and Light Company recommended the sale of the properties of the company "to public power agencies, the Grand Coulee Dam, the Bonneville Dam, and others, as the only way to protect the stockholders' interest." In a speech at a meeting of stockholders he "charged unfair competition from government-owned utilities" which "makes it impossible for public and private power distributors to operate side by side." A power company of the Government would, he said, "escape about $2,600,000 annually in Federal taxes and 1 million in State and local taxes paid by this company." He said, further, that "Government-subsidized competition has cut rates and earnings to the point where the company cannot expect to attract private investment capital."

All that sort of advantage to the monopoly of Government was shown of record in the case of the Tennessee Valley Authority, which case (297 U. S. 288) arose out of the attempt of the common stockholders of a private power company to sell part of its property to the Tennessee Valley Authority in order to save themselves from a competition which they knew would finish them. The preferred stockholders resisted, and lost in the Supreme Court.

The President's "yardstick" becomes a bludgeon

The Federal power companies are using as a bludgeon the "yardstick" of which President Roosevelt talked so much as a means of doing "justice." The Tenth Amendment forbids the United States to interfere thus in the field of local law. And, precedent to that, the Constitution forbids—by not authorizing—Congress to create a corporation for manufacturing and selling electric power, or doing any other business.

In the dissenting opinion in the case now to be examined, Justice McReynolds stated the purpose of the Socialists and Fascists who had "put over" the Tennessee Valley Authority:

"Public service corporations were to be brought to terms or put out of business."

It is manifest from the foregoing figures that they could not compete with a corporation which pays comparatively no taxes, and which operates on taxpayers' money, for which it pays no interest yearly. The Annual Report of the Secretary of the Treasury for 1945 shows that the United States (taxpayers) pays that interest for the money which it furnishes to the Authority.

When competing private power companies borrow money, they must pay interest at current rates, as they pay full taxes.

T.V.A. for power, not flood control

The analysis by the Edison Electric Institute of the reports of the Tennessee Valley Authority for 1946 shows these expenses for production:

for Electric Power	$6,198,023
for Navigation	2,309,548
for Flood Control	2,020,740

Those figures show that this corporation was created chiefly to manufacture and sell electric power. The pretense that it was primarily to control floods and develop navigation in an interstate river was pretense only.

On January 4, 1934, the Tennessee Valley Authority entered into an agreement with the Alabama Power Company for the purchase at more than $1,000,000 of some of its transmission lines and substations, for the purchase of some of its real estate, for the sale to the Power Company of "surplus power" of the Authority, and for (what used to be reprehensible) the division of territory between them.

Stockholders resisted entry of T.V.A.

Holders of preferred stock in the Alabama Power Company, believing the contract to be injurious to the company and also invalid, because beyond the power of the Federal Government, brought suit to have the performance of the contract enjoined, and thus save their property.

The United States District Court which heard the case granted an injunction on the ground that Congress had no constitutional power to engage in a permanent utility system.

The Circuit Court of Appeals reversed that decision. On appeal by the stockholders to the Supreme Court of the United States the latter decision was affirmed (297 U. S. 288) on February 17, 1936, Justice McReynolds writing a vigorous dissent.

Very pertinent to the holding of the trial court that the action of Congress was unconstitutional is this language of the opinion of the Supreme Court, written by Chief Justice Hughes:

"And the Government rightly conceded at the bar, in substance, that it was without constitutional authority to acquire or dispose of such energy except as it comes into being in the operation of works constructed in the exercise of some power delegated to the United States."

Case against T.V.A. perfectly clear

That is, it could not, independently of flood control or improvement of navigation in the interstate river, use the dam and the machinery connected with it for the sole purpose of manufacturing electric power for sale. In the control of floods and in improving navigation, the machinery might generate more power than was needed for the purposes stated. It would be unreasonable to let that go to waste. It could be legally sold, as the general purpose of the operations was not to manufacture power for commercial sale.

But the act of 1916, the beginning of the Wilson Dam, contemplated not only the manufacture of nitrates for war, a constitutional activity, but also the production of things "useful in the manufacture of fertilizers and other useful products," an unconstitutional activity. And the act of 1933, creating the Authority to take over the Wilson Dam, said that it was for "national defense," a constitutional activity, and also "for agricultural and industrial development," an unconstitutional activity.

The Supreme Court viewed the case through a narrow

slit and treated it as though it stood alone, whereas the record, as exhibited by Justice McReynolds, quoting from the pronouncements of the promoters, showed "no less a goal than the electrification of America." Since then the "goal" has been considerably attained.

In a dissenting opinion Justice McReynolds said that on the record the Court should have considered the truth of petitioner's charge that, while pretending to act within its powers to improve navigation, the United States, through corporate agencies, was really seeking to accomplish what it had no right to undertake—"the business of developing, distributing and selling electric power."

Justice McReynolds saw through the fraud

Justice McReynolds said, "Public service corporations were to be brought to terms or put out of business."

The Justice quoted from the report of the Authority for 1934:

" 'When we carry this program into every town and city and village, and every farm throughout the country, we will have written the greatest chapter in the economic, industrial, and social development of America.' "

That made plain how little were flood control and navigation involved in the adventure. Of course, that development was not the business of the United States, any more than the development of the country in the past has been.

On the findings of fact made by the trial court, which Justice McReynolds said were not controverted, he called the act of the Government "a deliberate step into a forbidden field, taken with definite purpose to continue the trespass."

President Roosevelt later confirmed view of Justice McReynolds

Precisely what Justice McReynolds stated of the purpose to continue a trespass in a forbidden field was admitted by President Roosevelt in a Press conference on November 14, 1944, shortly after he had been elected for the fourth time. This came in the dispatches from Washington (italics inserted):

"Of his seven water shed developments, Mr. Roosevelt said that the areas would center about a basic stream for each district. *Water control would be a minor phase of activity compared to power development."*

The need for secrecy and deception having passed, seemingly, the President let the cat out of the bag.

But there had been no cat in a bag except to the majority of the justices of the Supreme Court.[1]

And on May 11, 1948, the House of Representatives of the 80th Congress killed by a vote of 192 to 152 a bill of the bureau for the construction of a *steam* power plant in the Tennessee Valley to cost ultimately 84 million dollars.

---

[1] An advertisement by the Electric Light and Power Companies in United States News and World Report of March 3, 1950, shows a map of the United States in which are stuck 209 pins with white heads and 491 with black heads, over 44 of the 48 States. The white heads show where electric power plants are now operated or financed by the Federal Government, and the black pins mark the places where electric plants are under construction with taxpayers' money. The map presents a frightening picture. It goes to prove what Justice McReynolds said the record in this case established, that the Fascists had "no less a goal than the electrification of America." The United States is becoming Socialistic at top speed.

Flood control and navigation superseded by steam

Those facts go even further than President Roosevelt did when he admitted that the whole scheme was from the beginning for the manufacture of power by Fascist corporations aided by the money of the taxpayers. Of course, a steam plant manufacturing electric power is absolutely unrelated to flood control and the promotion of interstate navigation.

And the Supreme Court, notwithstanding what Justice McReynolds disclosed from the record, permitted itself to be taken in by the fraudulent pretenses of the promoters of Fascism!

In addition to that stupendous nongovernmental project, which has cost the taxpayers heavily every year—$41,839,062 in 1939, for instance—there are the Grand Coulee Dam Project of August 30, 1935, the Bonneville Project of August 20, 1937, on the Columbia River; the Fort Peck Project of May 18, 1938, on the Missouri River, and numerous other projects covering the map—all illegal power projects.

We were suffering from what General Eisenhower called "creeping paralysis" when those projects were pushed through!

Flood control fraudulent pretense of Fascism

The Federal Power Act of August 26, 1935, for the acquisition of power sites, plainly evidenced a comprehensive purpose of Government to manufacture and sell electric power, through Fascist corporations and with the money of the taxpayers, in competition with private investors and manufacturers and in violation of the Constitution.

The record raising the question whether the Government of the United States was bent on controlling floods in navigable rivers and promoting navigation in them, or whether it was in reality on an adventure in Socialism should have given pause to the Supreme Court.

Question should not have been decided by the Supreme Court

The question was for the Ultimate Court. It was for the Constituent Assembly, the people acting in their capacity as constitution makers, to say whether that business, stopped by the sound injunctive order of the United States District Court, should go further. It was the right of the people, passing on a proposal to amend the Constitution, to say whether they wanted their Government in the business of manufacturing and selling electric power, or in any other business. The departure from the law respecting the carrying on of business since the time of Magna Carta, 721 years before, was so radical that it was the duty of the Judiciary to stop it, as the trial court did, until the question could be carried to the people for decision.

That is what the court of Chief Justice Fuller did in 1895 with an income-tax law in disregard of a limitation stated in the Constitution. It told the proponents of the income-tax idea to take it to the people, as the Court would not try to rewrite the Fundamental Law.

A HISTORY OF LAWLESS GOVERNMENT

In later case Chief Justice stated principle correctly

And in a concurring opinion holding (298 U. S. 238) the Bituminous Coal Act of 1935 in conflict with the Constitution, this was said by Chief Justice Hughes:

"If the people desire to give Congress the power to regulate industries within the State, and the relation of employers and employees in those industries, they are at liberty to declare their will in the appropriate manner; but it is not for the Court to amend the Constitution by judicial decision."

It is lamentable that that principle was not applied by the Supreme Court respecting the Tennessee Valley Authority. For the time must come when the people will refuse to submit to taxation for money to be used in such ways. And it is fully as important that the tremendous and malign influences of such bureaus in the Government as propagandists be brought to an end.

With such forces pouring out "information" to the public all the time in torrents, it is, of course, impossible for the public to be *rightly* informed.

T.V.A. persistent danger to public opinion

The Tennessee Valley Authority has been a powerful and dangerous propagandist. The United States Government Printing Office put out "Progress in the Valley: T V A, 1947"—an 82-page book printed on heavy paper, with 7 costly pictures of the wonders accomplished for man, woman, and child in the Valley, and for invention, manufacture, and recreation.

On page 74 the book says that the average rate paid by "large industrial consumers" during the past year was 0.64 cents per kilowatt hour, in comparison with "0.93 paid by industrial consumers throughout the United States."

First, why should "large industrial consumers" be cared for by the American taxpayers?

Promptly upon the turning of machinery by the Tennessee Valley Authority, the Aluminum Company of America and the Monsanto Chemical Company, two of the largest manufacturers in the country, went down from the North and began business in the Valley under long-time contracts for cheap power at the cost of the taxpayers! They recognized a golden "yardstick" when it appeared.[2]

---

[2] A dispatch from Washington on April 5, 1949, showed that "big business" has taken over heavily the benefits of the cheap power provided by the taxpayers. In the Tennessee Valley are the Aluminum Company of America, the Monsanto Chemical Company, the Reynolds Metals Company, the Electro Metallurgical Company, the Victor Chemical Company, the Tennessee Copper Company, and the Reynolds Alloys, taking over 28 per cent of the total output.

In the Northwest the power generated at the Bonneville and Grand Coulee dams on the Columbia River by the taxpayers was taken by the Aluminum Company of America, the Pernamente Metals Corporation, the Reynolds Company, the Electro Metallurgical Co., the Pacific Carbide Company, and the Pennsylvania Salt Manufacturing Company, among others.

The "yardstick" which the President was so desirous of providing to show what rates to the consumer should be charged was evidently of the highest satisfaction to large corporations. Now the complaint at Washington is that the consumers in the homes and other small users are threatened with a shortage unless Congress will authorize the construction of steam plants—thus casting off altogether the cloak of navigation and flood control which Congress wore when it entered on this stage!

Mathematics proves private capital cannot meet taxpayers' money

Second, it is manifest that a rate by Government of 0.64 must drive out of business companies charging 0.93. Justice McReynolds found that to be the grand purpose.

On page 79 the book reveals that through the fiscal year 1945 the Authority purchased "facilities totaling $125,000,000." Those acquisitions brought in "some 345,000 consumers, or about half of those now served."

If that is not swallowing competitors alive, what expression would describe it?

The Supreme Court held that as the Constitution provides (Art. IV, Sec. 3) that "the Congress shall have power to dispose of . . . the territory or other property belonging to the United States," it could convert the water of the River into power and sell it as it disposes of coal or other minerals in the lands which it owns. But it does not own the water in the river. Besides, it sells from the public lands the coal or other mineral in its natural state. It does not, in competition with other manufacturers, convert potential into actual power. On that, Justice McReynolds said that the ownership of an iron mine by the United States would not "permit the construction of smelting works followed by entry into the business of manufacturing and selling hardware, albeit the ore could be thus disposed of, private dealers discomfited, and artificial prices publicized."

A great prophetic lawyer foresaw these cases

This decision upholding the Act of Congress creating the Tennessee Valley Authority, and the decision sustaining the National Labor Relations Act, and the decision sanctioning the Packers and Stockyards Act, bring to mind a passage from one of the lectures fifty years ago to the law students at Yale by John F. Dillon, who had sat on the Supreme Court of Iowa and on a Federal Bench, a great figure of that day. Dealing with the barriers set in the Constitution to keep Congress in its place—to keep it out of "a boundless field of power no longer susceptible of any definition"—with the barriers to keep a vaulting Chief Executive in his place, that great constitutionalist said:

"The value, however, of these constitutional guarantees wholly depends upon whether they are fairly interpreted, and justly and with even hand fully and fearlessly enforced by the courts. . . .

"If there is any problem which can be said to be *yet unsettled*, it is whether the Bench of this country, State and Federal, is able to bear the burden of supporting under all circumstances the Fundamental Law against popular, or supposed popular, demands for enactments in conflict with it."

The Judiciary, respecting which Judge Dillon had misgivings half a century ago, has certainly not grown stronger.

Whence authority to destroy productive land?

What overpowering necessity called for the drowning of 500,000 acres of cultivated land which the Farm Bureau of Tennessee found in 1941 to be producing each year crops valued at $14,415,300? Could the furnishing of cheap electric power by the President's new "yardstick" to powerful patrons of the Tennessee Valley Authority justify the destruction of this natural value of the Earth? When the Salt River Valley had recently been reclaimed by irrigation from the desert and made immensely fertile and productive, and when other reclamation projects had been carried out and more were in prospect, by what line of reasoning could any "planner" have concluded that it was desirable to submerge forever more than half a million acres of the rich bottom lands along the Tennessee River?

But that destruction of fertile lands displaced 13,433 families, or 56,000 persons, and sent them adrift, as the war in Europe displaced persons and sent them wandering. For those in Europe we have expressed much compassion and to them we have given much help; but there has been no sorrowing over the displaced persons in the Tennessee Valley. True, those who were displaced in that Valley were paid for their lands, so far as money can compensate for the loss of homes sanctified by long living and clustered with the memories of generations.

Irreplaceable loss of production from land

Yet, even if the compensation had been sufficient to cover every element of value entering into the worth of a long-established home, there still remained, and will forever remain, unpaid for, the yearly production of $14,415,300 of foodstuffs and other products given by the land and needed and consumed by the American people. And even if the displaced persons found employment in the electric power plants which the Government set up without authority from the Constitution, who on earth had authority to determine that it was better for those persons to exchange the independence and security of life on their lands for the uncertainty of subsistence from a pay roll which is liable to be suspended at any time without any explanation to them?

Fascism thrust upon Tennessee Valley

As previously indicated, the people of the Tennessee Valley did not ask for the submergence of their lands.

Those adventures by means of Fascist corporations are probably the worst aggressions by Congress and the President upon the liberty and the property rights of the Americans.

All who have become enthusiastic over the "success" of the Tennessee Valley Authority, and of the other projects of Government for manufacturing electric power for the commercial market by using the money of the taxpayers without asking their permission, should think again and carefully consider the warning given centuries ago by Authority, namely, that men may gain the whole world and still be heavy losers.

IX

IN MAY, 1933, CONGRESS, BY THE AGRICULTURAL ADJUSTMENT ACT, UNLAWFULLY PERMITTED THE PRESIDENT TO REDUCE THE GOLD CONTENT OF THE STANDARD DOLLAR

IT WAS WELL SETTLED LAW (293 U. S. 388) THAT THE power conferred on Congress by the Constitution cannot be delegated to another Department. That principle of the law of Agency was found by Bryce to be the best conception of the Constitutional Convention.

Yet the Legislative Department authorized the President, by a Senate amendment to the House Agricultural Adjustment bill, to reduce the content of the gold dollar, but not below 50 per cent. In 1936 the Agricultural Adjustment Act was held (297 U. S. 1) unconstitutional for taking money from one class for the benefit of another. But in the meantime the President had acted on the Senate amendment and cut the gold dollar.

Among the powers conferred on Congress by the Constitution is that "to coin Money, regulate the Value thereof, and of foreign Coin." At the time the Constitution was written there was much coin of other nations in circulation in America. The Spanish silver dollar was the coin of first importance. By the language quoted, recognition was given to the fact that governments had found it necessary to change the content of their standard coins, a course which conditions might make necessary in the New World.

President given no authority over money

But all the authority given by the Constitution was conferred, as the language quoted puts beyond question, on Congress alone. Neither in Article I, creating the Legislative Department, nor in Article II, establishing the Executive Department, is there even an intimation that the President should have anything to do with regulating the value of money. That is to say, the power was withheld from him. For another elementary rule of interpretation is that what is not granted is prohibited.

With the authority to regulate the value of coin limited by the Constitution to Congress, the President was, nevertheless, directed (or, what is more probable, allowed) by Congress to perform its task of fixing the value of the dollar. It was for Congress to determine whether the content of the dollar should be changed and, if so, to change it.

Constitutional power cannot be delegated

Delegation of *administrative* powers to fact-finding bodies which are guided, not by their own will or judgment, but by the specifications and limitations in the Acts of Congress creating them, has been common. The Federal Trade Commission, the Board of Tax Appeals, and many other agencies have been set up to relieve Congress of details *not legislative*.

But "the Congress, manifestly, is not permitted to abdicate, or transfer to others, the *essential legislative functions* with which it is invested," said the Supreme Court (293 U. S. 388) in 1934. (Italics inserted.) It pointed out the settled practice that Congress, in the act of delegating administrative powers, must declare a policy, establish a standard, and lay down a rule for its agent to follow in executing the Congressional (not its own) will.

In passing to the President an "essential legislative function," not a merely administrative function, second to none conferred by the Constitution on it, Congress did not itself, so far as the Act and the Joint Resolution show, determine anything—except that the Chief Executive might use his own judgment within a very wide range.

Here began the course of unconstitutional conduct by Congress which brought upon it and its successors the epithet of "rubber stamp."

The beginning of "directives" by the President

So, on January 31, 1934, the President "directed" that the standard gold dollar be reduced from 25.8 grains to 15-5/21 (15.238) grains.

On March 9, 1933, Congress had passed the Emergency Banking Relief Bill, which authorized the Secretary of the Treasury to require all persons to deliver to the Treasurer of the United States "any and all gold coin, gold bullion, and gold certificates" owned by them, and to accept therefor "an equivalent amount of any other form of coin or currency."

Here began the practice of the President and his rubber-stamp Congress of declaring an "emergency" when it seemed desirable to seize power not granted by the Constitution.

But "emergency does not create power," wrote Chief Justice Hughes (1934) in an opinion (290 U. S. 398) sustaining a law of Minnesota (1933) which extended the time for an owner of property to redeem it after sale under foreclosure of mortgage.

Congress repudiated its contract with the people

By a Joint Resolution of June 5, 1933, Congress proclaimed that the promises of the United States in the law under which the Second, Third, and Fourth Liberty Bonds were issued "are hereby repealed" so far as they pledged any payment except "dollar for dollar in any coin or currency which at the time is legal tender." The United States had borrowed money of the people for carrying on World War I and had issued bonds therefor payable as to both principal and interest "in the United States gold coin of the present [1918] standard of value." That is, in dollars containing 25.8 grains of gold nine-tenths fine.

The vastness of the debt repudiated

Just before this legislation, in 1932, the interest-bearing debt of the Nation was $19,161,273,540.[1]

At that time the States had submerged themselves in an interest-bearing debt of $17,589,515,000.[2]

Thus, the two governments of the American had loaded him in a time of peace with a burden of $36,750,788,540.

On the National Debt he was paying a yearly interest of $599,276,631, and the debt of his States cost him yearly in interest $527,685,450.

His interest load for the two debts was $1,126,962,081 per year, or $155,399,491 more than the National Debt the year before we entered World War I.

[1] Report Secretary of Treasury, p. 405.
[2] Financial Statistics States, pp. 52, 64.

A HISTORY OF LAWLESS GOVERNMENT 137

National and State governments had agreed with those who lent to them $36,750,788,540 to pay in dollars containing 25.8 grains gold. They had likewise promised to pay in such dollars yearly in interest $1,126,962,081.

But the governments would henceforward measure their debt to those who had lent money to them in time of need by a dollar containing 15-5/21 grains of gold instead of the promised dollar of 25.8 grains. Nor, as before said, would their creditors, under the decision of the Supreme Court, to be noticed presently, get the lesser gold dollar. They would be obliged to take paper money. Neither would they, the Supreme Court held, be entitled to enough additional paper money to compensate for the difference between the dollar lent and the dollar paid back.

The "profits" to governments from repudiation

The measure of value by which debtor and creditor had contracted was cut down not quite 41 per cent. If the debts of the Nation and the States just before given were to be cut down 40 per cent the debtor governments would gain over 15.7 billion dollars; and, of course, the people from whom they borrowed would be out of pocket that much, only a little less than the National Debt amounted to in 1931 after Secretary Mellon, by wise management, had reduced it almost 9 billion from the World War I peak of 25 billion, 234 million.

In like manner, all the other debtors in the United States, those not holding bonds or other obligations of Government, would receive in the depleted dollar from their creditors a forced forgiveness of 40 per cent of their debts.

That this was the effect of the performance was admitted of record by the Secretary of the Treasury in the report for the fiscal year ending June 30, 1946, where (p. 364), under *receipts* of money, there was entered "increment resulting from devaluation of gold dollar, $2,811,-375,756." Whether that amount was allocated to 1946, or to all the years up to that time, does not appear; but the "clip" on all the bonds of the United States outstanding was $7,760,315,773.

Chief Justice Marshall on honor in government

On the action of the Government in favoring debtors— and most of all itself and the States—by clipping the dollar 40 per cent, in one of the opinions of Chief Justice Marshall this is to be found:

"It may well be doubted whether the nature of society and of Government does not prescribe some limits to the legislative power; and, if any be prescribed, where are they to be found if the property of an individual, fairly and honestly acquired, may be seized without compensation." [3]

Hamilton on inviolability of governmental contracts

Long before that, Alexander Hamilton, who was Secretary of the Treasury in the Cabinet of Washington, stated with his characteristic clarity and force the position of a contracting Government, as ours was a contracting Government when it borrowed money from the people and promised to pay in dollars containing 25.8 grains of gold:

"When a government enters into a contract with an in-

---

[3] Fletcher v. Peck, 6 Cranch, 87, 135.

dividual, it deposes, as to the matter of the contract, its constitutional authority, and exchanges the character of legislator for that of a moral agent, with the same rights and obligations as an individual. Its promises may justly be considered as excepted out of its power to legislate, unless in aid of them. It is in theory impossible to reconcile the idea of a promise which obliges with a power to make a law which can vary the effect of it." [4]

Hamilton was a member of the Constitutional Convention, which "told the world" that the new Government would pay the creditors of the old.

Constitutional Convention for payment of all debts

Among the final words of the Constitution are these:
"All debts contracted and engagements entered into before the adoption of this Constitution shall be as valid against the United States under this Constitution as under the Confederation."

That provision gave the United States high standing and credit among the nations.

On the morality of government respecting its debt, Madison made this interesting observation (*The Federalist,* No. 43):

"This can only be considered a declaratory proposition; and may have been inserted, among other reasons, for the satisfaction of the foreign creditors of the United States, who cannot be strangers to the pretended doctrine that a change in the political form of civil society has the magical effect of dissolving its moral obligations."

[4] Hamilton's Works, 518.

The fine example set to the nations by the Constitutional Convention has not been accepted by them.

Once we upbraided governments of Europe for repudiating the obligations to us which they had incurred for World War I. But we can do that no longer.

Insolence attended repudiation of gold contracts

From the review which has been made of opinion on both sides of this subject, it is manifest that the Government of the United States, without adequate explanation to the people, took a step respecting their property of tremendous importance to them. The only pretense of explanation by the Government, as a Government, was in the authority given by a rider on the Agricultural Adjustment Act to the President to "fix the weight of the gold dollar . . . as he finds necessary . . . to stabilize domestic prices or to protect foreign commerce against the adverse effect of depreciated foreign currencies"; and in the Joint Resolution of Congress (June 5, 1933) declaring that "the holding or dealing in gold" had been disclosed by "the existing emergency" to "obstruct the power of Congress to regulate the value of money," for which reason "any obligation" purporting to give to the lender of money "a right to require payment in gold" was "declared to be against public policy."

But just how the cut by the President of 40 per cent from the gold dollar would stabilize domestic prices or protect foreign commerce, or how the repudiation by Congress of its promises to pay its bonded debts in gold, with the release of all other debtors from such promises, would help it "to regulate the value of money," was left without explanation beyond the bare recitals just quoted from the acts.

The opinions of some writers on finance

Some writers on finance had contended that the value of the gold in a dollar had increased in the market, and that therefore the creditor (the holder of bonds, the depositor of money, and some others) were receiving value above that intended by their contracts, for which reason a reduction of the content of the gold dollar was called for. But, as before indicated, the representatives of the Government said that the purpose was to increase the price of agricultural commodities, to stabilize American money against foreign currencies, and to make a profit for the Treasury of the United States.

While the depletion of the dollar quickly lifted the prices of wheat and other products in demand in foreign markets, it less quickly, but just as surely, increased the costs at home—of food, of clothing, of housing, of living. If the writers on finance were right, then the wearying burden of living costs carried by the American for fifteen years is in considerable part attributable to the devaluation of the gold dollar.

Supreme Court expounded repudiation

In one of the three Gold Clause Cases the Supreme Court held, on February 18, 1935, in an opinion by Chief Justice Hughes, that the Fourth Liberty Bonds of the United States, promising to pay the buyer (the lender of money to the Government) "in the United States gold coin of the present [1918] standard of value," could not be repudiated as to the *form* of payment. The bonds having been issued under the clause of section 8 of Article I of the Constitution authorizing Congress "to borrow money on the credit of the United States," and being affected by the provision of the Fourteenth Amendment that "the validity of the Public Debt of the United States authorized by law . . . shall not be questioned," those quoted expressions stating the sovereign will of the people, it was not within the power of Congress, a servant of the people with inferior authority, "to override their will thus declared," and by the joint resolution of June 5, 1933, to proclaim that the promises in the law under which the bonds were issued "are hereby repealed" so far as they pledged any payment except "dollar for dollar in any coin or currency which at the time is legal tender."[5]

Yet the bondholder won a Pyrrhic victory. He got nothing but a favorable judicial declaration that he should be paid in gold when the gold of the country had been seized and withdrawn from circulation.

The holder of Government bonds thoroughly "frisked"

Nor did he get in paper money the additional sum to equate the difference between the two gold dollars for the reason that "the plaintiff," the Court said, "has not shown, or attempted to show, that in relation to buying power he has sustained any loss whatever." Congress having withdrawn gold from circulation, it was unascertained what the new gold dollar would be worth to plaintiff in the "domestic and restricted market." He had not proved that, and as he had sued for damages for violation of contract, he failed for want of proof.

[5] Perry v. United States, 294 U. S. 330.

Dissenting Justices found the milk in the cocoanut

In the dissenting opinion in the Gold Clause Cases by Justices McReynolds, Van Devanter, Sutherland, and Butler, this was said (italics inserted):

"The Agricultural Adjustment Act of May 12, 1933, discloses *a fixed purpose to raise the nominal values of farm products*[6] *by depleting the standard dollar.* It authorized the President to reduce the gold in the standard, and further provided that all forms of currency shall be legal tender. The *result expected* to follow was *increase in nominal values* of commodities and *depreciation of contractual obligations.* The purpose of section 43, incorporated by the Senate as an amendment to the House bill, was clearly stated by the Senator who presented it. *It was the destruction of lawfully acquired rights.*"

Congress recognized damage by repudiation

That destructive result was admitted by the Government, for by an act of Congress of June 14, 1934, a credit of $25,862,750 was established on the books of the Treasury in favor of the Philippine Islands, that amount compensating for the cut in its gold-standard fund held by the banks in this country.

The fact deserves special emphasis that it was by an act of Congress taking *a course of avowed favor to agricul-*

---

[6] Where did Congress get authority "to raise the nominal value of farm products"?

This is one more support of the statement frequently made herein, namely, that those in places in Government have generally ceased to ask or raise the question: Does the Constitution warrant this action? Or, does the Constitution forbid it?

ture, as the dissenting justices stated in the foregoing quotation, that the President was empowered to reduce the gold content of the dollar. In the act the purpose of stabilizing "domestic prices or to protect foreign commerce against the adverse effect of depreciated foreign currencies" is recited. It is not clear why a dollar supported by the resources and productive power of this country could not stand up against foreign money. No explanation was vouchsafed by the prestidigitators of finance who drafted and put through the bill.

A senator clearly explained the trick

But this from the senator who incorporated section 43 as an amendment to the House bill, referred to in the foregoing quotation from the dissenting justices, is to a high degree lucid (italics inserted):

"The amendment has for its purpose the bringing down or *cheapening of the dollar,* that being necessary in order *to raise agricultural and commodity prices.* . . . The first part of the amendment has to do with conditions precedent to action being taken later.

"It will be my task to show that if the amendment shall prevail it has possibilities as follows: it may *transfer from one class to another* class in these United States *value to the extent of* almost *$200,000,000,000.* This volume will be transferred, first *from those who own the bank deposits.* Secondly, this value will be transferred from *those who own bonds and fixed investments."* [7]

There is nothing in that about cutting the value of the dollar over 40 per cent to protect it against "depreciated

---

[7] Congressional Record, April, 1933, pp. 2004, 2216-7, 2219.

foreign currencies," which Congress gave as one of its reasons, without saying how that would help against what.

Secretary of Treasury not concerned about foreign moneys

Justice McReynolds quoted from a radio address of the Secretary of the Treasury to the American people on August 28, 1934, the following unctuousness:

"But we have another cash drawer in the Treasury, in addition to the drawer which carries our working balance. This second drawer I will call the 'gold' drawer. In it is the very large sum of $2,800,000,000, representing 'profit' resulting from the change in the gold content of the dollar. Practically all of this 'profit' the Treasury holds in the form of gold and silver. The rest is in other assets.

"I do not propose here to subtract this $2,800,000,000 from the net increase of $4,400,000,000 in the National Debt, thereby reducing the figure to $1,600,000,000. And the reason why I do not subtract it is this: for the present this $2,800,000,000 is under lock and key. Most of it, by authority of Congress, is segregated in the so-called stabilization fund, and for the present we propose to keep it there. But I call your attention to the fact that ultimately we expect this 'profit' to flow back into the stream of our other revenues and thereby reduce the National Debt."

Usefulness of gold clause in American life stated

The dissenting justices pointed out that the gold clause in any agreement, employed by Americans for more than 100 years, "secures protection, one against decrease in the value of the currency, the other against an increase." Such clauses, they said, "have rendered possible our great undertakings—public works, railroads, buildings. . . . Furthermore," the dissenters wrote, "they furnish means for computing the sum payable in currency if gold should become unobtainable." Then the borrower pays "for each dollar loaned the currency value of that number of grains." He would thereby get, what was denied by the Supreme Court, enough additional currency to make up the difference between the value of the money lent by him and that paid back.

The whole case, as seen by the dissenting justices, was stated as follows:

"The fundamental problem now presented is whether recent statutes passed by Congress in respect of money and credits were designed to attain a legitimate end. Or whether, under the guise of pursuing a monetary policy, Congress has really inaugurated a plan primarily designed to destroy private obligations, repudiate National debts, and drive into the Treasury all gold within the country in exchange for inconvertible promises to pay, of much less value."

The President did not guard against foreign currencies

It was reported in the dispatches on March 15, 1941, that President Roosevelt told his conferees of the Press, whom he used as boosters of his exploits, that "the Treasury's $2,000,000,000 stabilization fund had made a profit of $22,000,000," which, he said, was "not such a bad record for what he called facetiously a bunch of rank amateurs in finance." The stabilization fund was established in 1934, the dispatch said, "from profits obtained from the devaluation of the dollar." It was the opinion of the President that he had given "a pretty good illustration of the fact that the American Government was not wholly amateurish in the financial part it plays in the country."

What the Government accomplished proceeded, not from its financial ability, but from an illegal and ruthless exertion of power.

Did predatory wealth or economic royalty ever "put over" anything comparable to that? Did either, even in its dreams, ever see such easy money picked from the gullible?

On "just compensation" for private property taken

Were Congress to authorize the Secretary of the Treasury to order all of the farmers in the country to drive in their herds and accept the pay offered by the Government, "just compensation" would be given for them under the command of Article V of the Bill of Rights. On whether gold could thus be called in and appropriated by the Government without paying grain for grain, the dissenting justices said:

"Congress has power to coin money, but this cannot be exercised without the possession of metal. Can Congress authorize appropriation without compensation of the necessary gold? Congress has power to regulate commerce, to establish post roads, etc. Some approved plan may involve the use or destruction of A's land or a private way. May Congress authorize the appropriation or destruction of these things without adequate payment? Of course not. The limitations prescribed by the Constitution restrict the exercise of all power."

On the point in the opinion of the majority of the Court, that as the holders of the bonds were forbidden to possess gold, it would do them no good to get payment in coin which they would be obliged to surrender immediately, and that consequently they were without damage, the dissenting justices said:

"Congress brought about the condition in respect of gold which existed when the obligation matured. Having made payment in this metal impossible, the Government cannot defend by saying that if the obligation had been met the creditor could not have retained the gold; consequently he suffered no damage because of the non-delivery.

Had an individual done such a thing

"Obligations cannot be legally avoided by prohibiting the creditor from receiving the thing promised. . . .

"If an individual should undertake to annul or lessen his obligation by secreting or manipulating his assets with the intent to place them beyond the reach of creditors, the attempt would be denounced as fraudulent."

The dissenting opinion concluded:

"Under the challenged statute it is said the United States have realized profits amounting to $2,800,000,000. But this assumes that gain may be generated by legislative fiat. To such counterfeit profits there would be no limit; with each new debasement of the dollar they would expand. Two billions might be ballooned indefinitely—to twenty, thirty, or what you will.

"Loss of reputation for honorable dealing will bring us unending humiliation; the impending legal and moral chaos is appalling."

X

FIVE MONTHS AFTER THE INCORPORATION OF TENNESSEE VALLEY AUTHORITY, IN 1933, TWO MEMBERS OF THE CABINET OF THE PRESIDENT, AND THE HEAD OF THE FEDERAL RELIEF ADMINISTRATION PROCURED A CHARTER IN DELAWARE FOR THE FEDERAL SURPLUS COMMODITIES CORPORATION, CAPITALIZED BY THE MONEY OF THE TAXPAYERS

THE NEXT EXCURSION OF GOVERNMENT BEYOND ITS CONstitutional domain was in October, 1933, after the Tennessee Valley Authority had been incorporated, and its aims were as general as human affairs.

Secretary of Agriculture Henry A. Wallace, Secretary of the Interior Harold L. Ickes, and Harry Hopkins, Head of the Federal Relief Administration, took out a charter under the ultraliberal law of Delaware for the Federal Surplus Commodities Corporation. The corporation, the charter recited, would have "perpetual existence."

Up to that time the "undesirable citizens," the persons of "predatory wealth," the "economic royalists," and others who became incorporators never thought of asking for their creatures more than half a century of life or, at most, 99 years. And if they organized under the laws of Dela-

A HISTORY OF LAWLESS GOVERNMENT 151

ware, they were, in the eyes of many, immediately suspect. But here the anointed in Government went to Delaware and took out a charter to last forever, until "the wreck of matter and the crush of worlds."

The tip-top corporation of Fascism

In part, the purposes of the charter were as follows (italics added):

1. "To relieve the existing economic emergency by the expansion of markets."
2. To "purchase, store, handle and process surplus agricultural *and other* commodities."
3. To perform "all functions" that may be "*delegated to it under acts of Congress.*"

(By not authorizing Congress to delegate any functions to any person or group, the Constitution thereby forbids delegation. Yet delegation was done.)

4. "To accept grants . . . of monies, commodities, lands or other property of any class, nature or description."
5. To "carry on any or all of its operations and business *without restriction* or *limit.*"
6. To "hold, own, mortgage, sell, convey" property of "every class."
7. To borrow money on the commodities in its possession.
8. "To encourage the farmers to co-operate in any plan which calls for the *reduction of acreage.*"
9. To engage in warehousing and exporting.

To incur debt in every conceivable way

10. "To borrow money," issue bonds and "all other kinds of obligations . . . without limit."

11. "To loan money, to buy, discount, sell or rediscount or otherwise deal in notes" and every sort of paper.

12. "To take and hold . . . by bequest, devise, gift, purchase, lease or otherwise" anything.

13. "To guarantee" or otherwise deal in shares of "any other corporation."

And so on for six more paragraphs of specifications and powers.

No engineers of high finance ever piled a pyramid of corporations with powers to match those in scope or absoluteness.

And, of course, none of those activities is any constitutional business of the United States.[1]

Some of the Fascist activities exhibited

Yet the corporation has been acting with devilish diligence. It has had a part of several grain crops deteriorating in storage, and it has released wheat—the prime food of man—to feed the pigs.

In July, 1944, the Associated Press reported the War Food Administration as saying that it had purchased

[1] In October, 1949, the Fairbanks Daily News-Miner published the secret draft of a charter for a Fascist company to be named The Alaska Development Corporation, which was in the main a copy of the Delaware charter of The Federal Commodities Surplus Corporation. The copy was taken to Alaska by an assistant secretary of the Interior and shown confidentially to a few persons, probably for consultative purposes.

The document went "all out" for everything—construction of electric power systems; loans of money of the taxpayers for any purpose; construction of railroads; operation of ships, docks, and all the equipment of the sea; aid to agriculture and to culture—nothing in the way of uplift is to be without provision. And, of course, the capital of the corporation (like that of the Commodities Corporation) will be taken by the United States out of the pockets of its taxpayers.

The plan for "the electrification of America" and the superseding of the Constitution by the Fascist corporations of Socialism is being driven with a vigor which the believers in the Republic lack.

10,500 carloads of eggs "for *price support* between January 1 and July 15."

No clause of the Constitution authorizes the support of prices by the Government of the United States for the benefit of farmers at the expense of the taxpayers. That point was passed upon by the Supreme Court when it held violative of constitutional limitations the original Agricultural Adjustment Act as an attempt to gather money for one class by taxing another.

In August, 1944, the dispatches told of the purchase in the Northwest by the War Food Administration of eggs at $9 a case of 30 dozen each, which it was obliged to sell at 20¢ to 50¢ a case. It dumped 14 railroad carloads of spoiled eggs. It was offering 14 more carloads to the trade. It had sold 26 carloads, about 16,000 cases, for hog feed at 5¢ a case. As stated above, the Government had paid $9 a case for them.

A consignment of 6 carloads was held in Chicago for orders from Washington to destroy them, until freight charges had accumulated to $4,200. But it was the money of the taxpayers!

The egg in its relation to great Government

The Associated Press reported in 1944 that a deputy director of War Food Administration testified before a committee of Congress that he "wished he knew" what could be done "with between $100,000,000 and $150,000,000 worth of eggs bought this year."

"Do you mean to say that the American taxpayers have invested between 100 and 150 million dollars in eggs we have no use for?" demanded the Chairman of the Committee.

"That's right," answered the witness.

Losses of taxpayers' money on ventures of the kind described were reported as to nearly every agricultural commodity. The Federal Surplus Commodities Corporation and its subsidiaries became possessed, by using the money of the taxpayers, of many surpluses of enormous—almost fabulous—cost, which they had to dump. The "ever-normal granary" of Henry A. Wallace, one of the incorporators of the Federal Surplus Commodities Corporation, turned out upon trial to be an instrumentality for feeding wheat to pigs. And Harry L. Hopkins, another of the incorporators, never made any apologies, probably because of the belief which he once expressed that "the people are too damned dumb to understand."

A potato famine resulting from abundance

On December 31, 1946, the Associated Press reported from Washington that "millions of bushels of frozen and rotten potatoes will be dumped under Government instructions." The Department of Agriculture had underwritten the 1946 crop up to 90 per cent of parity. The crop turned out to be 100,000,000 bushels larger than the "planners" had expected. Then prices tumbled. The Department loaned money to the growers at the guaranteed price and asked them to store the potatoes until the price should rise. It did not rise. The great loss came from those loan-stored potatoes. The dispatch carefully did not tell what price the Government guaranteed. Here is an illustration of the worst feature of centralized authority—its deceit, its adroit concealment of facts, its purposeful misleading of the public.

The loss from damp, vermin, and deterioration of wheat and other grains which the Corporation ordered held in storage for better rates, the while paying out of the pocket of the taxpayers unjustifiable prices to the farmer, was enormous, and the true extent of it will probably never be known.

One of the great "plungers" in debt

The Federal Surplus Commodities Corporation had a capitalization of $100,000,000, and all the stock was owned by the United States—which has no authority from the Constitution to own stock in any corporation. By the acts of 1938 and 1945 it was empowered to borrow up to $4,750,000,000 on obligations guaranteed by the United States, which has no authority from the Constitution to guarantee the borrowings of any corporation.

The Associated Press reported from Washington on May 23, 1949, that the total of subsidies provided for favored classes by the taxpayers without their permission for 17 years amounted to $15,571,060,000, of which $10,300,000,000 went to farmers. No clause in the Constitution authorizes Congress to appropriate money for such purposes.

Unquestionably the farmer has been put in a very serious predicament by the high costs of help on the land, and the high costs of labor going into farm implements, machinery, fertilizer, and all the other things that he has to buy. Those costs were increased out of all reason by the aid of the administration at Washington to the monopoly of organized labor, now so powerful at the polls that it holds the President captive.

Rejection of external government needed

But the cure for the grievances of the farmer, and of every other citizen weighted down by the operation of indefensibly high wages, is not the bestowal of subsidies from the taxpayers of the country, but the removal of the cause—the rejection for the future of the external government of the United States, and the exclusion of the President from the field of low politics.

And the Federal Surplus Commodities Corporation is only one of a number, the magnitude of the spending of which nobody certainly knows. At least, that is what is gathered from the reports of Senator Byrd on his efforts to find out what is doing by the spenders and wasters.

Congress, by setting up such activities in competition with man, assailed his liberty to live, unhampered and unannoyed, which it was its duty to safeguard.

No such corporation in Jackson's administration

On the proper and only place of Government in the affairs of men, President Andrew Jackson said more than a century and a decade ago:

"The duty of Government is to leave Commerce to its own capital and credit, as well as other branches of business, protecting all in their legal rights, giving exclusive privilege to none."

That cogent statement contains the American philosophy laid down in the Declaration of Independence, that Government is limited strictly to giving protection to men from men and to men from Government, and it is entirely without grant from the Constitution of any paternal authority.

A HISTORY OF LAWLESS GOVERNMENT

The idea of President Jackson and other right-thinking Americans, that Government has no place in business, is sustained by the report of the Commodity Credit Corporation for the last fiscal year. A dispatch from Washington dated September 26, 1949, and sent by the United Press, said that the fund for the support of prices of farm commodities for the year had been set at $500,000,000. That was altogether wiped out, and an additional "red" expenditure was made of $170,000,000.

The "planner" and the bagatelle

The loss of cash in price support was	$254,000,000
Inventory losses were	416,000,000
Losses on potatoes were	203,886,000
Losses on peanuts were	23,000,000
Losses on corn were	99,000,000
Losses on cotton were	36,000,000

On wheat there was written off as lost $56,000,000, of $529,000,000 invested.

Of $81,000,000 in eggs, $38,000,000 was written off.

Of $191,000,000 in linseed and other oils, $73,000,000 was written off.

The dispatch stated, without figures, that the report showed inventory losses on wool, peas, beans, barley, resin, turpentine, prunes, raisins, grains, sorghums, and tobacco.

Wires of the bureaus crossed

Under a multilateral agreement at Geneva in 1947, large imports of potatoes at half tariff rates came to the United States in 1949. That action of the Department of

State was negatived by the Department of Agriculture in buying 90 million bushels of domestic potatoes in 1948 to make prices higher—keeping them out of consumption.

In like manner, 60 million pounds of butter imported from Denmark in 1949 was checkmated through the purchase by the Department of Agriculture, for price support, of 93 million, 305 pounds of domestic butter!

A recent dispatch from Washington quoted a member of the Government as saying that its business has become so large that it is next to impossible to handle it. But if the Government would abandon nongovernmental activities and consider the Constitution before taking up something new, its work would be cut by three fourths or more.

Former Secretary Morgenthau considers the situation

Contemplating the enormous volume of foodstuffs kept back from consumers in the United States by the "planning" of the Federal Surplus Commodities Corporation and other bureaus, Henry Morgenthau Jr., former Secretary of the Treasury, wrote an article in October, 1949, advocating the outright gift of the great quantities in storage to the needy in the Far East and the Near East. He gave a "partial listing" of the stocks of goods in possession of the Federal Surplus Commodities Corporation, which, after taking over all the available storage room in the country, must now "finance the building of much new storage capacity." He wrote that "the quantities of farm products which have been bought and paid for with the taxpayers' money, and which continue to be stored in warehouses at the taxpayers' expense, are so tremendous as to be almost beyond belief."

"It costs the United States Government," he added, "$237,000 a day just for storage and carrying charges on these commodities." Those charges now aggregate, he said, $76,281,725.

A table showing unconstitutional prodigality

The following are "partial listings" by Mr. Morgenthau of commodities in storage, which will be increased, he thinks, from the harvests of 1949 and 1950:

Commodity	*Quantity*	*Value (Cost)*
Wheat	190,600,000 bu.	$451,722,000.00
Corn	75,000,000 bu.	132,000,000.00
Linseed Oil	212,889 tons	119,218,153.32
Eggs, Dried	65,558,257 lbs.	84,786,714.83
Butter	87,378,000 lbs.	55,048,140.00
Beans	4,950,000 cwt.	40,639,500.00
Barley	27,700,000 bu.	39,334,000.00
Milk, Dried	204,167,000 lbs.	26,541,710.00
Oats	13,250,000 bu.	10,997,500.00
Mexican Meat	34,691,585 lbs.	9,832,679.39
Dried Prunes and Raisins	36,036,330 lbs.	3,646,226.68
Cheese	16,250,000 lbs.	5,525,000.00
Rice	431,000 cwt.	2,439,460.00
Soybeans	580,000 bu.	1,450,000.00
Rye	850,000 bu.	1,351,500.00

The Vice President summarizes those figures

Speaking at Chicago on August 18, 1949, Vice President Barkley said that "the Democrats have done more in 17 years for the farmers than ever was done before by any party."

In his campaign speeches in 1948 President Truman

appealed directly to agriculturists to remember what had been done for them by his administration. They did.

Government of that sort must be put at end through a return by the States to the exercise of their police power and to the constitutional appointment of presidential electors.

XI

THE NATIONAL LABOR RELATIONS ACT OF 1935 WAS A VICTORY FOR CAESARISM OVER THE STATES AFTER A CONTINUOUS BATTLE FOR TWO DECADES

THE MOST COMMON DISREGARD BY CONGRESS AND THE PRESIdent of the Tenth Amendment, forbidding the Nation to usurp powers not granted to it, and especially to stay away from the governmental field of the States, has been in its persistent attempts, under the cloak of the Commerce Clause and of the General Welfare Clause, to invade the police field of the States—for the protection and care of the health, safety, morals, education, and general wellbeing of the people—and take jurisdiction of the liberties and living of men.

The Commerce Clause authorizes Congress "to regulate commerce with foreign nations, and *among* the several States"—not within the States. The General Welfare Clause is discussed in another section.

By NLRA Congress displaced a Union of States by a Nation

After half a century of notable failures and some burrowing successes, that invasion won completely through the National Labor Relations Act of 1935. By that act Congress usurped police control of all workers in the United States.

Could Hamilton have foreseen that, he would have been dumbfounded.

"I confess," he wrote in No. 17 of *The Federalist*, "I am at a loss to discover what temptation the persons intrusted with the administration of the General Government could ever feel to divest the States of the authorities of that description"—legislation "for the individual citizens of America."

Briefly, the act declared an "emergency" to exist because of the "burdening" of commerce and the "obstructing" of it by strikes arising out of labor disputes; and, to keep the "flow" of commerce—not alone interstate commerce covered by the Commerce Clause, but *all* commerce—uninterrupted, it set up a Labor Board to which disputes between workers and employers should be taken for hearing and decision. As there could be no suspension of production by any strike that would not "affect" or "obstruct" both intrastate and interstate commerce at least a little, all workers and employers were thus brought under the Commerce Clause, written respecting interstate commerce only, as its language so plainly shows.

Before that only a small part of the workers of the country were within reach of Congress by virtue of the Commerce Clause—those employed by railroad companies, telegraph and telephone companies, and aviation companies. The great body of them lived and worked subject to the police power of the States.

Representatives of the States in Congress, by passing the act, disparaged and diminished their commonwealths.

By a complete about-face Supreme Court sustained Congress

Overriding its own decisions for half a century, on the powers of Congress over interstate commerce, and reversing the judgments of four Circuit Courts of Appeals of three judges each, the Supreme Court of the United States, in an opinion by Chief Justice Hughes, Justices McReynolds, Van Devanter, Sutherland, and Butler dissenting, upheld (301 U. S. 1) on April 12, 1937, two months after the President proposed to "pack" the Court, and while the proposal was still before Congress, the National Labor Relations Act as a valid exercise of the granted power to Congress to regulate commerce "among the several States." The very title gives the lie to the strained recitations in the Act in a make-believe that it is a regulation of commerce and not a labor law. The promise was in those recitations that the operation of the Act would put an end to strikes and the disorders and losses which had attended them, which was not, of course, a subject of national jurisdiction.

Legislation had numerous precedents

The National Labor Relations Act had been preceded by many acts for the usurpation by Congress and the President of power over concerns of the States. The tyrannies spawned by the Labor Board in applying the National Labor Relations Act were a long time in coming.

When Franklin D. Roosevelt was Governor of New York, he protested in behalf of the States against the dishonest and lawless use of the Commerce Clause by Congress and the President to occupy forbidden ground in the States. Speaking on July 16, 1929, before a conference of governors at New London, Connecticut, he condemned the "stretching" of the Commerce Cluase by Congress to cover cases not embraced by grants of power to it in the Constitution (italics inserted):

**Governor Roosevelt declared against
such legislation**

"Our Nation has been a successful experiment in democratic government because the individual States have waived in only a few instances their sovereign rights. . . .

"But there is a tendency, and to my mind a grievous tendency, on the part of our National Government, to encroach, on one excuse or another, more and more upon State supremacy. The elastic theory of interstate commerce, for instance, has been stretched almost to the breaking point to cover certain regulatory powers desired by Washington. But in many cases this has been due to a *failure of the States, themselves,* by common agreement, *to pass legislation necessary* to meet certain conditions."

Importance of commerce in history

The Commerce Clause, for the strict observance of which Governor Roosevelt was rightly solicitous, contains a principle dating back as far as Magna Carta (1215), when King John, faced by armed men, signed an agreement not to interfere in the right of Englishmen to go to and fro in commerce, and abroad and return, except only in an exigency of war.

Englishmen in commerce were "in pursuit of happiness," which the Declaration of Independence later denominated a right from the Creator, for the protection of which "governments are instituted among men."

The speeches and writings of Edmund Burke in behalf of the American colonists make clear that the restrictions on commerce by the government of England were far more burdensome and intolerable than was "taxation without representation," usually given as the cause of the American Revolution. All products for sale had to go to England—in English ships. All things that they had to buy they were obliged to buy in England—for transportation in English ships. Raw material ready for manufacture had to go to England for that purpose. This interference with commerce (only one of many hard regulations) destroyed shipbuilding, which had become of great importance, put an end to manufacture, and cut off commercial communication with other countries.

Constitution designed to make commerce free

It was obstruction by States of this right to engage in commerce that contributed much to the breakdown of the government under the Articles of Confederation. And the third grant of power to Congress in the Constitution which followed (after taxing and borrowing) is "to regulate commerce . . . among the several States."

Congress is authorized to regulate commerce so that it will not be obstructed as it was before—that is, it is to *promote* commerce. It is not to obstruct it affirmatively, any more than the early States could rightly do so, by legislation like the Norris-LaGuardia Law, which cripples men in commerce in the maintenance in court of their constitutional rights—and their inherent rights. It is not to obstruct commerce negatively by failure to guard the rights of those engaged in it, as in the toleration of costly and destructive strikes.

Commerce most important activity of man

The history of commerce makes clear that legally it is the most important right of men, not to be trifled with by kings or others in power. Nevertheless, for a third of a century obstructions to commerce have been so nearly continuous as to condemn the Government at Washington for default of duty under the Commerce Clause.

Five years before the National Labor Relations Act of Congress, Governor Roosevelt condemned illicit ideas which he afterwards sanctioned as President. In a radio address in 1930 he again took up States' rights and home rule and said that with "a great number . . . of vital problems of Government, such as the conduct of *public utilities,* of banks, of *insurance companies,* of *agriculture,* of *education,* of *social welfare,* and of a dozen other important features . . . *Washington must not* be encouraged to *interfere.*" (Italics inserted.)

But Roosevelt, like Supreme Court, did turn-around

With every one of those "features," Congress, taking orders from President Roosevelt, *did* interfere, to the denial of the liberty of man to engage unhampered by his Government or by his fellows in pursuits which had never before been regarded in the United States as subjects for political meddling. Never before regarded, because no fancy had ever found in the Constitution anything even suggesting the power in Congress to engage in or control such activities.

Yet, during the first eleven years of the Act, from 1935 to 1945 inclusive, there were 37,383 work stoppages, involving 16,827,305 workers and the loss of wages for 175,896,235 man-days.

N.L.R.B. failed of purpose proclaimed

For the eleven years *before* the National Labor Relations Act, 1924 to 1934, inclusive, the work stoppages were 11,565, affecting 5,829,339 workers, about one-third of the number involved in stoppages during the 11 years following the Act.[1]

Even more deplorable than those losses to the workers was the brake put on production of food, clothing, housing, and other things required by a people in sore need, who had shown every willingness to do their part in the conduct of the war.

Many of those strikes were attended by the worst disorders, sometimes by bloodshed. Plants were seized by strikers and the owners excluded from them. Picketing was of the most violent sort.

Against those manifestations of lawlessness, which appeared in all parts of the country, the authorities of the States did nothing, or next to nothing. The United States looked on. There was generally a breakdown of law.

---

[1] For the six years from 1940 to 1945, inclusive, covering the whole time of World War II, strikes took place as follows:

In 1940 there were	2,508 strikes
1941	4,288
1942	2,968
1943	3,752
1944	4,956
1945	4,750
Total	23,222

A picture of countrywide performances

What was going on all over the country all during the war is illustrated by this official statement of the Employment Relations Board of the State of Wisconsin, issued on December 27, 1946 (italics added):

"It *can no longer be assumed,* as it was when the first order of this board was made in May of this year, that the *leadership* of the organization now *on strike intends to be law-abiding citizens.*

"Events transpiring since the entry of the order and its enforcement by a judgment of the Circuit Court of Milwaukee County clearly indicate that *the leadership of this union entertains no respect for the law,* agencies designated to administer it, *or the courts,* but *intends to prevent by any methods,* legal or illegal, *the use of the company's premises by the company,* or the pursuit of work by employees of the company desiring to work."

Previous orders of the Board had been disregarded. As the quotation shows, the strike at the plant of Allis-Chalmers had been on since May preceding. All the powers of unionism had been concentrated on Allis-Chalmers to compel it to establish the closed shop and thereby deny to Americans the liberty to work under conditions of their own choosing.

Was the conduct described in Wisconsin treasonable?

The Constitution defines one of only two acts of "treason against the United States" as "adhering to their enemies, giving them aid and comfort."

Were not the unceasing strikes which were waged in essential industries from one end of the war to the other of great "aid and comfort" to Germany and Japan?

What did the Department of Justice of the United States do to protect the Government in its war endeavor and the American in his liberty?

Nothing.

Not until the head of the United Mine Workers notified the Secretary of the Interior, who was operating the coal mines under one of the many illegal seizures of property, without compensation, committed by Government during the war, that it would terminate its working agreement at midnight, November 20, 1946, did the United States show mettle befitting such an occasion. This time it had been put on the spot.

Government of great Republic driven to corner

The United States could not say that the duty to act was on the States, or use any other of the evasions which it had employed as encouragement to strikes against private industries. So it had its Department of Justice bring a suit on November 18 for injunction in the United States Court in the District of Columbia, which immediately issued an order restraining the head of the union and the miners from carrying out the notice. Nevertheless, a gradual walkout of miners began on November 18, and by November 20 "a full-blown strike was in progress," the Supreme Court said in sustaining the action of the trial judge in fining for contempt the head of the union $10,000 and the miners as a body $3,500,000. It authorized the reduction of the fine imposed on the miners to $700,000 on condition that they permanently obey the order of the court.

Simple case pointed way to managing labor disputes

That shows how nicely those disputes could be handled if Congress and the States (which have really fostered labor troubles) would remit them to the courts, where all other people having disputes are obliged to go. Congress does not interfere in controversies between individuals, or between corporations, or between corporations and individuals, or between States, or between associations of men. Why should it interfere in disputes between employee and employer?

The questions in dispute are justiciable (for the Judiciary) where negotiation or arbitration fails and the next step is the strike, with suspension of production for the needs of the people and the country, and disorder, sabotage, and personal peril. At that point society must assert its paramount interest, as it did in the instance just described, and require the adjudication of the dispute in its courts.

Labor decisions show courts afford remedy

Since the decision of the Supreme Court of the United States in 1923 holding (262 U. S. 522) invalid a statute of Kansas setting up an Industrial Court to hear and decide controversies between employee and employer, including differences over wages, the interest of the public in the continuity of service has become more and more recognized. The National Labor Relations Act of July, 1935, brought all of the employees of the country within the Commerce Clause of the Constitution under the pretense that it was necessary to prevent strikes from interrupting the free flow of commerce to the discomfiture and damage of the people. And in 1934 the Supreme Court sustained (291 U. S. 502) a law of New York setting up a Milk Control Board to fix maximum and minimum prices for milk, thus taking away the right of the parties to contract. The welfare of the public and the interest of the Nation have been so grossly disregarded during the last two decades that views on "the liberty of contract," and on "the right to strike" and plunge society into confusion and distress, have undergone change. The act of the legislature of Kansas setting up the Industrial Court would probably be sustained today.[2]

Labor controversy has ceased to be personal to parties

When, for illustration, employment was on a small scale, the law was that an employee assumed the risk of injury by the carelessness of a fellow worker and he was therefore not entitled to damages from the employer. But as employment became stupendous, laws making the employer liable (as an operating cost) for injuries to a worker, whether there was negligence or not, were upheld by the courts as valid exercise of the police power of the States

---

[2] Long after that part of the text was written, the Supreme Court of the United States, in an opinion rendered on January 3, 1949, sustaining a law of North Carolina and a constitutional provision of Nebraska forbidding employers to enter into contracts obligating themselves to exclude persons from employment because they are or are not members of labor unions, examined the case of the Industrial Court of Kansas and said that hours and wages can be fixed by law in the public interest. That fulfills the prophecy of the text.

in the interest of society. So the controversy between employee and employer is no longer a matter exclusively personal to them.

Congress should get out of labor politics, in which it has too long performed a discreditable as well as an unconstitutional part.

Government now conducted with respect to elections

The capers that have been cut at Washington during the last three decades make one wonder whether sight has been entirely lost of the purpose of Government as laid down in the Declaration of Independence, namely, to secure man against his fellows, and more especially against those whom he has chosen for his servants in public office. The activities of administrations have been plainly to favor, in view of the next election, great voting blocs like the labor organizations, the people on the farms (who, subsidized for years, turned the Presidential election in 1948), and the political bosses who "deliver" the votes of many corrupt cities. The platforms of both parties have offered shamelessly to "give every thing to every body" in those classes.

Meanwhile, the people, who set up Government "to secure these rights" which came to them from the Creator, "among which are life, liberty and the pursuit of happiness," are stripped of their possessions with a system of ruthlessness rarely exampled in the history of tyranny.

Although the Criminal Code of the United States provides that a fine of $100 and imprisonment for six months, or both, shall be imposed upon anyone who shall "knowingly and wilfully obstruct the passage of the mail," and although the opening of mail is severely punished, the Executive Department of the Government took no action respecting the obstructing and opening in 1937 of mail addressed to Americans engaged in their work and surrounded by pickets trying unlawfully to deny to them this liberty.

The nonaction by the Chief Executive, who is enjoined by the Constitution to "take care that the laws be faithfully executed," looked to the beholder like sanction of the illegalities.

Washington friendly to the sit-down strike

While the Government at Washington assumed to legislate by the National Labor Relations Act respecting all labor, regardless of whether it might be engaged in interstate commerce (of which only it has jurisdiction), a spokesman for the White House let it be known that sit-down strikes in various parts of the country, by which owners were forcibly dispossessed of their property by their employees, were matters of concern, not to the Nation, but to the States! As before indicated, the debilitated States generally concurred in such strikes.

The Secretary of Labor was reported by the Press to question at first whether the seizure and detention of plants by sit-down workers was illegal!

While employees of a steel manufactory at Canton, Ohio, were working under siege by an army of pickets, airplanes dropped leaflets to discourage the workers, saying, "Our members are well fed and happy. Relief is being arranged for their families. Four departments of the United States Government are fighting for our side."

On March 23, 1947, the Associated Press reported from

Milwaukee that "the Allis-Chalmers strike, one of the most bloody and turbulent in recent history, ended today when the striking UAW-CIO Local 248 voted to return to work without a contract."

That shows that the workers themselves had tired of the long misleading by their officers.

Communism in strikes in United States

As the chief principle of the tactics of Communism is to provoke disorder and profit by it, the foregoing record, made mostly while the Republic was in the perils of war, compels the question whether Communist influences guided that disgrace to "government under law."

Earl Browder, for years head of the Communist Party in the United States, and twice a candidate for the Presidency of this Nation, reported to the Congress of the International Communist Party in Moscow on July 18, 1935:

"How was our party able to penetrate the masses and emerge from isolation? A great role was played by leaders in the strike movement and in the work of the party among the unemployed. In some of the most important strikes, the San Francisco general strike for one, the Communist Party had a decisive, determining influence."

And the great Government of the United States was not only unable to deport the alien who fomented and led that strike, but it also came around to issuing citizenship papers to him!

In *What Is Communism?* it is made clear (p. 163) by Browder, a native of the United States, that the plan of Communism is to take away liberty and property by armed force:

"The Revolution is carried out by the great masses of the

A HISTORY OF LAWLESS GOVERNMENT 175

toilers. The Communist Party, as the vanguard of the most conscious toilers, acts as their organizer and guide."

And again (pp. 164, 165):

"In the revolutionary situation the Communist Party . . . wins some of the armed forces to its side, and leads the effective majority of the population to the seizure of State power. . . . Above all, they need the armed forces."

An attempt to destroy an industry

Although not so wide in its reach to people as the National Labor Relations Act of 1935, the law of Congress of 1886, forty-nine years before (amended and extended in 1902), taxing oleomargarine ¼¢ a pound, and 10¢ a pound when colored, was fully as bad an invasion of the police field of the States. Agriculturists, a voting power, put the bills through Congress in protection of dairy butter. In addition to the destructive tax on the colored article (while colored butter was not taxed), the heavy license tax on manufacturers, on wholesalers, and on retailers, and the regulations regarding packing, labeling, and permits were obstructive and costly. The manufacturers abandoned coloring and left that to the consumers. Notwithstanding the handicap, oleomargarine grew steadily in favor. It was used in the navies of the world, including our own.

Those laws, attacked as intended to destroy an industry, as an encroachment upon the police field, and as working a deprivation of property without due process of law, were sustained (195 U. S. 27) in 1904 by the Supreme Court of the United States in an opinion by Justice White, with dissent by Chief Justice Fuller and Justices Brown and Peckham.

In 1888 the Supreme Court had upheld (127 U. S. 678)

a law of Pennsylvania (1885) which forbade the making and selling of anything to be used as butter, or in lieu of it, out of any substance "other than unadulterated milk or cream." Justice Field dissented from the opinion written by Justice Harlan chiefly on the ground that the Court had lost the distinction between regulation and prohibition. To be sure, a State may *regulate* the manufacture of foods so as to secure purity and prevent fraud. But Pennsylvania had no more right or power to suppress the manufacture of oleomargarine, made and sold without deception, than it had to prevent the making of marmalade. Wide as the police power is, it must be exerted with regard for rationality, liberty, and the right to property.

Of the case arising in Pennsylvania, Judge Dillon, once on the Federal Bench, wrote in *Municipal Corporations* and also in *Law and Jurisprudence in England and America* this sound and complete comment:

"The record of the conviction of Powell for selling without any deception a healthful and nutritious article of food makes one's blood tingle."

If the police power of Pennsylvania could not extend that far, how could Congress, without any police power at all, get a seat in the game of politics?

In March, 1950, a discreditable record of 64 years was ended by Congress when it repealed the legislation by a vote of 202 to 106 in the House and 59 to 20 in the Senate.

The unbelievable guilelessness of the American

In all worlds of fabulists and fictionists no state of things is exhibited which is at once so preposterous and so potentially calamitous as that there should be tolerated a party against freedom and possessions in a land where the Constitution twice guarantees security to Liberty, Property, and Life!

Why have Senators and Representatives, who have been sent by the people of the States through the years to represent them in the Congress of the Union of States, failed to maintain their States in their constitutional position in that Union? They have made the State a kind of satrapy of the central power.

What Congressmen and Governors have done to sovereign States

The degraded position to which the States have descended in the estimation of our Government was shown by a meeting in 1944 in St. Louis of the governors of 26 States, who deplored the fact that for 11 years not a Governor had been called to the White House for consultation.[3]

When President Truman took office in 1945, the Republican members of Congress proceeded to the White House

[3] The bill of particulars drawn by the governors proposed the resumption by the States of their constitutional functions. It condemned the acquisition by the United States of the lands of the States, the usurpation by Washington of unemployment insurance and unemployment services, the derogatory "conditions" fixed by the Federal Government to grants in aid of States for public works, the attempt of the Administration "to undermine and abandon our traditional National Guard," the entry of the United States into competition with insurance companies, the plans to control from the National Capital the field of medicine, the development of water resources without any recognition of the superior rights of the States, and some other acts of total indifference to the existence of local governments, as leaving for ten years "entire regions of our country" without "representation in the Cabinet or administrative agencies of the Federal Government." The crowning insolence was the failure of the President to invite any governor to the White House for an exchange of views.

Of course, the things complained of were brought about by the incompetence or delinquency of members of Congress from the States.

to tell him that they would help him in all ways consistent with their political beliefs. On leaving the White House, the Republican leader in the Senate said to newsmen that he had not been on the premises since the party in power took office in 1933.

Well, the governors complaining at St. Louis were not heard in protest when the representatives of their States in Congress were originating or supporting bills for weakening their commonwealths and widening the authority of the National Government. And as for the treatment of members of Congress by the White House, they had let go of their constitutional reins.

At the 42nd annual convention of the governors of the States, at White Sulphur Springs, West Virginia, on June 19, 1950, there was a quite general expression of the view that "Federal aid" should be relied upon by the States to carry their projects of flood control, reclamation, irrigation, electric power, and the like.

The presiding governor sought to prevent "stump speeches on the obligation Washington has in the development of the West." But the governor of California thought it "perfectly logical to ask the Federal Government for help in irrigation, reclamation, and power projects: we repay every cent and pay interest on Federal moneys going into such projects."

No one rose to inform him that the Constitution gives no authority to Congress to lend money at interest or otherwise for any purpose. Nor was he reminded that banks, and others having the right to lend, provided the necessary money for all great projects in the building of the United States from the beginning down.

The governor of New Jersey protested the proposal for

Federal aid. He could not understand how any governor could "go on record for a balanced Federal budget and at the same time have his hand out for millions for reclamation, irrigation, and public power." He said that "New Jersey would have nothing to do with Washington, that it can and does finance its own projects, and at cheaper interest rates than the Federal Government can borrow money."

It is somewhat reassuring that one governor out of 48 had been sufficiently educated to declare for constitutional procedure.

The meeting of governors revealed the great need, not so much for "Federal aid," as for a school for giving constitutional instruction to the executives of the States. Such a school might accept members of Congress. Something *must* be done toward teaching those in office.

In the days of the horse and buggy

In the autobiography of Senator Hoar it is said that if any group went to the White House and brought back directions on policy, they would be made to regret it. For sixteen years or more the White House has been permitted by Congress to usurp direction of policy.

The States must back-track to where the writers of the Constitution set them—or where they set themselves, for they made the Constitution.

And the schools must so teach the Constitution that governors of States will know better than to resign their great offices to take inferior seats in Congress.

And the President must be elected by the constitutional method.

When the States have exercised the power which they

reserved to themselves by section 2 of Article I, to prescribe the qualifications of voters for members of Congress as well as for candidates for local offices, by making a certificate of graduation in the study of the principles of our constitutional system a condition of registering for voting, then we shall have a better situation in Congress and out.

And in the days ahead

And when the States have abolished the straight ticket by restoring or putting into effect the Australian ballot, which was emasculated for the aid of the illiterate followers of political leaders or bosses, then American elections will express the competence of the people for self-government.

And when the States have brought back the constitutional election of the President and put him in his place to stay, and thereby removed the need for Corrupt Practices Acts of Congress, our country will then be again "the land of the free."

The States, which intended when they wrote the Constitution to manage the country largely, should return to that duty.

XII

BY THE SOCIAL SECURITY ACT OF AUGUST, 1935, FOLLOWING THE NATIONAL LABOR RELATIONS ACT OF JUNE, THE REPRESENTATIVES OF THE PEOPLE IN CONGRESS STRIPPED THEIR STATES ALMOST ENTIRELY OF POLICE AUTHORITY

It is difficult to tell which of the half score of Socialistic acts of Congress of the Roosevelt Revolution was the most far-reaching in its threat to the Republic. But the competition for evil lies between the Fascist Tennessee Valley Authority of May 18, 1933, and the Social Security Act of August 14, 1935.

When President Roosevelt signed A Bill to Alleviate the Hazards of Old Age, Unemployment, Illness, and Dependency, to Establish a Social Insurance Board in the Department of Labor, to Raise Revenue, and for Other Purposes, he made this comment:

"If the Senate and House of Representatives in this long and arduous session had done nothing more than pass this bill, the session would be regarded as historic for all time."

Most complete abandonment of constitutional principle

It will certainly stand apart forever as a complete departure from the Constitution as expounded by its writers, notably Madison, afterward President, and James Wilson, later a Justice of the Supreme Court of the United States; by President Monroe in a celebrated veto message of a bill for "public improvements," the beginning of the most wasteful of all squanderings by Congress of the money of the taxpayers; by President Jackson, who vetoed every appropriation bill not clearly for *national,* as distinguished from *personal,* welfare; by Presidents Tyler, Polk, Pierce, Grant, Arthur, and Cleveland.

The "hazards of old age, unemployment, illness and dependency" are subjects (if of any government) for the police power of the States, which has been defined as having to do with "the health, morals, safety, education, and general well-being of the people."

"The Federal Constitution forms a happy combination in this respect," wrote Madison in No. 10 of *The Federalist;* "the great and aggregate interests being referred to the National, the local and particular to the State legislatures."

No police power was granted by the people through the Constitution to Congress.

And "Congress is not empowered," wrote Chief Justice Marshall in 1824 (9 Wheaton 1), "to tax for those purposes which are in the exclusive province of the States." [1]

States cannot abdicate their police power

It was held by the Supreme Court (219 U. S. 270,282) as late as January, 1911, that the police power inhering in the States cannot be surrendered by them.

---

[1] While the Social Security Act gathers money from the employer and the employee, it provides that money so collected shall go into the funds of the United States and that bonds shall be issued against it. Of course, it is the taxpayers who must eventually redeem such bonds.

There is no stronger principle of American constitutional law than that forbidding the delegation of power. For a decade and a half the Newspaper has told us of powers granted by Congress to the President. It has no powers that it can grant or give away. The reports by the Newspaper were constitutionally nonsensical. Yet they affected the public mind, untaught in the Constitution, to accept as valid the abdication—not the delegation or grant—of powers by what came to be known as "a rubber-stamp Congress."

Abdication of constitutional duties by Congress

Congress permitted the President and his nonelected advisers to write bills, as George III sent bills to Parliament against the American Colonies, and Congress passed them. But that was abdication of power by Congress, not delegation or grant.

So, too, the States cannot part with their powers or any portion of them. Their power of police, especially, over the welfare of the people they cannot surrender, as the decision of the Supreme Court just before cited shows. Therefore, the rush of the States, like children in the street to whom a handful of coins has been thrown, to enact compliant legislation in order to get "gifts" of their own money from Washington under A Bill to Alleviate the Hazards of Old Age, Unemployment, Illness, and Dependency, to Establish a Social Insurance Board in the Department of Labor, to Raise Revenue, and for Other Purposes, was an unconstitutional abdication by the States of their obligations to the people. The liberties of the people were grossly transgressed.

On the police power resident in the States, Judge Cooley,

recognized half a century ago as the leading constitutionalist of his time, had this to say in volume 2 of the 8th edition of *Constitutional Limitations,* page 1232:

"In the American constitutional system the power to establish the ordinary regulations of police has been left to the individual States, and it cannot be taken from them, either wholly or in part, and exercised under legislation by Congress."

States and Congress join in unconstitutional action

Yet that is exactly what was brought to pass by a usurping Congress and abdicating States when the scheme for social security through Washington was set up.

On the same page Judge Cooley said further:

"Neither can the National Government, through any of its Departments, or offices, assume any supervision of the police regulations of the States."

When, in September, 1787, the Constitutional Convention sent the new Fundamental Law to the States for ratification, only one of them was opposed to it from the start—or before the start. New York convoked a convention headed by Governor Clinton which was three fourths against the proposed form of government. Some able men in other States were not wholly satisfied with the Constitution. The objections which they expressed in the ratifying conventions resulted in a Bill of Rights in addition to the limitations on power amounting to a Bill of Rights written in the original Instrument. Several delegates to the Constitutional Convention went home without signing the new form of Government. Alexander Hamilton was the only signer for New York.

A HISTORY OF LAWLESS GOVERNMENT

Elbridge Gerry of Massachusetts, one of the ablest men in the Convention, did not sign. Edmund Randolph of Virginia and George Mason of Virginia, the author of The Virginia Bill of Rights, did not sign. Nor did William Houstoun of Georgia.

Most important of original objections to Constitution

The commonest and strongest objection was that the identity and sovereignty of the States were not sufficiently guarded. It was this objection that brought out the Tenth Amendment, to prevent Congress from invading the States.

In the convention in New York the point here under discussion was most strongly urged, namely, that the General Welfare Clause gave to Congress powers without limit. The States would eventually be swallowed by the central Government, which properly could deal only with subjects strictly national and international.

Yet the Housing Act of 1937 declared the policy of Congress to be to provide for the general welfare of the Nation by employing its funds and credit to assist the States to relieve unemployment and to safeguard health, and for other like purposes. In 1945 the Supreme Court, in an opinion by Justice Roberts (none dissenting), held (323 U. S. 329) that legislation constitutional!

Thus the objection which chiefly evoked the Bill of Rights, and especially the Tenth Amendment, went for naught.

And in 1941 the Court, in an opinion by Chief Justice Stone (none dissenting), held (312 U. S. 100) that under the Fair Labor Standards Act of Congress of 1938 the Nation can exercise police power in the States! That overruled a great decision (247 U. S. 251), rendered in 1918, that Congress is prevented by the Tenth Amendment from regulating labor conditions in the States.

The first and most important grant of power

The very first grant of power is this:

"Congress shall have power to lay and collect Taxes, Duties, Imposts and Excises to pay the Debts and provide for the common Defence and general Welfare of the United States."

In the convention in New York it was argued that the power to tax and spend for "the general Welfare of the United States" was a grant without limitation at all. That was answered by James Madison, the reporter of the Constitutional Convention, from whose notes day by day we get most of our knowledge of the course of deliberations. In the history of governments and in general fitness for his task he was second to no other man in the Convention.

Madison, along with Hamilton and Jay, was writing a series of 85 papers explanatory of the Constitution and addressed "to the people of the State of New York" to convince them that their objecting convention should ratify the new form of government. Those papers became known as *The Federalist,* the most brilliant work on our Constitution. They have been translated into French, German, Spanish, and Portuguese.

Objections of States cleared away by Madison

Of the argument in New York, which was made in other States too, that power in Congress for "the general Welfare" was authority to do its will throughout the land, Madison wrote, evidently in anger:

"No stronger proof could be given of the distress under which these writers labor for objections than their stooping to such a misconstruction."

By "stooping" Madison plainly meant that they knew better and were unfair in their opposition to the General Welfare Clause of the Constitution.

Then he proceeded to explain the language under the established rules of interpretation. Had no other enumeration of powers been made than for taxing and spending, he said, then there might be some color to the objection that Congress would be without restraint—though that would be an "awkward way of describing an authority to legislate in all possible cases."

"But what color can the objection have," he asked, "when the specification of the objects alluded to by these general terms immediately follows, and is not even separated by a longer pause than a semi-colon?"

Limitation on power of Congress to spend

That is, the grant of power to tax and spend for the "common Defence and general Welfare" is followed in the same sentence by all the other grants—to borrow money, to regulate commerce, and so on. The first grant of all—to tax and spend—is inseparable in the context from all the other grants.

The power to tax and spend was granted to effectuate all of the seventeen succeeding paragraphs of clauses as well as the one in which it appears.

Madison met this question again in the very first Congress of the new Government, in which he was a member of the House of Representatives, and where he assembled and formulated twelve of the leading objections to the Constitution that came in from the ratifying conventions in the States for submission as amendments, ten of which were ratified and became known as the Bill of Rights.

First appearance of the "Subsidy"

A bill was introduced by a member from New England to pay a bounty to cod fishermen, to subsidize a private interest, as agriculture and many more private interests have been subsidized by the "New Deal." He spoke at length with great vigor against the bill. Stating that those who wrote the Constitution and those who ratified it conceived it to be not an indefinite Government, but a limited one, "tied down to the specified powers, which explain and define the general terms," he added:

"If Congress can employ money indefinitely to the general welfare, and are the sole and supreme judges of the general welfare, they may take the care of religion into their own hands; they may appoint teachers in every State, county and parish and pay them out of their public treasury; they may take into their own hands the education of children, establishing in like manner schools throughout the Union; they may assume the provision of the poor. . . . Were the power of Congress to be established in the latitude contended for, it would subvert the very foundations, and transmute the very nature of the limited Government established by the people of America."

The consequences of the misapplication by Congress of the money of the taxpayers—a scourge of mounting debt and cumulative deficits—establish Madison as a major prophet.

Hamilton, as well as Madison, rejected the contention strongly urged against the Constitution, that it left the National Government with unlimited power to do its will, and in No. 83 of *The Federalist* he said (italics his):

"The plan of the Convention declares that the power of Congress, or, in other words, of the *National Legislature*, shall extend to certain enumerated cases. This specification of particulars evidently excluded all pretension to a general legislative authority, because an affirmative grant of special powers would be absurd, as well as useless, if a general authority was intended."

Article I, Section 8 sets boundaries to constitutional power

There is no power in Congress beyond the boundaries of those eighteen paragraphs of clauses.

Certainly James Madison and Alexander Hamilton should have known what the purpose of the Constitutional Convention was. New York, by ratifying the new form of government, accepted what they said. Other States doubtless ratified on their explanation.

Abraham Baldwin of Georgia, a member of the Constitutional Convention, said in Congress in 1798 that "to provide for the common Defence and general Welfare" had "never been considered as a source of legislative power, as it is only a member introduced *to limit* the other parts of the sentence." That is, it limits the purposes for which Congress can "lay and collect taxes" and exert its other granted powers.

**The legal scholar of the
Convention speaks**

But there was another man in the Constitutional Convention, the ablest lawyer, as Madison was the ablest historian—James Wilson, a scholar from Edinburgh and from one of the Temples in London, who explained the taxing and spending power in a course of lectures to what afterwards became the University of Pennsylvania, as Madison had done. He said in part:

"The National Government was intended to promote the 'general Welfare.' For this reason Congress have power to regulate commerce . . . and to promote the progress of science and of useful arts by securing for a time to authors and inventors an exclusive right to their compositions and discoveries."

In this way he proceeded from the Patent and Copyright Clause to explain all the other clauses in section 8 granting power. He made it very clear that Congress was to "provide for the common Defence and general Welfare" by exerting the powers granted to it in the seventeen paragraphs following the first, by which it was authorized "to lay and collect taxes."

Thus, three members of the Constitutional Convention have spoken on this point—Madison, Baldwin, and Wilson—and none of them thought that the General Welfare Clause, which has been construed as a limitation on the activities of Congress rather than a grant of power, authorized the Legislative Department to get into anything even remotely resembling a Quixotic adventure "To Alleviate the Hazards of Old Age, Unemployment, Illness, and Dependency, to Establish a Social Security Insurance

Board in the Department of Labor, to Raise Revenue, and for Other Purposes."

General Welfare brilliantly defined by Jefferson

Although Jefferson was in Paris while the Constitutional Convention was sitting, he was in close communication with Madison and other delegates. He knew the Constitution. In a profoundly able letter to Albert Gallatin in 1817 he discussed the General Welfare Clause on which the Social Security Act was based (italics inserted):

"You will have learned that an act for internal improvement, after passing both Houses, was negatived by the President. The act was founded, avowedly, on the principle that the phrase in the Constitution which authorizes Congress 'to lay taxes, to pay the debts and provide for the general welfare,' was an *extension* of the powers *specifically enumerated* to whatever would promote the general welfare; and this, you know, was the Federal doctrine. Whereas our tenet ever was, and, indeed, it is almost the only landmark which now divides the Federalists and the Republicans, that Congress had not unlimited powers to provide for the general welfare, but was *restrained to those specifically enumerated;* and that, as it was never meant that they should provide for that welfare but by the exercise of the enumerated powers, so it could not have meant that they should *raise money* for *purposes which the enumeration did not place under their action;* consequently, that the *specification* of powers *is a limitation* on the purposes for which they may raise money.

"I think the passage and rejection of this bill a fortunate incident. Every State will certainly concede the power; and this will be a national confirmation of the grounds of appeal to them, and will settle forever the meaning of this phrase, which, by a mere grammatical quibble, has countenanced the General Government in a *claim of universal power*. For in the phrase 'to lay taxes, to pay the debts and provide for the general welfare,' it is a mere question of syntax, whether the two last infinitives are governed by the first, or are distinct and co-ordinate powers; a question unequivocally decided by the exact definition of powers immediately following."

That early interpretation should have been conclusive

That exposition by Jefferson, applied to a practical case in legislation, is perhaps the most illuminating that has been made.

Six years later, Jefferson returned to the subject (italics inserted):

"I have been blamed for saying that a prevalence of the doctrine of consolidation would one day call for reformation or revolution. *I answer by asking if a single State of the Union would have agreed to the Constitution had it given all powers to the General Government? If the whole opposition to it did not proceed from the jealousy and fear of every State* of being subjected to the other States in matters merely its own? And if there is any reason to believe the States more disposed now than then to acquiesce in this general surrender of all their rights and powers to a consolidated government, one and undivided?"

Jefferson's reasoning applied to present-day legislation

That is to say, it was inconceivable to Jefferson that the representatives of the people in Congress could ever so far disregard our constitutional history and purpose as to strip their States of local authority by abdicating their police power through such acts as these:

The Agricultural Adjustment Act	of May 12, 1933
The Tennessee Valley Authority	of May 18, 1933
The National Industrial Recovery Act	of June 16, 1933
The Federal Surplus Commodities Corporation	of October, 1933
The Bituminous Coal Act	of May, 1935
The National Labor Relations Act	of July, 1935
The Social Security Act	of August, 1935

Not a State would have ratified the Constitution, Jefferson declared, had it thought such a "revolution" possible.

We have suffered a constitutional revolution without use of amendments in accordance with Article V. That has come about through what Senator Thomas H. Benton of Missouri used to call "latitudinarian construction." That form of construction has been applied to the Commerce Clause and the General Welfare Clause. No other clause in the Constitution, even with the gross twisting which the ardent "progressists" employ, could be used by them in the framing of a bill for flouting the Tenth Amendment, the great bulwark of the States.

Did President Cleveland foresee present-day unconstitutionalism?

In 1888, President Cleveland, evidently noticing the tendency of representatives of the States in the Congress of the Union to favor measures for degrading their commonwealths, gave them in his fourth annual message this lesson in constitutional law:

"The preservation of the partitions between the proper subjects of Federal and local care and regulation is of such importance under the Constitution, which is the law of our very existence, that no consideration of expediency or sentiment should tempt us to enter upon doubtful ground.

"We have undertaken to discover and proclaim the richest blessings of a free Government, with the Constitution as our guide. Let us follow the way it points out—it will not mislead us."

In the next year President Cleveland vetoed a bill appropriating money from the National Treasury for the purchase of seed wheat *to relieve the farmers in a drought-stricken area.* In that message he defined the meaning of the General Welfare Clause as Madison and the others hereinbefore quoted interpreted it (italics inserted):

"Under the limited and delegated authority conferred by the Constitution upon the General Government the statement of the purposes for which money may be lawfully raised by taxation in any form *declares also the limits of the objects for which it may be expended.* . . . This 'general welfare of the United States,' as used in the Constitution, can only justify appropriations for *national* objects and for purposes which have to do with the prosperity, the growth, the honor, or the peace and dignity of the *Nation*."

What would Mr. Cleveland think could he know that the Federal Government now subsidizes the farmer, pensions everybody, and plans to medicate and hospitalize the whole population? And no amendment to the Constitution authorized the change!

Supreme Court ignored history and learning on General Welfare

Notwithstanding all that members of the Constitutional Convention had written in explanation of the General Welfare Clause, which they had drafted with the care that marked every line of the Constitution, the Supreme Court of the United States, on May 24, 1937, three months after the President had attacked the Judiciary as inefficient and obstructive and asked Congress to recast it to his liking, in an opinion (301 U. S. 548) by Justice Cardozo, with dissents by Justices Sutherland, Van Devanter, McReynolds, and Butler, used this language:

"It is too late today for the argument to be heard with tolerance that in a crisis so extreme the use of the moneys of the Nation to relieve the unemployed and their dependents is a use for any purpose narrower than the promotion of the General Welfare."

That expressed the popular notion of the party in power, that a "crisis," or an "emergency," or an "extraordinary emergency," such as the President[2] was given to declaring

---

[2] The field of the President's authority is very limited. It does not include the States, to say nothing of the external world. In No. 75 of *The Federalist* Madison pointed that out:

as difficulties unfolded, and as Congress had declared in the National Industrial Recovery Act and its companion pieces, confers on Congress powers which the Constitution did not and which it therefore withheld. The Constitution withheld more powers from Congress than it granted. Besides that precaution, the Tenth Amendment was added to warn Congress not to "grab" power in any circumstances whatsoever, especially against the States.

Two fundamental errors in decision of Supreme Court

In the opinion by Justice Cardozo it is *assumed* that because Washington could give relief it had the *power* to do so. It points out that for a given time Washington gave emergency relief to the amount of $2,929,307,366, while the States expended only $689,291,802 and local subdivisions $777,675,366.

But official figures assembled by the United States News for June 18, 1938, showed that for five years the people of the States had paid to the National Government in taxes $20,411,347,208 and received in "benefits" from their own money $18,267,527,000.

They gave to Washington more than 2 billion over what was returned to them. Those figures are absolute disproof of the statement of the Court, that "the fact developed quickly that the States were unable to give the requisite relief."

But even had the States been unable to give relief, that fact would not have conferred power on Congress to take

---

"The execution of the laws and the employment of the common strength, either for this purpose or for the common defence, seems to comprise all the functions of the Executive Magistrate."

A HISTORY OF LAWLESS GOVERNMENT

over police jurisdiction in the States, which the Constitution had not granted.

Instead of the first American *coup d'état,* which was executed by the Federal Emergency Relief Act of May 12, 1933, Congress should have repealed the Income Tax Law and the Estate Tax Law, by which it had been draining the States of their resources, and let the States, in close contact with the needy, go ahead and perform their police duties of relief. It chose revolution.

Rapid spread of the evil of subsidies

"Federal aid" to States for relief, for schools, and for what you will has grown worse and worse. In a report by the floor leader of the House of Representatives on January 8, 1950, to the Ways and Means Committee it was shown that for the fiscal year ending June 30, 1949, the people of the States paid in Federal taxes $41,864,542,295, while they got back in "aid" from their own money $5,551,054,046.

As just before stated, for the *five years* ending June 30, 1938, the States paid in Federal taxes $20,411,347,208, or less than one half of what they paid in the last *one year.* That is what may be described as "going some." The "grants in aid" for the five-year term averaged 3 billion, 653 million, while for the last one year they were 5 billion, 551 million—and all unconstitutional.

Arkansas, Mississippi, and New Mexico are the only States that got back anything near to half what they had paid.[3]

---

[3] A vigilant reporter for the United Press discovered that the king of the Hoboes was visiting a friend in Pittsburgh and he interviewed His Highness for the edification of the country. The King, who has made several trips around the world, has concluded that modern travel is at-

The situation is fantastic, for it has often been shown in Congress that there is not a State in the Union that is not in a stronger financial position than the National Government. The States need no "aid" from Washington—except for political purposes. That's what is going on, reminding of the "bread and circuses" which the politicians provided for the populace of sinking Rome.

Finally, on the decision in the Social Security case, it was based not only on the erroneous assumption of the inability of the States to perform their duties in giving relief, but also on what Justice Cardozo termed "a cyclical depression." To be sure, permanent legislation is not justified by a cyclical depression.

Constitutionality of Social Security Act not for Supreme Court

In the light of the reading of "general Welfare of the United States" which was given by Madison and other members of the Constitutional Convention, and by Jefferson, who was in constant communication with members while the Convention was sitting, and by several Presidents, it was not for the Executive Department, the Legislative Department, or the Judicial Department, or all of them together, to give the words a different meaning.

---

tended by too many risks, and he has therefore concluded to become a lobbyist for "Federal aid" to young men possessed by the urge to wander. He believes that all such young men should have each year a vacation of two weeks at the expense of the Government. "Then they could travel safely and in style," he said.

Is that any more absurd than that the wealthy State of Kansas, which, up to an act for pensions to its sons who served in World War I, had no debt at all, should receive "Federal aid" in 1950 for the benefit of its needy in the amount of $18,000,000? The supervisor of welfare reported that fact in June.

Kansas does not differ from the other states. Degeneracy is general. To them the Constitution is a dead letter.

As in 1895 the Supreme Court, refusing to strike out a limitation in the Constitution on taxation, referred the proponents of the Income Tax Law of 1894 to the Ultimate Power, to the people as the only Constitution makers, to write an amendment if they should deem that expedient, so in the Social Security case the Supreme Court should have held the act of Congress unconstitutional and referred the "planners" and their project to the people for disposition. Then a proposal to let Congress "into a boundless field of power no longer susceptible of any definition" would have brought the answer from those who alone had it.

That course would have been what Justice Brandeis called "procedural regularity," which he said must always be followed in resolving constitutional problems.

Where authority over welfare resides

It is within the police power of the State to protect the farsighted, the frugal, and the temperate from the tax burden of caring for the indifferent, the unthrifty, the profligate, and the handicapped when they become unable to care for themselves. It may require persons not voluntarily carrying insurance in standard companies to do so, if they cannot show resources making insurance unnecessary. And it can compel employers of such persons to make payroll deductions for the payment of insurance premiums through the working years of the employees.

The United States has no constitutional interest in this subject.

This discussion may well be closed by a quotation from a sound decision of the Supreme Court on January 6, 1936, holding the Agricultural Adjustment Act unconstitutional as not authorized by the General Welfare Clause. Later, on May 24, 1937, the Court, as seen, sustained the Social Security Act as within the General Welfare Clause—on two erroneous conceptions: (1) that the States could not care for the people in need (which would not confer authority on Congress), and (2) that "a cyclical depression" gave power to Congress to take control forever.

An admirable view of history

In the Agricultural Adjustment case the Court, speaking through Justice Roberts, said:

"Until recently no suggestion of the existence of any such power in the Federal Government has been advanced. The expressions of the Framers of the Constitution, the decisions of this Court interpreting that Instrument, and the writings of great commentators will be searched in vain for any suggestion that there exists in the Clause [General Welfare] under discussion, or elsewhere in the Constitution, the authority whereby every provision and every fair implication of that Instrument may be subverted, the independence of the individual States obliterated, and the United States converted into a central Government exercising uncontrolled police powers in every State of the Union, superseding all local control or regulation of affairs or concerns of the States.

"Hamilton himself, the leading advocate of broad interpretation of the power to tax and appropriate for the general welfare, never suggested that any power granted by the Constitution could be used for the destruction of local self-government in the States. Story countenances no such doctrine. It never seems to have occurred to them, or to those who have agreed with them, that the general welfare of the United States (which has aptly been termed "an indestructible Union, composed of indestructible States") might be wrecked by obliterating the constitutional members of the Union."

Justices Stone, Brandeis, and Cardozo dissented.

That decision shows the ground we have since abandoned, with Congress "in a boundless field of power, no longer susceptible of any definition."

XIII

THE CONSERVATION OF SOIL IN FARMING STATES BY THE FEDERAL GOVERNMENT IS NOT AUTHORIZED BY THE CONSTITUTION

WITH THE TRICKINESS IN THE USE OF LANGUAGE WHICH characterized the National Industrial Recovery Act, the Agricultural Adjustment Act, and the Bituminous Coal Act (all three held unconstitutional), to make believe that they were not what they were, Congress passed the second AAA and called it an act for "Soil Conservation," proceeding thereunder to irrigate the farming land with money of the taxpayers which it had been prevented by the decision of the Supreme Court from distributing under the first act. The second AAA was as lawless as the first.

For more than a decade Congress has been sending money to the farmers ostensibly to help them conserve their soil, an obligation resting upon them in the first instance, and upon the State when the erosion (or whatever is the matter) is so widespread as to call for the exertion of the police power, of which power the United States has none.

Illegal subsidies to agriculture of appalling magnitude

The magnitude of this drain upon the taxpayers of the country may be understood from the fact that in 1946

Washington gave to the farmers for "soil conservation" $57,000,000.

The total of subsidies to agriculture in 1947, as reported (1948) by the Secretary of the Treasury (p. 429), was $2,299,000,000. Yet in the Presidential campaign of 1948 the candidates of all parties promised the farmer more! The returns indicated that he voted for the party that had delivered.

And that misuse of money favored a powerful voting class who were marketing wheat at $3 a bushel, corn at about the same price, oats at a similar price, and livestock at rates so high that restaurants were charging their patrons $4 for a sirloin steak!

Through the years, $1 a bushel for wheat, 75¢ for corn, and the same price for oats were regarded on the land as good prices.

Of course, as before said, the conservation of soil is none of the business of the United States. It is the obligation of the landowner to take care of his land. He had done that from the time the Pilgrims cleared away the timber in the Massachusetts Colonies. He mastered rivers without knowing that he should have the help of a Big or Little T.V.A., and he opened roads wherever they were needed without a Federal Highway Act.

Why Constitution for independent individual

The men who wrote the Constitution being of that kind, they never gave authority to Congress to take the money of one class by taxation and pass it along with a bow and a smile to another group of great voting power. By Magna Carta their forebears made the King promise to keep hands off industry and trade, except under the necessity of war. Hence, the Constitution contains no grant of power to Congress to pass anything of even the remotest resemblance to the National Industrial Recovery Act. And as they extracted a pledge from King John to let trade alone, the Constitution authorizes Congress only to *"regulate"* commerce carried on by *men,* not to *engage in* commerce by any branch of government, or by a Fascist corporation set up by it. The early American tilled his land without expecting any help from anybody, and he had no idea that Government could by either punitive or predatory taxation place any limit on the fruits of his industry. Accordingly, no grant for paternalism or imperialism was given by the Constitution to Congress.

Soil conservation important, but not to Washington

To be sure, the conservation of the soil of the farmer may become in some localities of so burdensome a nature that it ceases to be the obligation of the individual. Where erosion or some other peril is so widely extended and affects so many owners and so much property that it cannot be dealt with successfully by individuals or by a group of them, then it becomes the duty of the State, either to assist in the task of prevention or take it over altogether. But the United States has no police power. And the Tenth Amendment was designed to prevent it forever from usurping any.

"Soil conservation" is a deceiving term, like "commerce" in the National Labor Relations Act. It is a cover for subsidies from the pockets of the country to those on the land, a transfer of money from one class to another which the Supreme Court held could not be made when it pronounced the first Agricultural Adjustment Act unconstitutional.

As mentioned in a preceding chapter, the farmer has been put in a bad situation by the mismanagement in Government which ballooned his costs and those of everybody else beyond all endurance. But that must be mended by removal of the cause, not by subsidies, which the taxpayers cannot carry indefinitely, even if they were legal.

Procedure provided by Constitution adequate for conservation

In a condition of erosion, or of a "dust bowl," involving several States, they have open to them the "Agreement or Compact with another State" authorized by the closing words of Article I of the Constitution, with "the Consent of Congress." The seven States in the basin of the Colorado River made use of this provision to work out an agreement for a fair division of the valuable water of that stream. So when the erosion or other trouble is beyond the ability of the landowner, it becomes the duty of the State to take hold. And when the difficulty belongs to more than one State, there is a constitutional way to solve the problem.

But the subject is as far beyond the constitutional field of Congress as are the sands of the Sahara.

On July 22, 1947, the Associated Press reported that the House of Representatives "had voted twice to eliminate the benefit-payment program for 1948 and sharply cut back payments on this year's crops." The Senate-House conference group agreed "to continue the main farm program into 1948." In addition to that, it agreed to a fund of $265,000,000 "to make the benefit payments and meet other costs of the farm crop program on the 1947 crop."

The "other costs" were $24,000,000 to pay the bureaucrats "for expenses of farmer committeemen who plan and check the programs"!

The farm bill compromise would provide $960,000,000 "for agricultural purposes during the fiscal year 1948 in comparison with last year's expenditures of $2,275,000,-000." President Truman asked for $1,188,000,000.

National government without feeling for taxpayers

The disrespect for the rights and property of the people in general, in order to favor highly organized voting groups, is, in addition to being unconstitutional, morally wrong. In the Congress for the last decade and a half, in the White House, in the legislatures, in the city councils, everywhere in public office where there is authority to spend, there has developed, through indifference or incompetence of those who should have been on guard, the grossest unconcern for the taxpayer. As a capital illustration of this, there is cited the veto by the President of a tax-reduction bill passed by the new Congress in 1947 which had been voted into power on a platform promising relief from exorbitant taxation.[1]

In the concluding chapter of this work it is shown that we must take the President out of this kind of politics by returning to the strictest observance of the method of election prescribed by the Constitution.

---

[1] The ruthless course of the Government at Washington respecting the taxpayers brings to mind the denunciation by Saint Simon of the Bourbon monarchy, which brought on by taxes the French Revolution, that it "has scourged, rather than governed, the state."

XIV

THE EXPANSION OF THE CONSTITUTION BEYOND ITS LETTER AND SPIRIT THROUGH JUDICIAL LEGISLATION BY THE SUPREME COURT OF THE UNITED STATES IS, BECAUSE INSIDIOUS, THE WORST THREAT TO LIBERTY AND PROPERTY

THIS CHAPTER DEALS WITH THE ATTEMPTS OF THE SUPREME Court of the United States to "construe" into the Fourteenth Amendment—restraining the States—what was not written in it, what the writers of it did not have in mind, that is, "freedom" of religion, freedom of speech, and freedom of the Press.

The writers of the Amendment had under consideration (1866) the recently (1865) liberated Negro, to whom the Amendment would give citizenship in both his State and the United States; and it forbade the States to "abridge the privileges or immunities of citizens of the United States," or to deprive any person in a State of "life, *liberty*, or property without due process of law," or to deny to him "the equal protection of the laws" of his State.

Freedom of religion, freedom of speech, and freedom of the Press were safeguarded (1789) against denial by the National Government 77 years before by the First Amendment, the first article of what we call the Bill of Rights, in protection of the States and the people against interference by the National Government.

The search for the unperceivable

The Supreme Court has held in recent years that the word "liberty," italicised in the foregoing quotation from the Fourteenth Amendment, against the States, is the equivalent of, or connotes, or contains, the "freedoms" of religion, speech, and Press, written against Congress in the First Amendment.

That reading ignores two cardinal rules of interpretation: (1) that the plain language must be followed, without addition or subtraction; and (2) that there must be kept in mind the evil which the writing was being made to cure.

First, the Fourteenth Amendment makes no mention of religion, speech, or Press. They cannot be drawn into it and be made a part of it by an expansive "construction" of the word "liberty."

Second, the writers of the Amendment were dealing only with the Negro and his "liberty" and prospective rights, which were to be protected. Religion, speech, and Press were as far away from their thoughts as the poles are apart.

Judicial deviation from Constitution most serious

When Congress, cloaking itself with the Commerce Clause of the Constitution, makes an enactment like the National Labor Relations Law, which shows by its name that it is not an act to regulate commerce among the States,

A HISTORY OF LAWLESS GOVERNMENT

the educated American is alerted. He should immediately do something about it. But at that time he didn't. He should have driven out of Congress every man that voted for the degradation of his State from its place in the Union of States.

But when, by specious reasoning, or no reasoning at all, by "assumptions," the Supreme Court makes application of constitutional provisions where they do not belong, the departure from principles is less likely to be noticed.

For a good many years the Supreme Court has had trouble with "due process of law" in the Fifth Amendment to the Constitution, restraining the Nation, and in the Fourteenth, curbing the State. It has been perplexed about the application of "the privileges and immunities of citizens of the United States" in the Fourteenth.

Chief Justice Marshall on following the text

That has been owing to its failure to adhere to the text. On adhering to the text the great Chief Justice Marshall, in a dissenting opinion, gave these directions in 1827 (12 Wheaton, 213):

"To say that the intention of the Instrument must prevail; that the intention must be collected from its words; that its words are to be understood in that sense in which they are generally used by those for whom the Instrument was intended; that its provisions are neither to be restricted into insignificance, nor extended to objects not comprehended in them, nor contemplated by its powers, is to repeat what has been already said more at large, and is all that is necessary."

The tragic effort of the Supreme Court has been in trying to make the Fourteenth Amendment bring down against the States prohibitions in the Bill of Rights written against National power *only*.

Of course, if the people should want the First Amendment, for example, applied against State power, they can say so by action under their amending Article V. But it is not for the Judiciary to do the amending.

Could the States have intended to restrain themselves?

When, upon the submission by the Constitutional Convention to the States of the proposed new form of government, they complained that it did not contain restrictions enough on power, did they mean that they themselves would not be sufficiently curbed? Certainly not. The question is self-answering.

If the States could not have intended by the First Amendment to curb themselves, why should the Supreme Court take authority to bring against them that Article of *their* Bill of Rights?

The question with the States was: would the over-all government eventually become *absolutely* over-all? They were determined that it should not. They got protection through ten amendments, the Bill of Rights, not one prohibition in which restrains the States in any way.

From the beginning both the States and the Nation proceeded on that fact. Many of the States abandoned the grand jury which the Nation is required (Amendment V) to employ and dispensed with the indictment. In some States if the accused does not take the witness stand to explain, that may be used against him before the jury, a practice forbidden in the Federal courts. Some States permit the trial of criminal cases without a jury, a practice forbidden to the Nation. Others employ a jury of fewer than twelve. The unanimous verdict has been succeeded by the majority verdict of the jury in some States. The jury in suits for money (Amendment VII) is not called in many States.

States provide protection for their people

Most if not all of the constitutions of the States have their own provisions, like those in the Bill of Rights (Amendment VIII) against excessive bail, excessive fines, and cruel and unusual punishment.

But the Bill of Rights is strictly a barricade against the exertion of National power. It was so treated down to about the time (1926) that an inquiry by the American Bar Association revealed that out of 25 leading university law schools only 8 required a course in the Constitution as a condition to a degree! That may have been the origin of scrambled brains in the law of the Constitution.

Since the States demanding the Bill of Rights did not intend it to be operative against themselves, and since the States and the Nation so accepted it for near a century and a half, how in reason can a court now make an unintended application of any provision of it and act as pedagogue to a State?

States are Republics, independent in most respects

It is to be kept in mind that by section 4 of Article IV of the Constitution "the United States shall guarantee to every State in this Union a Republican form of Government." Every one of the forty-eight States is a Republic, has a Constitution of its own, with an Executive Department, a Legislative Department, and a Judicial Department, fully equipped to manage its own internal affairs. Fear that the National Government would not let those republics alone, made the original States add to the Constitution the Bill of Rights against it.

The first sentence of the Fourteenth Amendment is this:

"All persons born or naturalized in the United States, and subject to the jurisdiction thereof, are citizens of the United States and of the State wherein they reside."

That dual citizenship had always existed except as to those in slavery. In the Constitutional Convention that was expressed by James Wilson of Pennsylvania, the leading lawyer of the body, afterward a justice of the Supreme Court of the United States:

"A citizen of America is a citizen of the general government, and is a citizen of the particular State in which he may reside."

Citizenship intended by Civil War Amendment

The Fourteenth Amendment was intended to give to the liberated Negro both citizenships, but the language is broad enough to include others, and it has been so applied.

The second sentence of the Fourteenth Amendment, which has become a Pandora's Box of evils, is this, with insertions in brackets to show how it had been read by the Supreme Court down to recent times:

"No State shall make or enforce any law which shall abridge the privileges or immunities of citizens of the United States [springing from National citizenship]; nor shall any State deprive any person of life, liberty or property without due process of law [of the State]; nor deny to any person within its jurisdiction the equal protection of the laws [of the State]."

The meaning of "liberty" considered

In the Fifth Amendment that language precisely as to "liberty" had been written *against the Nation*—"nor be deprived of life, *liberty* or property without due process of law." The writers of the Fourteenth Amendment, *against the States*, 76 years later, copied that language from the Fifth. The rule is that language thus borrowed carries into the later position the meaning that it expressed in the earlier position.

As the First Amendment deals openly and specifically with the "freedom" of religion, speech, and Press, those subjects are certainly not contained again in the Fifth *concealed* in the word "liberty." The writers of that time were given to clarity, rather than redundancy and confusion.

The set-up in 1789 of the First and Fifth Amendments in the Bill of Rights refutes the theory that "liberty" in the Fifth carries again the *freedoms* (of religion, speech, and Press) of the First. If, therefore, "liberty" in the Fifth does not connote or contain freedom of religion, speech, and Press, then those subjects are not embraced in the "liberty" borrowed from the Fifth and inserted in the Fourteenth.

Accordingly, to read into "liberty" in the Fourteenth what was not in the "liberty" which the writers of it borrowed from the Fifth is to be guilty of "latitudinarian construction."

The purpose of the Fourteenth Amendment

The language of the Fourteenth Amendment is so clear that it does not need the interpretation just given to it. The meaning is that the Nation cannot enter a State except to enforce a right of National citizenship, as, for example, the right to travel at will throughout this land, which California was prevented (314 U. S. 160) from abridging by a law (1941) excluding from ingress indigent persons.

Second, it means that the Nation cannot enter a State in protection of "life, liberty or property" unless the State (not individuals) denies *its* due process in protection of a right springing from National citizenship, as the right of the Negro to possess property and exercise suffrage.

Third, it means that the Nation cannot enter a State to secure "the equal protection of the laws" *of that State* unless those laws are being administered to deny a right of National (not State) citizenship, as a law denying suffrage to the Negro, while others enjoy it.

What Fourteenth Amendment did not contemplate

Nothing in the language of the Fourteenth Amendment just quoted indicates an intention of the writers in 1866 to recast or rewrite the First Amendment (1789) by inserting after "Congress shall make no law" the words "nor shall any State," making the Amendment since 1868 read thus:

"Congress shall make no law [nor shall any State] respecting an establishment of religion, or prohibiting the free exercise thereof; or abridging the freedom of speech, or of the press; or the right of the people peaceably to assemble, and to petition the Government for a redress of grievances."

Nothing in the Fourteenth Amendment just quoted imports an intention that we should take the word "liberty" (written after Emancipation) to mean the "free" exercise of religion, or the "freedom of speech, or of the Press," dealt with by the writers of the First Amendment seventy-seven years before.

When it comes to blending thus the First Amendment in the Fourteenth, or mingling the provisions of the two, that can be done, not by assertions of the Supreme Court, nor by the authority of Congress, even, but only by the Constituent Assembly, the people exerting sovereign power as constitution makers.

In all the years of litigation and argument respecting this matter no one has ever dared to propose to the States an amendment for their ratification which would emasculate them as they have been broken by decisions of the Supreme Court.

Non-National subjects occupying Supreme Court

It is with matters which are of no constitutional concern to the Nation that the Supreme Court has been overbusy of recent years, to the great confusion of thought respecting our Fundamental Law.

It may be well to illustrate the manner and extent of this before taking up the constitutional and judicial history which is to be the service of this chapter. Parents of different religious denominations in Illinois arranged with the board of education to have their children receive in the school building, but out of class, from special teachers, religious instruction for half an hour once or twice a week. The regulation was attacked as a violation by the State of this clause of the First Amendment:

"Congress shall make no law respecting an establishment of religion, or prohibiting the free exercise thereof; or abridging the freedom of speech, or of the Press."

To be sure, Congress never passed any such law. But it was *assumed*, without any attempt at demonstrating, a practice which the Supreme Court had been employing for many years, that the Fourteenth Amendment, just before quoted in pertinent part, brought down against the States the First Amendment, originally written, with all its companion articles in the Bill of Rights, against action by the Nation *only*.

Illinois passed no law respecting religion

Accepting for the moment (but no longer) the assumption of the Court that the First Amendment *had* been brought down to block action by Illinois, the answer is that neither did Illinois pass any "law respecting an establishment of religion, or prohibiting the free exercise thereof."

Consequently, no constitutional question could exist under the First Amendment. And the Supreme Court of Illinois so decided.

On the simple facts given before on the use of the schoolrooms the Supreme Court of the United States, speaking (1948) through Justice Black (333 U. S. 203), said:

"This is beyond all question a utilization of the tax-established and tax-supported public school system to aid religious groups to spread their faiths. It falls squarely under the ban of the First Amendment (made applicable to the States by the Fourteenth) as we interpreted it in Everson v. Board of Education, 330 U. S. 1."

A HISTORY OF LAWLESS GOVERNMENT 217

In the Everson case it was said:

"No tax in any amount, large or small, can be levied to support any religious activities or institutions, whatever they may be called, or whatever form they may adopt to teach or practice religion."

How the law should have been stated

What the Supreme Court should have said in the Everson case (after taking jurisdiction of it when without authority to do so) is that Congress gets no authority from the Constitution to spend money in the States for any school purpose. And that schools, being within the inherent police jurisdiction of the States, are entitled to support by the States—public schools, private schools, and religious schools—provided only that a State constitution does not speak in some respect to the contrary.

First, the Fourteenth Amendment did not make the First applicable to any conditions in Illinois.

Second, no tax was levied for religious purposes. The use of rooms apart from school classes could be no more objectionable than the use of them for a meeting of a club or other local organization, a use very commonly enjoyed in every town and city. It is too bad if the people cannot use their own buildings for what they deem to be their own advantage—and that in an educational way.

The Supreme Court "mystified" the subject

The inaccuracy of the language of the Court, and its inapplicability to any constitutional provision, brings to mind what was said in an opinion (100 U. S. 393) by Justice Bradley, a judicial stalwart, seventy years ago:

"We may mystify anything. But if we take a plain view

of the words of the Constitution, and give to them a fair and obvious interpretation, we cannot fail in most cases in coming to a clear understanding of its meaning. We shall not have far to seek. We shall find it on the surface, and not in the profound depths of speculation."

That is to say, all that the Supreme Court had to do in the Illinois case, *assuming* that the First Amendment had any bearing on it, was to examine the record and find whether Illinois had passed a "law respecting an establishment of religion, or prohibiting the free exercise thereof." That, and that *only*, was forbidden. As shown in the quotation hereinbefore made from Chief Justice Marshall, the Court had no right to extend the language of the Amendment to something else.

When Judge Thomas M. Cooley was recognized as the constitutional authority of this country he stated the rule that the court should keep in view the conditions which caused the language to be written, else it will be made to say something that the writers never thought of, and thereby may work great harm.

How to get meaning of First Amendment

The conditions which caused the First Amendment to be written in its brief and clear language were those of law and practice in England which drove the Pilgrims to Holland and thence to America, which made the Puritans set sail for Massachusetts, which made William Penn take his fellow Quakers to Pennsylvania, which caused Lord Baltimore to settle Maryland with his coreligionists; and the conditions in America which drove Roger Williams and Anne Hutchinson from Massachusetts to Rhode Island, and the law of Virginia which set up a State

Church supported by taxation, a law which Jefferson and Madison caused to be repealed.

Cooley told us in effect that when we consider the First Amendment we must, in the words of St. Paul, "think on these things." Were any of those things in Illinois? If not, then neither was the First Amendment operative there, even though we "assume," as the Supreme Court did, that the Fourteenth Amendment brought it down against the State.

Justice Reed, adhering to the text, dissented on the ground that the question was on "an establishment of religion," forbidden by the First Amendment, although he erroneously thought "the First Amendment . . . made effective as to the States by the Fourteenth." But he was right that "an establishment of religion" by Illinois must necessarily appear to work a violation by it of the Constitution, admitting for the moment the "assumption" of the Supreme Court.

The wide effect of the decision

The record in the case disclosed that in all but two of the States about 2,000 communities provided, by the use of school buildings or rooms, religious instruction to more than 1,500,000 pupils. That work was upset without reason—and contrary to law. The Republic of Illinois, one of the oldest, was highly competent to manage constitutionally its own affairs, and the Republic of the United States should have kept out of its jurisdiction.

In 1931, seventeen years before the decision in the case from Illinois, the Supreme Court (283 U. S. 697) made a similar misapplication of the provision in the First Amendment for the "freedom of the Press," Chief Justice Hughes writing the opinion, and Justices Butler, Van Devanter, McReynolds, and Sutherland dissenting. As that decision may have given some parentage to the one in the school case, promulgated by younger and less experienced justices, it, too, will be examined preceding the Judicial history to be made.

The first definite trespass on State autonomy

The Republic of Minnesota, with a provision in its Constitution for the freedom of the Press (as every other State has in its basic law), enacted that the continued publication of libelous and scandalous matter would be regarded as a nuisance and might be stopped by the writ of injunction. The law was a valid exercise of police power by the State, and the Supreme Court of Minnesota so held. The case was taken by appeal to the Supreme Court of the United States, without jurisdiction to receive it, and the decision of the court of last resort in Minnesota was reversed. The law provided for the suspension of the libels only, not the periodical.

At the opening of the opinion the Chief Justice begged the main question, as follows (brackets and italics inserted):

"It is no longer open to doubt that the liberty [a word not in the First Amendment] of the Press, and of speech [in the First Amendment], is within the *liberty* safeguarded by the Due-Process Clause of the Fourteenth Amendment [nor shall any *State* deprive any person of life, *liberty*, or property, without *due process* of law] from invasion by State action."

That is, the Fourteenth Amendment makes applicable

A HISTORY OF LAWLESS GOVERNMENT

against the States the prohibitions of the First against the Nation.

In support of his proposition the Chief Justice cited:

Gitlow v. New York (1925), 268 U. S. 652 (666), by Justice Sanford

Whitney v. California (1927), 274 U. S. 357, by Justice Sanford

Fiske v. Kansas (1927), 274 U. S. 380, by Justice Sanford

Stromberg v. California (1931), 283 U. S. 359, by Chief Justice Hughes.

Not one of those citations supports by reason the proposition stated.

The "authorities" of the Court examined

In the Gitlow case, sustaining a conviction by a jury for violation of the Statute of New York against criminal anarchy, Justice Sanford began (italics inserted):

"For the present purposes *we may and do assume* that freedom of speech and of the Press—which are protected by the First Amendment *from abridgement by Congress* —are among the fundamental personal rights and 'liberties' protected by the due process clause of the Fourteenth Amendment *from impairment by the States.*"

An *assumption* contrary to a demonstrable historic fact cannot stand as the foundation of a departure from a long-settled reading of a constitutional provision.

In the Whitney case, under the Syndicalism Act of California, the main contention was that the legislation was directed against a class and that therefore "equal protection" was denied. The Supreme Court of California was reversed. The opinion contained no attempt to show that free speech or Press is protected against the State by the Fourteenth Amendment.

The Fiske case, reversed, dealt with due process under the Syndicalism Act of Kansas, not free Press. There was no showing as to how due process, protected from the beginning in all the constitutions of the States, had been converted into a right dependent upon National citizenship to be protected by the Fourteenth Amendment.

The Stromberg case arose under the criminal statute of California forbidding the display of the red flag. The judgment of conviction was reversed on the ground that the law was too vague in its prohibition for a criminal statute.

Thus, not one of the four cases cited by the Chief Justice in support of the interference by the United States with the Constitution and laws of the Republic of Minnesota showed how that could be constitutionally done. The Constitution of Minnesota gives protection to a free Press, and the free Press guaranteed by the First Amendment against National (not State) interference was absolutely alien to the case, which the Supreme Court of Minnesota had correctly disposed of.

Every one of the four cases was a bald invasion of a sovereign State.

Even had each of the three States named denied freedom of speech, of Press, and of religion, that would not have been violative of the First Amendment, which says only that "Congress shall make no law," and which is not, therefore, a command to the States. It was so taken at its plain words by both Nation and States during the 79 years that the Fourteenth Amendment did not exist. This Amendment did not purport to make the First applicable to the States. It was the *liberty,* the property, and the general rights of the Negro that were under consideration when the Fourteenth Amendment was written—not speech, not Press, not religion.

The legislation of Minnesota was sound

The law of Minnesota granting relief by injunction from continuous libels was sound. It was not at variance with the provision in the Constitution of the State for the protection of a free Press. The first ground of equity jurisdiction is that the complainant has no speedy and complete remedy at law. That is, if he were to recover judgment for damages in an action at law, the defendant might not be financially able to respond; and if he were financially able, the injured party would be obliged to bring an action for each libel. That is the second ground of equity jurisdiction, to prevent a "multiplicity of suits." The court of equity or chancery simply stops by its writ of injunction what the legislature properly denounced as a nuisance. The law does not suppress the periodical—it stops the libeling.

In the dissent by Justice Butler and three associates—Justices Van Devanter, McReynolds, and Sutherland—it was said:

"Confessedly, the Federal Constitution prior to 1868, when the Fourteenth Amendment was adopted, did not protect the right of free speech or Press against State action. Up to that time the right was safeguarded solely by the constitutions and laws of the States and, it may be added, they operated adequately to protect it."

That being so, why should the National Government attempt to take over after three quarters of a century?

Chief Justice Marshall on relation of State and Nation

In support of their appeal to history, the dissenting justices cited a case (7 Pet. 243) decided in 1833 by Chief Justice Marshall, which involved a claim for damage to property done by the City of Baltimore in improving the harbor. The claim was made under the Fifth Amendment, which requires "just compensation" from the Nation for property taken for public use. That case of 116 years ago may be the first in which the principle under discussion here came up. The language of the Chief Justice suggests that it was new. He laid out the whole subject with the clarity and completeness that marked his work (italics inserted):

"The question thus presented is, we think, of great importance, but not of much difficulty.

"The Constitution was ordained and established by the people of the United States for *themselves,* for their own government, and *not for the government of the individual States.* Each State established a constitution for *itself,* and, in that constitution, provided such limitations and restrictions on the powers of its particular government as its judgment dictated.

"The people of the United States formed such a government for the United States as they supposed best adapted to their situation and best calculated to promote their interests. The powers they conferred on this government were to be exercised *by itself;* and the *limitations on power,* if expressed in general terms, are naturally and, we think, *necessarily applicable to the government created by the Instrument.* They are limitations of power granted by the

A HISTORY OF LAWLESS GOVERNMENT 225

Instrument itself; *not of distinct* [State] *governments*, formed by different persons and for different purposes. If these propositions be correct, the Fifth Amendment must be understood as restraining the power of the general government, and *not as applicable to the States."*

State not commanded by Bill of Rights

In brief, a disregard by a State of any prohibition in the Bill of Rights, from the First Amendment down, is not remediable in a proceeding against the State, *for the State is not commanded to obey it.*

In the Minnesota case Chief Justice Marshall would rule that the First Amendment on the freedom of the Press could not be applied against the Constitution and laws of Minnesota. And he would make like ruling in the Illinois school case, namely, that the "establishment of religion" forbidden by the First Amendment was not forbidden to Illinois. And, anyway, Illinois made no law respecting an establishment.

The dissenting justices cited some other decisions to similar effect, but there is nothing to be said after Marshall.

In 1936 the decision in the case in Minnesota was cited and followed where a law of Louisiana imposed an excise tax on the proceeds of advertising in newspapers "for the privilege of engaging in such business." Collection of the tax was enjoined by the United District Court. Appellant contended, correctly, that the Fourteenth Amendment does not prohibit States from infringing freedom of the Press, citing Cooley to the point that the Amendment is to prevent hostile legislation by States against the "privileges and immunities" of citizens of the United States as distinguished from those of citizens of the States. The Supreme Court held (297 U. S. 333) the act "unconstitutional under the Due Process-of-law Clause [of the Fourteenth Amendment] because it abridges the freedom of the Press." There, again, it was assumed that the Fourteenth Amendment brings down the First against the States.

In 1883 the Supreme Court held (110 U. S. 516,535) that due process in the Fourteenth Amendment "refers to the law of the land in each State," not to the law of the United States. The State does not have to afford due process under National law—under the Fourteenth Amendment in case of the Press or of religion.

Cases examined respecting Bill of Rights

Now for "the strange, eventful history."

In 1867, the year before the Fourteenth Amendment became a part of the Constitution, the Supreme Court of the United States passed on a law of Nevada levying a tax of $1 on every person leaving the State by railroad or other vehicle. It was held in an opinion by Justice Miller, the lion of the Judiciary of that day, that the levy was invalid (6 Wallace, 35) as a restraint by a State upon a *right* of National citizenship, the right to go at will throughout the country, to Washington on business with the Government, to the land office of the United States, to go abroad, and so on.

The decision followed one by Chief Justice Marshall (12 Wheaton, 419) in 1827, that when the importer paid the duty levied by the United States he received *from* the United States a *right* to sell the imported packages, for which reason the license law of Maryland on importers was unconstitutional, a levy on a *National right*.

A HISTORY OF LAWLESS GOVERNMENT

In 1872, four years after the Fourteenth Amendment became a part of the Constitution, the most memorable decision that has been written respecting it was rendered (6 Wallace, 36) by the Supreme Court of the United States in a group of cases heard together and known as the Slaughter-House cases. A law of Louisiana authorizing the centralizing of livestock handling and butchering at a designated place outside of New Orleans was attacked by a number of butchers as abridging their "privileges and immunities" under the Fourteenth Amendment, and as denying the "due process" and "equal protection" guaranteed by that Amendment. Equal protection was not denied because the law required that the slaughter-house be open to all butchers.

The two American citizenships made plain

In the opinion of the Court, by Justice Miller, he returned to the discussion of the dual citizenship which he had considered in the Nevada case, previously examined:

"It is quite clear, then, that there is a citizenship of the United States, and a citizenship of a State, which are distinct from each other, and which depend upon different characteristics or circumstances in the individual."

On the meaning of "the privileges and immunities of *citizens of* the several *States*," Justice Washington was quoted:

"They may all, however, be comprehended under the following general heads: protection by the [State] government, with the right to acquire and possess property of every kind, and to pursue and obtain happiness and safety, subject, nevertheless, to such restrictions as the government may provide for the general good of the whole."

Up to the time of the three Civil War Amendments (Thirteenth, Fourteenth, and Fifteenth) no claim or pretense was made that these rights depended upon the Federal Government for their existence or protection, beyond the very few express limitations imposed by the original Constitution on the States—against *ex post facto* laws, bills of attainder, and laws impairing the obligation of contracts.

"But with the exception of those and a few other restrictions," said the Court, "the entire domain of the privileges and immunities of the citizens of the States, as above defined, lay within the constitutional and legislative power of the States, and *without that of the Federal Government*" (italics inserted).

Some privileges of National citizenship named

Thus, holding that the privileges and immunities asserted by the plaintiffs in the cases with respect to slaughtering belong to citizens of the States and are to be protected, not by National but by State government, Justice Miller enumerated some privileges and immunities proceeding from National citizenship: to go from place to place throughout the land, to assert any claim against government, to share in its offices and affairs, to free access to seaports, to the land offices and courts of justice, to demand care and protection on the high seas and abroad, to have the privilege of the writ of habeas corpus, the right to use navigable waters, to have the benefit of treaties and of the War Amendments.

A HISTORY OF LAWLESS GOVERNMENT 229

The holding was that the rights and privileges claimed by plaintiffs were not those of citizens of the United States within the Fourteenth Amendment.[1]

The theory which the Court rejected

A dissent was written by Justice Field and joined in by Chief Justice Chase, and Justices Swayne and Bradley, chiefly on the ground that an unlawful monopoly had been granted. The dissenters sought to bring within National cognizance every right of man—whereas the majority opinion by Miller was that the right to slaughter or to pursue any other occupation existed before the Fourteenth Amendment, and therefore did not spring from it—a right under State, not National, citizenship.

It was the belief of some that the writers of the Fourteenth Amendment intended to enfeeble all the States for what the Confederate States had done. But the opinion just reviewed came from master minds in statesmanship as well as in law.[2] They knew that it would be fatal to

[1] The cases presented no Federal question and were dismissed. A Federal question, essential to the jurisdiction of the Supreme Court, is, briefly, one arising under the Constitution, under an act of Congress, under a treaty, or under an action by a State against a right accruing from National citizenship.

[2] On the importance to the American people and the Republic of the able jurist, Senator Hoar wrote in his memoirs (vol. 2, p. 391) of the illustrious Chief Justice Shaw of the Supreme Judicial Court of Massachusetts:

"He possessed, beyond any other American judge, save Marshall, what may be termed the statesmanship of jurisprudence. He never undertook to make law upon the Bench, but he perceived with a farsighted vision what rule of law was likely to operate beneficially or hurtfully to the Republic. He was watchful to lay down no doctrine which would not stand this test. His great judgments stand among our great securities, like the provisions of the Bill of Rights."

liberty to take from the supreme court of a State the final word respecting rights emanating from or existing under State citizenship. What that would mean—what they divined—we have seen in the Minnesota Press case and in the Illinois School case.

The very next case (16 Wallace, 130) was decided by Justice Miller and it was held that Mrs. Myra Bradwell, who had been denied a license to practice law in Illinois, had not been deprived of a right of National citizenship:

"The right to control and regulate the granting of a license to practice law in the courts of a State is one of those powers which are not transferred for its protection to the Federal Government and its exercise is in no manner governed or controlled by citizenship in the United States in the party seeking such license."

Chief Justice Chase dissented.

Next great case of applicability of amendments

In 1908 the case next to the Slaughter-House cases in importance in distinguishing between State citizenship and National citizenship was decided (211 U. S. 78), Justice Moody writing the opinion. Twining was on trial in New Jersey on a criminal charge. By the practice in that State comment was permitted before the jury on the fact that a defendant did not take the witness stand to clear up the accusations. He claimed that the Fifth Amendment, forbidding that a person "be compelled in any criminal case to be a witness against himself," was violated by New Jersey, as his right to be silent had been turned against him. It was held that the Amendment is not applicable to State citizenship—that the first eight amendments[3] affect the United States Government only. For 79 years before the Fourteenth Amendment immunity from self-incrimination was afforded by the constitution of the State, if it was enjoyed at all in State tribunals.

Counsel for Twining made frequent reference to "fundamental rights," but he drew no distinction between fundamental rights of State citizenship and rights fundamental to National citizenship.

Marshall on power of people in States

The decision in the Twining case was in conformity with what Chief Justice Marshall had explained (4 Wheaton, 122) 89 years before:

"When the American people created the National Legislature, with certain enumerated powers, it was neither necessary nor proper to define the powers retained by the States. These powers proceed, not from the people of America, but from the people of the several States; and remain, after the adoption of the Constitution, where they were before, except so far as they may be abridged by the Instrument."

That goes to what has been before mentioned, that there is a National Republic and a State Republic, each operating "on its own." The State Republics existed before the National Republic—they created it, not to manage their affairs, but to do certain duties which they carefully assigned to it; later, in fear, more clearly circumscribing its activities by a Bill of Rights.

---

[3] The Bill of Rights is usually spoken of as the first ten amendments, but sometimes as the first eight. The Ninth and Tenth are the final warnings to Congress to keep within its boundaries, whereas the first eight are protective to men. But men could not be fully guarded without the Ninth and Tenth.

Supreme Court avoided applying First Amendment

In 1906, the year before the Twining case, the Supreme Court passed by the question, in a Denver newspaper case (205 U. S. 454), whether in the Fourteenth Amendment is to be found "prohibition similar to that in the First." [4] It had left the question open in 1902 (187 U. S. 71), Justice Harlan dissenting in both cases.

But in 1937 a law of Georgia against insurrection, or inducing others to join in resistance to government, was held (301 U. S. 242) repugnant to the Fourteenth Amendment in an opinion by Justice Roberts, who *assumed* that the Amendment let the United States into the Republic of Georgia for managerial purposes. Justices Van Devanter, McReynolds, Sutherland, and Butler dissented.

Supreme Court followed Slaughter-House cases

In the same year (1937) it was stated (302 U. S. 319) in a case of murder done in Connecticut that "there is no such general rule" that "whatever would be a violation of the original Bill of Rights (Amendments I to VIII) if done by the Federal Government is now equally unlawful, by force of the Fourteenth Amendment, if done by the State." Justice Cardozo said that "the conviction of appellant was not in derogation of any privileges or immunities that belong to him as a citizen of the United States." Citizenship of the United States could not have been involved

---

[4] However, in the case of contempt against the Denver newspaper Justice Holmes said that it raised "questions of local law, which are not open to re-examination here." No Federal question was raised and therefore an order of dismissal was entered.

unless Connecticut had denied to him the "due process" of *its* laws or the "equal protection" of *its* laws. If it thus disfavored him by denying the practice due and given to others under its system, then the "no-State-shall-make-or-enforce-any-law" of the Fourteenth Amendment would be in control. As a citizen of the United States he was guaranteed the due process and equal protection of the *law of his State.* If it did not appear at the opening of the record in the Supreme Court that he charged denial of the law and procedure available to all others in his State, there was no "Federal question," and the appeal should have been dismissed, leaving the case where Connecticut closed it.

Where the Fourteenth Amendment was applicable

In 1940 the Supreme Court reversed (310 U. S. 573) the United States District Court and the Circuit Court of Appeals, which had held that the method established by Texas for regulating the production of oil made the owners of large areas diminish pumping while small adjoining owners drained the large holdings. That presented a proper question of the denial of "equal protection" by a State to a citizen of the United States, which the Fourteenth Amendment forbids as to the white man as well as the black.

In 1947 the Twining case was followed and it was held that the law and practice of California permitting comment before a jury upon the fact that the defendant in a criminal case did not take the witness stand to explain accusations denied no constitutional right. The opinion, by Justice Reed, said (332 U. S. 46) that "the Due Process

Clause of the Fourteenth Amendment, however, does not draw all the rights in the Federal Bill of Rights under its protection." Justices Black, Douglas, Murphy, and Rutledge dissented, showing the radical difference of opinion on this point.

The question that embarrasses the Justices

If the Fourteenth Amendment "does not draw all the rights," which ones *does* it draw? And if it draws any at all, why and how? That is what troubled Justice Frankfurter, who wrote a concurring opinion and said that *if* the Fourteenth Amendment makes the Fifth operative against the States, then it must so effectuate all the others of the Bill of Rights. To be sure, that is the only logical conclusion.

An authority on constitutional construction

Thus, for 150 years the States—and for most of the time the Nation—had in their daily lives construed the first ten amendments to the Constitution, the Bill of Rights, as having no application to local governments. The States have established legal and procedural systems strikingly at variance with the requirements of the amendments. In striving for the meaning of a constitutional provision or a law, a court always inquires: How was it construed from the beginning by those whose duty it was to apply it in government?

By that rule the First Amendment, respecting religion, press, and speech, is in no way binding on any State. It was misapplied in the Minnesota Press case and in the Illinois School case.

Due process of law is enjoined by the Fifth Amendment on the Nation and by the Fourteenth on the States. That is, there is due process of law in each of the Republics, each enforcing its process.

"Due process of law," wrote Chief Justice Chase (92 U. S. 90) in 1875, "is process according to the law of the land. This process in the States is regulated by the law of the States." It was there held that "trial by jury [Seventh Amendment] in suits at common law pending in the State courts is not, therefore, a privilege or immunity of National citizenship which the State is forbidden by the Fourteenth Amendment to abridge."

Due process of law made clear

Justice Moody explained in the Twining case the meaning of due process:

"These principles grow out of the proposition universally accepted by American courts on the authority of Coke, that the words 'due process of law' are equivalent in meaning to the words 'law of the land,' contained in that chapter of Magna Carta which provides that 'no person shall be taken, or imprisoned, or disseized, or outlawed, or exiled, or in any wise destroyed; nor shall we go upon him, nor send upon him, but by the lawful judgment of his peers or by the law of the land.'"

A denial of any of those rights guaranteed by King John at Runnymede is a denial of due process, a denial of the law of the land.

Another explanation of Due process of Law

A better definition of due process for the nonlegal scholar may be built upon an expression by Justice Brandeis in a dissenting opinion in which he said substantially that fully as important as the constitutional or statutory provision for protecting the right of man is "procedural regularity" in the adjudication of his claim.

Thus, an accused must have (1) inquiry of the charge by a Grand Jury in a Federal case. If a true bill be returned he must have (2) a copy of the indictment with a list of the witnesses who testified respecting him. He must have (3) adequate time to prepare his defense. He must have (4) the assistance of counsel, and if he cannot employ counsel the Government must appoint a competent attorney to defend him. He must have (5) a trial in public before (6) a petit jury of twelve, fairly drawn, deciding for or against him unanimously. He must be (7) confronted by the witnesses against him. Should he be convicted, he must have (8) appeal to a court of review, if he desire it.

States require due process of law

In civil proceedings in the courts of States involving money or realty or estates in probate or damages, there is like "procedural regularity" provided. A denial of any element of this procedure is a denial of the due process of law enjoined upon the Nation by the Fifth Amendment and upon the States by the Fourteenth.

Many cases appear in the judicial reports in which some factor in this process due to the defendant or the litigant was denied, and in each the appellate court reversed the judgment and remanded the case to the trial court to proceed again, and correctly.

Those are some of the safeguards to "life, liberty and property" set up by the profound historians in the Constitutional Convention, who knew so well what has been insufficiently taught to us, that, in the words of William

Ellery Channing, "the state is too often the grave of the man."

Justice Field said in 1885 (113 U. S. 27) of the Fourteenth Amendment, of late being misapplied against the States:

"But neither the Amendment—broad and comprehensive as it is—nor any other amendment, was designed to interfere with the power of the State, sometimes termed its police power, to prescribe regulations to promote the health, peace, morals, education, and good order of the people."

In that case a municipal ordinance regulating the operation of laundries at night was upheld. The case is an example of the unimportant litigation which has been taking the attention of the Supreme Court in recent years, and about which Justice Miller wrote (96 U. S. 97) in 1877 (brackets inserted):

Justice Miller on misuse of due process clause

"It is not a little remarkable that while this provision [due process, Fifth Amendment] has been in the Constitution of the United States, as a restraint upon the authority of the Federal Government, for nearly a century, and while, during all that time, the manner in which the power of the Government has been exercised has been watched with jealousy, and subjected to the most rigid criticism in all its branches, this special limitation on its powers has rarely been invoked in the judicial forum or in the enlarged theater of public discussion.

"But while it has been a part of the Constitution [in Fourteenth Amendment], as a restraint upon the power of the States, only a very few [9] years, the docket of this Court is crowded with cases in which we are asked to hold that the State courts and the State legislatures have *deprived their own citizens* of life, liberty or property without due process of law.

"There is here abundant evidence that there exists some strange misconception of the scope of this provision as found in the Fourteenth Amendment."

In that case an assessment for the drainage of swamp lands in Louisiana was under attack. Unless the complainant was denied the procedure under the law of Louisiana which was given to everybody else, he had been deprived of no right under the Fourteenth Amendment.

What would that constitutionalist think could he know of the decisions in recent years exhibiting a "strange misconception of the scope of this provision as found in the Fourteenth Amendment?"

A review of some leading cases

In 1884 the Supreme Court held (110 U. S. 516) that California did not violate the Fifth Amendment, requiring indictment by a grand jury, by employing instead the "information" of the prosecuting attorney. Certainly not. The requirement was written against the United States Government only.

In 1897 a man spoke on Boston Common without a permit, for which he was apprehended. It was held (167 U. S. 43) that the regulation was not in conflict with any constitutional provision respecting National citizenship.

That decision should have been *stare decicis*, the controlling precedent, for a large number of late cases overturning local regulations of States or their municipalities for cleanliness and order.

In 1900 it was held (176 U. S. 581) that Utah, in setting up a jury of 8 in criminal cases, was not bound by the Sixth Amendment requiring the United States to have a jury of 12 deciding unanimously. To be sure, not one of the ten amendments touches the States.

A State law tending to disorder

In 1921 the Supreme Court held (257 U. S. 312) that a law of Arizona exempting strikers from civil or criminal liability while all others remained liable for breaches of duty (torts) denied the "equal protection of the laws" of the State which the Fourteenth Amendment forbids. Of course, the Fourteenth Amendment was written against the States, while the First to Tenth, inclusive, were to protect the States from the National Government, which is now busy taking over, notwithstanding. Judicial "liberalism" appeared here. Justices Holmes, Pitney, and Brandeis dissented in the belief that the State could leave persons injured by strikers to remedy in actions at law for damages.

The doctors of law in disagreement

In 1939 an ordinance of Jersey City forbidding the leasing of a hall without permit for a meeting to advocate the obstruction of government was held (307 U. S. 496) in an opinion by Justice Roberts to violate the free speech provision of the First Amendment. A permit was denied to an organization of Communists. The United States District Court had enjoined the City from enforcing the ordinance, the Circuit Court of Appeals affirmed that, and the Supreme Court gave final affirmation, all three National courts applying to the Republic of New Jersey the Freedom-of-Speech Clause of the First Amendment, written against the Nation only. Justice McReynolds dissented on the ground that the plaintiffs should have sought relief in the courts of New Jersey, which alone had jurisdiction. Justice Butler also dissented, saying that the Boston Commons case, previously mentioned, should have been the guide.

Great States toppled in groups

In the same year again Justice Roberts wrote the opinion (308 U. S. 147) which overturned the courts of last resort in the sovereign States of California, Wisconsin, Massachusetts, and New Jersey upholding municipal ordinances forbidding the distribution of handbills in the streets. The Supreme Judicial Court of Massachusetts pointed out the fundamental fact that there was no interference with speech or publication anywhere in the city except in the streets. There is probably not a municipality in the United States, down to the smallest, that has not some such police ordinance, which is for good order—and constitutional.

In 1940 the Supreme Court of Connecticut was reversed (310 U. S. 296) for sustaining an ordinance requiring a permit for authority to solicit for a religious or other cause, Justice Roberts writing the opinion.

A large number of the cases overturning municipal ordinances prohibiting uses of the streets for different purposes were instituted by Jehovah's Witnesses under the claim that the religious freedom and the free speech protected by the First Amendment had been denied. They spoke in the streets and used sounding instruments to give recorded addresses, and they disturbed residents by knocking on the doors and urging the purchase of books and pamphlets. They were not forbidden to hire a hall and carry on there, or to go to some open place. But if they had been prevented by State or municipal law from activity anywhere, that would not have violated the First Amendment, a restriction on National action only.

From 1937 down, there have been more than thirty cases of the kind reviewed before the Supreme Court of the United States. They belonged for final decision in the tribunals of the States. It would be iteration and reiteration to go over any more of them.

Delinquency of American lawyer

The American Bar—local, State, and National—stood tongue-tied during the years that a quartet of great Justices—Van Devanter, McReynolds, Sutherland, and Butler—resisted steadily and brilliantly the pressure of swelling centralism against our system of widely divided powers.

Although the hour is very late, the organized Bar of each State should make ready to admonish the senators from its State to refuse to confirm any appointment by the President to any Federal Court—the Supreme Court, the eleven Circuit Courts of Appeals, and the hundred and a half District (trial) Courts—if the appointee is not a seasoned jurist of repute or an attorney who has won distinction as a practitioner in the field of constitutional law. Constitutional scholars, not sociologists or politicians, must make up those courts.[5]

---

[5] When Franklin D. Roosevelt became President, the Supreme Court of the United States numbered 5 Republicans and 4 Democrats. The policy

Highly experienced judicial material abundant

The courts of last resort in the forty-eight States, and the appellate courts below those, offer an abundance of highly competent jurists for appointment to the Federal courts. They are entitled to recognition by promotion. The Judiciary of States and of Nation would be strengthened by that course.

By remaining dumb and inactive for a decade and a half or more while judicial appointments have gone to low politics and inexperience, the American lawyer has discredited himself.

The Press, because the schools failed the writers, was of little use, where it was not a contributor to the confusion.

Long ago a European writer on our system declared the Judiciary to be the keystone of the American arch. The writers of *The Federalist* said that it is the least able of the three Departments to defend itself, and that it would be in peril from the other two. The Executive Department has not made the best appointments, and the Legislative Department has sanctioned such appointments.

A thorough-going reform as to appointments and confirmations is imperative.

---

had been to have each party fairly represented, although the subject is not political. Yet, when Congress turned over the general management of the country to the President, and his "policy" was Socialism, how could the American expect to secure in courts under such appointment the rights of free enterprise?

In 1949 the Court contained 8 Democrats and 1 Republican, the last mentioned having been a colleague in the Senate of Mr. Truman, who appointed him.

Of the 192 appointees to all Federal courts by Presidents Roosevelt and Truman, 184 are Democrats and 8 are Republicans. Not one of these appointees, from top to bottom, had gained any measurable experience as a jurist on any of the State supreme courts, or had achieved distinction at the Bar as a constitutional lawyer.

A HISTORY OF LAWLESS GOVERNMENT 243

Will a packed court "deliver"?

On June 23, 1947, the Supreme Court of the United States, in a suit brought by the Attorney General against the State of California, held (332 U. S. 19) that "California is not the owner . . . and that the Federal Government, rather than the State, has paramount rights in and power over that belt, an incident to which is full dominion over the resources of the soil under that water area, including oil."

The "belt" is a three-mile strip of land lying under water seaward from low-water mark and called tideland. The belt of water is the boundary line between a nation and the open sea. Vessels of foreign countries entering those waters become affected by the maritime laws of the country. But the land under the waters is the property of the State.

Three decisions of the Supreme Court had held this.

California had been giving leases on this tideland to drillers for petroleum under an act of its Legislature of 1921. Many valuable wells have been found under the deep water. Similar valuable production of petroleum has been carried on along the Gulf Coast within the three-mile limit.

On October 27, 1947, Chief Justice Vinson entered a decree giving effect to the decision of the Court by Justice Black, declaring that the United States is now and has been "possessed of paramount rights and powers over the lands, minerals and other things underlying the Pacific Ocean lying seaward of the ordinary low-water mark on the coast of California, *and outside of inland waters,* extending seaward three nautical miles. The

United States is entitled to injunctive relief" (italics inserted).

What the United States went after

The petition of the Government (original in the Supreme Court) asked for a decree of ownership and for a writ enjoining the State and persons from continuing the trespass complained of.

Neither the decision of the Court nor the decree deals with *title* to the land. Each is with respect to "paramount rights" of the United States, implying inferior rights in the State, but without any discussion as to how either got its rights or precisely what those rights are. In a dissenting opinion Justice Frankfurter asked how the United States got its "rights"—by conquest, or how.

In the ordinary lawsuit a claimant of land must exhibit a deed, or a lease showing a right to occupy, or a will transmitting, or a line of inheritance, or prescription by adverse possession. Otherwise, his suit will be dismissed.

Baseless claim of U.S.A. to "right"

Here the United States appeared with empty hands with respect to documentary evidence of title. And it appeared with unclean hands, which is ground for dismissal in a court of equity. For California had held possession of the land for 100 years, since its admission under the Constitution of 1849 laying claim to the tidelands. Thus California had documentary evidence of its title. But without the provision in its Constitution accepted by the Congress which admitted it to the Union, its adverse possession for that time would have ripened into title. And, by that token, the United States would be denied relief for laches, long sleeping on its "rights."

The decision ambiguous and far-fetched

Not only was the defense of California brushed aside as of no effect, but the United States made no motion, as before said, to show how it got *title* (not "paramount rights"), which Justice Frankfurter urged as necessary. The decision was cluttered with citations of what Justice Frankfurter called "the tenuous writings of publicists," to the disregard of judicial decisions on the subject and the constitutional provisions governing. Referring to a decision (262 U. S. 100) respecting rum running at sea during the term of the Eighteenth Amendment, the opinion said:

"That the political agencies of this Nation both claim and exercise broad dominion and control over our three-mile marginal belt is now a settled fact."

Freedom of seas not muniment of title

But that had no bearing on the title to lands under the tidewaters. The opinion lugged in also "the freedom of the seas"; but as the decisions on the subject point out, the ownership of the land by the State is subject to navigation. There is no record that the ownership of tidelands by States ever interfered with the operations of the United States in peace or war. Even if there were interference, the United States would have to *acquire* title, not seize possession.

In a decision of the Court written by Chief Justice Taney in 1842 the law was stated (16 Peters 367) as follows, and it has remained unchanged (italics inserted):

"When the Revolution took place the people of each State became themselves sovereign; and in that character hold the absolute right to all their navigable waters *and the soils under them* for their own common use."

Law respecting tidelands long undisputed

In 1873 the Supreme Court, Justice Field writing (18 Wallace 57), followed the decision of Taney in stating the rights of California itself (italics inserted):

"Upon the admission of California into the Union upon equal footing with the original States, *absolute property in,* and dominion and sovereignty over, *all soils under the tide-waters within her limits* passed to the State," subject only to navigation.

The cases cited here, and others urged by California, were not overruled. They are still the law. Justice Black gave much attention to a case decided (3 Howard 212) in 1845 respecting tidelands in Mobile Bay and said that the principle applying to "inland waters" could not be extended seaward. The decree entered by the Chief Justice against California was made to deal with lands "outside of inland waters," which seems to show the only reason that the Court could find for not following the decisions by Taney and Field just before presented. However, the subject matter is tidelands, not waters inside or outside. Whether inside or outside, the land belongs to the State when the tide of the ocean covers it.

International law rewritten by the Court

Justice Black and those concurring were in what is known in the American vernacular as "a hard row of stumps." They left unexplained where the Court got authority to rewrite international law—defined in the administration of George Washington between England and the United States—by drawing a distinction between tidelands in the open and tidelands in an arm of the ocean.

As international law has been a build-up under practices by the executive departments of governments, and by treaties covering points agreed to, the making of it necessarily lies beyond the jurisdiction of courts.

Constitutional limitations also by-passed

The wise men at Philadelphia wrote into the Constitution their objections to the ownership of lands in a State by the United States except in instances specified. In next to the last paragraph of section 8 of Article I, carefully specifying and limiting the powers to Congress, the Legislative Department is given the right "to exercise like authority [as over the District of Columbia] over all Places purchased by the Consent of the Legislature of the State in which the Same shall be, for the Erection of Forts, Magazines, Arsenals, dock-Yards, and other useful Buildings."

It was undoubtedly with reference to that language that the Supreme Court said (3 Howard 212) in 1845 (italics inserted):

"The United States has *no constitutional capacity* to exercise jurisdiction, sovereignty, or eminent domain *within the limits of a State* or elsewhere, except in the cases in which it is expressly granted."

Tenth Amendment supported title of California

Following that forceful implication in the first article of the Constitution, that territory even for the governmental purposes of the Nation can be acquired in a State only by its consent, the Tenth Amendment, the last article in the Bill of Rights, added this buttress against National encroachment:

"The powers not delegated to the United States by the Constitution, nor prohibited by it to the States [as are powers of coinage, treaties, war], are reserved to the States respectively or to the people."

In the States is a vast reservoir of powers not surrendered, and the Sovereignty is withholding many more.

The official report of the decision in the case against California does not show that the Court was asked to explain how the National Government could vault those obstructions to its getting title—or even "paramount rights" —in a State. The first question that should have been elucidated—Where did the United States get any "rights," and how, to tidelands in California?—remains a deep mystery.

What "precipitated" this conflict of Republics?

In the opinion of the Court it is said that by giving leases to these lands, California "precipitated this extremely important controversy."

"Precipitate" imports sudden action. But the law of California authorizing the leasing was passed in 1921, a quarter of a century before the United States awoke to the invasion of its "paramount rights." The conflict between the States—for interior as well as maritime States intervened in support of California and the Constitution—and the Nation was "precipitated" in 1936 by the introduction of a bill by a senator destitute of any conception of the constitutional position of the States in the Union.

Near mania of Congressmen to break States

As often pointed out herein, members of Congress have long seemed to be possessed of a near mania to break down their States. To be sure, the schools and universities gave them no constitutional education, and to a degree they are to be pitied rather than blamed.

The bill of the unschooled senator declared the tidelands to be part of the public domain of the United States. Title by *ipse dixit!* It was remodeled into a joint resolution directing the Attorney General to assert and establish the title of the United States to tidelands and petroleum deposits. The resolution passed the Senate by unanimous consent, but the House took no action. The Secretary of the Navy, whose Department got a sniff of petroleum during the dispute about the Teapot Dome in the Harding and Coolidge administrations, filed a brief in the Senate in support of the movement. While a number of maneuvers immaterial here were in progress, this suit was brought, and the attorneys general of 46 States filed a brief in opposition to it. That was an amazing awakening of the States from protracted slumber.

Two Presidents encouraged the illegal scheme

A joint resolution of Congress of July, 1946, quieting title in the States was vetoed by President Truman, who, as a recent senator, had been favorable to the action against the States.

The Secretary of the Interior testified before a congressional committee that in a talk with President Roosevelt in April, 1937, the Chief Executive raised the question of the ownership of oil in the tidelands. That was shortly after the senator had "precipitated" the controversy. He authorized the litigation. After his death in April, 1945, President Truman did likewise.

Thus, the whole administration, the Executive Department, the Legislative Department, the Navy, and the Judicial Department, all concurred in this attempt upon the property of the States.

The worst imaginable can happen here

The facts related show the origin and development of a plot by one Republic to seize illegally the lands of other Republics, such as might have been hatched in Moscow against Poland. Administrations calling themselves the "New Deal" and the "Fair Deal" did that!

Quite a change in the American governmental mind has taken place since England attempted to "move over" and occupy some gold-bearing lands in Venezuela and was stopped by the Cleveland administration.

What has been shown is a demonstration that anything may happen here.

But, of a certainty, it is within the power of the States in Congress to override this startling decision and clear their lands of the cloud which it put upon title to them.

Interpretative amendments to the Constitution suggested

Chisholm sued the State of Georgia and recovered a judgment which the Supreme Court sustained (2 Dallas, 419) in 1793. As it is against ancient principle for sovereignty to be sued without its consent (as the United States consents to be sued in specified instances in its Court of

Claims), a great commotion followed the decision, and in the next year what became the Eleventh Amendment was proposed to the States for ratification. It provided, briefly, that "the Judicial power shall not be construed to extend to any suit in law or equity" against a State.

Again, in 1933, what became the Twenty-first Amendment, repealing the Eighteenth (Prohibitory) Amendment, was proposed and it was adopted in the short space of nine months and fifteen days. After 13 years and .10 months of trial and controversy, the Prohibitory Amendment went out and carried with it the coercive legislation and some fantastic judicial decisions which it had engendered. In one case it was held that a man on an interstate journey by railroad with a flask of liquor in his valise was "transporting" intoxicating drink in "interstate commerce" in violation of governmental command!

In like manner, curative amendments should be proposed to the States revoking all the acts of Congress and the judicial decisions applying the Taxing Clause, the Commerce Clause, and the General Welfare Clause of the Constitution where they were not intended to be operative. It may be asked, for example: How can the National Labor Relations Act and all that has been done under it be unscrambled? The answer is that the States can resume the police power which they abandoned, but of which they could not divest themselves constitutionally, over their labor conditions and over all the needs of the people. Already that sentiment has found expression in many States.

In December, 1949, the State of Michigan had formally "seceded" from the District of Columbia. Its legislature had enacted a law forbidding strikes until a vote of the workers has been taken in accordance with specifications laid down. In the month named, the Department of Justice went into the Supreme Court of the United States to ask that the law of Michigan be restrained from operation, as the National Government had "preempted" that field, having reference to the unconstitutional National Labor Relations Act of Congress. But it has been shown from the Constitution and other authorities that the United States cannot take over a field inherently in the States and not susceptible of surrender by them.

The battle of the States for taking back their Union is opening up. They can win it easily. The whole power respecting the subject resides in them.

The interpretative amendment or amendments might declare that the grant of power to Congress by section 8 of Article I "to lay and collect . . . Taxes to pay the Debts and provide for the common Defence and general Welfare of the United States" shall be strictly construed as limiting expenditures for the Nation, at home and abroad, as a member of the family of nations, and shall not be taken to authorize the Government to engage in the manufacture of electric power, or to provide rural electrification, or to engage in any kind of industry or trade, or to provide aid to any class of individuals, who are protected by the inherent police power of the States.

Two clauses most wrongfully used

Second, the Commerce Clause shall be strictly construed to mean *regulation* of interstate (not intrastate) commerce as commerce was understood in the Constitutional Convention and as the word was applied by the courts and the Interstate Commerce Commission down to the 1930s; and it shall not be held to give jurisdiction to Congress of workers throughout the country except those engaged in commerce across State lines and with foreign countries; and it shall not be construed to authorize the engaging in commerce of any kind by Government by any means, direct or indirect.

Third, the General Welfare Clause shall be strictly construed to mean the welfare of the United States as a political entity, and as specified in the grant of powers in section 8 of Article I; and it shall not be taken to mean the welfare of persons as to health, safety, morals, education, and general well-being, matters of which the States have inherent jurisdiction by virtue of their police power, no part of which they surrendered to the Nation when they drew the Constitution. They adopted the Bill of Rights in further protection of that power.

Those suggestions are merely outlines of what should be developed in thorough detail in Congress for amendments to restore the Union to the States comprising it.

XV

THE COURSE OF PRESIDENTIAL ELECTIONS DURING THE LAST FORTY YEARS HAS MADE CLEAR THAT THE SAFETY OF THE REPUBLIC REQUIRES RETURN TO STRICT CONFORMITY WITH THE DIRECTIONS OF THE CONSTITUTION

IN THIS CHAPTER MAY BE FOUND THE ANSWER TO THE QUEStion of James Bryce (1 *The American Commonwealth*, 77) as to why our Presidential Office has not been oftener filled by the most competent men. He wrote that Europeans ask and Americans do not always explain "how it happens that this great office, the greatest in the world, unless we except the Papacy, to which any one can rise by his own merits, is not more frequently filled by great and striking men."

That it should be so filled always, was the careful design of the Constitutional Convention.

Let us proceed to search out the causes of the condition which seemed strange to Bryce and which we have tolerated too long.

The constitutional government of the United States is scientific. Science is defined as classified knowledge, or the conclusions which the classification compels. The causes of all the breakdowns of governments in history were gone over in the Constitutional Convention and it was concluded that law making, law enforcing, and law interpreting must be definitely in different hands.

All national and foreign concerns were assigned to the Nation and all others were retained by the States or the people.

All officials, State and National, were put under oath to support the Constitution and observe the boundaries to power specified in it. As far as could be, men with power were chained.

Education in this science is indispensable. It is badly lacking.

An early prophecy respecting the President

"The Executive of our Government is not the sole—it is scarcely the principal—object of my jealousy," wrote Jefferson from Paris, urging upon Madison the need of amendments making a Bill of Rights additional to the twelve provisions already in the Constitution; "the tyranny of the Legislature is the most formidable dread at present, and will be for many years. That of the Executive will come in turn, but it will be at a remote period."

The tyranny of the Executive has come.

The field of the President's authority under the Constitution is very limited. It does not include the States, to say nothing of the external world. In No. 75 of *The Federalist* that was pointed out by Hamilton:

"The execution of the laws and the employment of the common strength, either for this purpose or the common defense, seems to comprise all the functions of the Executive Magistrate."

The guilelessness of the Press

Yet the Press, instead of dealing with the great committees of the Senate and the House—on Ways and Means, on Banking, on Foreign Relations, and others—unwittingly abandoned Congress as the constitutional General Manager of the United States and gave itself over to the President as a sounding board for him to proclaim his "plans" and "policies." Dispatches from Washington daily refer to the President as "the administration." To be sure, an inferiority complex in the Congresses which brought upon them the description of "rubber stamp" contributed to this unfortunate situation.

To illustrate what a change has come in the strength of constitutional Government, a quotation is made from the *Autobiography of Seventy Years* of Senator George F. Hoar of Massachusetts (vol. 2, p. 46):

"The most eminent senators—Sumner, Conkling, Sherman, Edmunds, Carpenter, Frelinghuysen, Simon Cameron, Anthony, Logan—would have received as a personal affront a private message from the White House expressing a desire that they should adopt any course in the discharge of their legislative duties that they did not approve. If they visited the White House, it was to give, not to receive, advice. Any little company or coterie who had undertaken to arrange public policies with the President and to report to their associates what the President thought would have rapidly come to grief."

They ask him for guidance now.

A witness of Congressional deterioration

Maurice Francis Egan, our Minister to Denmark during World War I, noticed this change in the Congress when he returned home in 1918. Mentioning in *Recollections of a Happy Life* the change which he had found in the city, in the clubs, in the offices, and elsewhere, he added:

"The quality of our Legislature seemed to have deteriorated greatly. One had only to go to the Senate or the House and compare the speeches of Senators and Representatives with what one heard in the seventies and eighties to feel strongly that there was something radically wrong with the American people if these men were their voluntarily chosen delegates. A recent visit to Milwaukee and an examination of the Wisconsin legislators, as expressed in their speeches, has corroborated this impression."

Too much "democracy" and not enough republicanism. Those who promised to cure the evils of democracy by "more democracy" propagated more evils.

Jefferson wrote to Francis Hopkinson that even with a Bill of Rights added to the Constitution, "it would still have one fault in my eye, that of perpetual re-eligibility of the President."

Through absence of mind, especially on the part of the Bar, which, by reason of its education, should have known better than shirk the duty accepted in its oath, the election of the President of the United States has descended to what too closely resembles the popular vote for party nominees, the very course which the Constitutional Convention employed all its ability to prevent.

President has become in politics virtual chief

By force of the evil machinery which has been developed, the President, as it has several times been demonstrated since 1904, is able, through the use of patronage and other pressure, to control the National Nominating Convention of his party and renominate himself or pick his successor.[1]

It being in the nature of unchecked power to spread itself, conditions eventually enabled the President to step with impunity over the strong customary law of the American people against a third term. With that step, "new powers," as he called them, were accumulated so that nomination and election for a fourth term were even easier than they had been in the previous adventure. For the President had raised the number of nonelected Federal executive employees throughout the States from about 500,000 in 1932 to 3,121,153 [2] on June 30, 1944.

[1] This quotation from an article in a magazine in July, 1949, by one of the personal secretaries of President Franklin D. Roosevelt, is not so humorous as the writer thought it. One of the great perils of the times is revealed:

"Hannegan [Democratic Chairman] had a lengthy palaver with the Boss, and when he came out of the President's sitting room he was carrying the letter [of the President] naming Douglas or Truman as an acceptable running mate.

" 'Grace, the President wants you to retype this letter and switch these names so it will read "Harry Truman or Bill Douglas." ' The reason for the switch was obvious. By naming Truman first it implied that he was the preferred choice of the President. The Convention took it that way and Truman was nominated."

So have gone the safeguards set up by the Constitutional Convention for selecting the two chief Officers of the Republic.

[2] Report Joint Congressional Committee on Reduction Non-Essential Federal Expenditures.

On which side the bread is buttered

It is in human nature that such a body of appointees will support the appointing power to which they are indebted for their pay envelopes. Those men and women, and their children of voting age, must have cast 5,000,000 ballots in November, 1944, when ambition achieved its fourth term. In addition to that, many of the big cities to which Washington had been lavish in the unconstitutional granting of the money of the taxpayers for "relief" and for "development" supported the President for the fourth term.

From 13 Northern and Western cities he received 2,280,000 votes of his plurality of about 3,500,000. It is therefore manifest that, without the vote of those who were beholden to the President for personal favors, he would have been defeated.

"A power over a man's support," wrote Hamilton in No. 73 of *The Federalist,* "is a power over his will."

In 1948 the electoral conditions were so extravagantly bad that they should convince the most enthusiastic advocate of "democracy" that a popular election of the President and the Vice President would be the worst blow possible to our *representative* form of Government, and that the design of the Constitutional Convention, "that every practicable obstacle should be opposed to cabal, intrigue and corruption," has been proved by our experience to be sound.

History disproves need for National Nominating Convention

The first eleven Presidential elections took place without the help of the spectacular National Nominating Convention. There was no "campaign" supported by contributors expecting something.

That successful history shows that the National Nominating Convention is unnecessary—we can get along without it. The record which it has made discredits it.

Washington (twice) was chosen without a National Nominating Convention, so were Adams (once), Jefferson (twice), Madison (twice), Monroe (twice), and Jackson the first time. The convention for the second term of Jackson was rather a popular gathering to ratify his course during his first term, and not the Nominating Convention which we know.

So the American people and the Republic had a very good line of Chief Executives without the aid of machinery external to Government.

And during that half century Congress enacted no Corrupt Practices Laws.

After the ratifying convention mentioned, in 1832, Van Buren was nominated by a Democratic Convention in 1836. But the Whigs did not hold a convention.

For the first nine elections there was no platform and there was no popular vote.

And the people lived through those years in content without long platforms promising that Government would "give every body every thing." They were then so close to the Declaration of Independence that they still believed the Government to be a protector and not a provider.

States can resume control of Constitutional Election

Their experience proves to us that it would be very practicable for the States to resume control of their Union by returning to the constitutional election of the President and the Vice President.

And our latter-day experiences prove beyond argument that the National Nominating Convention will no longer do.

In "Thirty Years' View" the National Nominating Convention was condemned (1859) by Senator Thomas Hart Benton of Missouri thus:

"An irresponsible body (chiefly continued, and mainly dominated by professional office-seekers and officeholders) have usurped the election of the President (for the nomination is the election, so far as the party is concerned); and always making it with a view to their own profit in the monopoly of office and plunder."

In 1872 Charles Sumner spoke of the Convention as "the engine for the nomination of the President, allowing the people little more than to record its will" and becoming "the personal instrument of the President when elected, giving him dictatorial power, which he may employ in reducing the people to conformity with his purposes and promoting his re-election, all of which is hostile to good government, and of evil example."

Sumner favored the popular election of the President, but recent elections have demonstrated that the officeholders beholden to the Chief Executive would then control—there would be no real "popular" choice.

Direct election of President would be governmental suicide

In the Executive Department there were more than 2,000,000 on the pay rolls in 1948. In 1933, when Franklin D. Roosevelt took office, there were 575,123 on the rolls.

At his next inauguration, in 1937, there were 859,668. At his third inauguration, in 1941 (before World War II), there were 1,164,463 payrollers. At the fourth inauguration of President Roosevelt, in 1945, the number on his pay rolls was 3,465,420 (figures from Senate Committee Print No. 53, May-June, 1948). His plurality at the election was 3,596,227.

Thus, the payrollers alone, with the voting members of their families, could give him victory.

But in the election of 1948, giving the regime of Socialism, miscalled the "New Deal," the embryo of Communism, its fifth term, there were receiving checks from Washington, in addition to the 3,000,000 pay rollers, 2,500,000 beneficiaries of the Social Security Law, 3,500,000 farmers enjoying unconstitutional subsidies from the taxpayers of the country, 6,500,000 veterans, and 1,500,000 in the armed services.

The Presidential Office must be dissevered from that situation.

Customary law, made not by legislatures or constitutional conventions, but by the people themselves in daily life, has always been recognized in England and America as the very strongest form of legislation. Yet the customary law against a third term for the President went down in the election of 1940. That levee broken, the flood of Socialism took the land. In 1944, and again in 1948, it was, of course, irresistible.

Elections so foreign to Republic's welfare people cease voting

It cannot be said that those elections were turned in the best interests of the United States by the best sections of the people. Indeed, at none of them was a representative poll made. In 1948 the votes for all candidates aggregated 47,500,000. The Bureau of the Census informs us that in the country there were 95,000,000 eligible to vote.

Did the half of the voters who remained away from the polls do so from disgust or from despair?

It may have been a feeling of discouragement that they could accomplish anything against the multitude that kept them away from the polls in 1948, as they had been staying away for many years. Bryce wrote in *The American Commonwealth* (vol. 2, p. 331) on "the fatalism of the multitude" and "the tyranny of the majority" as they appeared to him in our country:

"Thus, out of the mingled feelings that the multitude will prevail, and that the multitude, because it will prevail, must be right, there grows a self-distrust, a despondency, a disposition to fall into line, to acquiesce in the dominant opinion, to submit thought as well as action to the encompassing power of numbers."

There never was a stronger statement made in support of the conclusion reached by the Constitutional Convention, namely, that the President and the Vice President should be selected and elected, not by the people at large (democracy), but by *representatives* of the people "appointed" as directed by the Fundamental Law.

Road back to Constitution is very plain

We have only to return to the barricades which the Constitution erected and which delinquent States, for one reason or another, or for none, abandoned. When the legislatures of the States take hold of the subject as the Constitution directs and *themselves* "appoint" electors to choose the President and the Vice President, the Corrupt Practices Acts as to the Presidential election will become dead letters, and the power of the pay rollers and the donees will be extinguished.

Then we shall have the Government of the days of George Washington.

Greatest fear of Constitutional Convention nearly realized

It was of the direct popular vote, liable to "cabal, intrigue, and corruption," that the Constitutional Convention stood in most fear. Our election of late years has given demonstration that they were right. From the fourth day of the Convention, when Edmund Randolph of Virginia presented a plan for a Constitution under which "a National Executive" was provided for, "to be chosen by the National Legislature," until the last day of the sessions, the subject of a Chief Executive was under almost continuous discussion. To no part of the Constitution did the Convention of able men at Philadelphia give so much patient care as they bestowed upon the plan to keep the choice of the first two officers protected from possibility of corruption, and also from domination by Congress.

The members of the Convention intended that the States would choose the chief officers of the United States, or, as someone has well put it, "the States united." This is a Government of States resulting from a Union of States which had won their independence as States by the prosecution of a Revolutionary War. The conception was that the States should pick and choose the Chief Executive of their Union.

On July 31, 1787, "the questions not yet settled" were

referred to a Committee of Eleven, which brought back on September 4 substantially what went into the Constitution for the choice of President. The Committee introduced to the Convention the idea of a Vice President. Its report was worked over from day to day until this second paragraph of Article II finally resulted (italics inserted):

States put imperative duty on themselves

"Each State *shall* appoint, in such manner as the legislature thereof may direct, a number of electors, equal to the whole number of Senators and Representatives to which the State may be entitled in the Congress: but no Senator or Representative, or person holding an office of trust or profit under the United States, shall be appointed an elector."

It is an erroneous idea that whatever the Legislature of a State may do, or permit, with respect to the appointment of electors is valid.

Clearly, the language quoted commands that the electors be agents of the State as an entity of the Union which they, as States, established. For the plan of the Constitutional Convention, as extensively shown later herein by Hamilton, was that the States should themselves select and elect the two chief officers of their Union.

"Although the spirit of an instrument, especially of a Constitution, is to be respected not less than the letter," said Chief Justice Marshall for the Supreme Court (4 Wheaton, 122) in 1819, "yet the spirit is to be collected chiefly from the words."

It was the spirit of the Constitutional Convention, acting as States, that the States should, as governmental entities, select and elect the President and the Vice President. Then that spirit was expressed in the plainest words, emphasized by the imperative *shall*—"Each State shall appoint."

If the Legislature does not wish to make the appointment itself, as legislatures did from the beginning down through many years, Colorado so appointing them when it came into the Union in 1876, then any other mode that it may establish must operate as an organ of the State so that the result will be the appointment *by the State*. Any other reading is disregardful of both the spirit and the letter of the provision of the Constitution quoted.

In view of the importance given to Statehood from the Declaration of Independence—"that these United Colonies are, and of Right ought to be, Free and Independent States"—down through the Articles of Confederation—"each State retains its sovereignty and independence"—and the closing words of the Constitutional Convention—"Done in Convention by the Unanimous Consent of the States present"—ending with "Each State *shall* appoint" electors to select and elect the President, the idea is wholly untenable that the legislatures of the States can turn over the choice by States of the Chief Executive to political groups or parties.

No roving commission to legislatures

In the provision just before quoted there is no roving commission to legislatures to have their will in the choice of electors of the President, or to abandon to political parties, or to conventions of parties, or to Presidential primaries, their constitutional duty. Electors appointed for a State by a committee of a political party, or by a convention of the party in the State to send delegates to a National Convention to nominate a Presidential ticket, or by primaries designed to express a choice of President, are not constitutional electors. They are not constitutional electors even where their names have been put on the national ballot of the party, as the practice was long ago, now largely abandoned through the "short ballot," and the people vote for them at the polls. For the voters are powerless to validate, *as an appointment by the State*, an appointment by a political committee or party, or by any other political machinery.

The mess for which legislatures are responsible

According to Beard's *American Government and Politics*, a number of States—not half—allow voters at primaries for choosing delegates to the National Nominating Convention of the party to express preference for Presidential nomination. That tends toward selection and election by the people directly, who were excluded by the States in the Constitutional Convention from such a direct participation in the choice of President. Their direct action was to be at the polls choosing legislators to appoint electors. An expression at the primaries is an introduction of "more democracy" against the representative structure.

In some States a list of the Presidential aspirants is printed on the primary ballot of each party and the voter may indicate at the polls his choice for President. That, also, tends toward the prohibited popular choice, and against the constitutional action of the people in voting for legislators to appoint electors.

In other States, candidates as delegates to the National Nominating Convention of the party may specify on the ballot whom they will favor in the convention for President.

"Thus," wrote Beard, "the voters may disclose their will indirectly." But the will of the voters cannot be legally so expressed. The constitutional expression of the will of the voters is given in their ballots for the members of the Legislature which is to choose the electors. At that election the people participate (or were intended to) in the election of the President. Their will so expressed constitutionally cannot be expressed again along the way to introduce "democracy" or "populism" against the representative system.

The effect of the short ballot

The early appointive system of the States, by which only the Governor and other top officers were elected by the vote of the people, gave way to "democracy," until all persons in public service, down to the least important, were named on the ballot. In one Congressional district in Chicago the voter was perplexed by the names of 334 nominees on the ticket. The evil had become so great and general that an agitation was begun for return to the appointive method, and the short ballot resulted. It struck from the ticket all the names of the Presidential electors, leaving the voter to cast a ballot directly for the President and Vice President named at the head of the ticket, which the Constitution plainly does not permit.

The short ballot was adopted by States with 350 of the 531 electoral votes. "The Book of States" for 1948-1949 says that 70 per cent of the voters ballot for the two candidates named at the head of the ticket. This, it should be repeated, they have no right to do. And so electors not appointed by the Legislature, or by any constitutional organ set up by it, and not voted for in most of the States, meet and vote for the nominees of the party and report the result to the President of the Senate!

Here is the most censurable default of the States in constitutional obligation. They can easily get right, and reduce the President from Imperator to constitutional Executive with limited powers.

Officeholders prevented from participating in Presidential elections

Members of Congress and all holders of office or trust were carefully prevented by the provision just before quoted from participating in election of the President. The Constitutional Convention seemed to have fear of the time when it would become to the interest of members of the Senate and the House, and of Federal officeholders generally, to control the choice of the President. With the introduction of the unconstitutional National Nominating Convention, at times overrun by members of Congress, members of the Cabinet, postmasters, and other Federal payrollers executing the will of the President by renominating him or nominating his pick for a successor, the very evil feared was brought to pass.

Although section 1 of Article II sternly commands that "no Senator or Representative, or Person holding an Office of Trust or Profit under the United States, shall be appointed an Elector," the spirit of that has many times been disregarded by National Nominating Conventions controlled in whole or in part by members of Congress and other Federal officeholders.

Convention's fear of Government
in politics becomes fact

The Constitutional Convention foresaw that the separation of powers which it designed would be undone if the Executive Department should become the creature of the Legislative Department and the officeholders. Both Madison and Jefferson expressed fear of the combining of powers in one hand or in one group.

In Henry L. Stoddard's *It Costs to Be President*, published by Harper & Brothers in 1938, it is shown that in the Republican National Convention of 1920 there were 18 Senators who had themselves chosen as delegates from nine States, and 4 more who were chosen singly from different States.

The Senators represented, or assumed to represent, 400 of 984 delegates.

Senator Lodge of Massachusetts was Chairman of the Convention.

Senator Watson of Indiana headed the Committee on Resolutions.

Senator Harding of Ohio was nominated for President.

Senator Lenroot of Wisconsin was almost nominated for the Vice Presidency, but the best heads thought that that would be going too far. So Governor Coolidge of Massachusetts was given second place.

While those Senators were not acting as the electors of the Constitution, they influenced the naming of, if they did not name, the two men for whom, under our degenerated system, the electors would be obliged to vote. Virtually they were acting as the forbidden electors. In *operate* in the choice of the person to whom so important a trust was to be confided. This end will be answered by committing the right of making it, *not to any pre-established body, but to men chosen by the people* for the special purpose, and at the particular conjuncture.

"It was equally desirable that the immediate election should be made by men most capable of analyzing the qualities adapted to the station, *and acting under circumstances favorable to deliberation,* and to a judicious combination of all the reasons and inducements which were proper to govern their choice. A *small number of persons,* selected by their fellow citizens from the general mass, will be most likely to possess the information and discernment requisite to such complicated investigations.

"It was also *peculiarly desirable* to afford as little opportunity as possible to tumult and disorder."

If Hamilton and his coworkers in the Constitutional Convention could have foreseen the "tumult and disorder" of our National Nominating Convention, what might they have done to prevent its coming!

"This evil," he went on, "was not least to be dreaded in the election of a magistrate who was to have so important an agency in the administration of the Government as the President of the United States. But the precautions which have been so happily concerted in the system under consideration promise an effectual security against this mischief."

Speed desired to prevent cabal and intrigue

On the need for prompt action and security from interference and what we call "pressure," Hamilton wrote:

"And as the electors chosen in each State are to assemble

and vote in the State in which they are chosen, this detached and divided situation will expose them much less to heats and ferments which might be communicated to them from the people than if they were all to be convened at one time in one place."

That is to say, any such aggregation as the National Nominating Convention would be abhorrent to Hamilton and his coworkers.

Addressing himself to what in time brought about the Corrupt Practices Acts of Congress, Hamilton said:

"Nothing was more desirable than that every practicable obstacle should be opposed to cabal, intrigue, and corruption. . . .

"But the Convention have guarded against all danger of this sort with the most provident and judicious attention. They have not made the appointment of the President to depend on any *pre-existing bodies of men* who might be tampered with beforehand to prostitute their votes; but they have referred it in the first instance to an *immediate act of the people of America,* to be exerted in the choice of persons for the temporary and sole purpose of making the appointment.

Convention sought to prevent officials from controlling election

"And they have *excluded from eligibility to this trust* all those who from situation might be suspected of too great devotion to the President in office."

Pointing out that members of Congress and others holding office cannot be electors, Hamilton continued:

"Thus, without corrupting the body of the people, the immediate agents in the election will at least enter upon the task free from any sinister bias. Their transient existence and their detached situation, already taken notice of, afford a satisfactory prospect of their continuing so to the conclusion of it. *The business of corruption, when it is to embrace so considerable a number of men, requires time as well as means. . . .*

"Another and no less important desideratum was that the Executive should be independent for his continuance in office on all but *the people themselves.* He might otherwise be tempted to sacrifice his duty to his complaisance for those whose favor was necessary to the duration of his official consequence."

About the second term, Hamilton said:

"This advantage will also be secured by making his re-election to depend on a *special body of representatives deputed by society* for the single purpose of making the important choice."

That would prevent him from renominating himself, as he does now.

Convention saw statesmen, not politicians, in Presidential office

Passing over some details as to the casting and counting of the votes of the electors, we come to this:

"The process of election affords a moral certainty that the office of President will never fall to the lot of any man who is not in an eminent degree endowed with the requisite qualifications. . . . It will not be too strong to say that there will be a constant probability of seeing the station filled by characters pre-eminent for ability and virtue."

Quotation has been made at some length to show with

what care the Constitutional Convention considered the choice of the two Chief Officers of the Republic, a subject which was under discussion from the opening of the Convention until near its close. The electors spring from the people. Recently elected legislators take immediate steps to carry out the will of the voters under the direction of the Constitution.

**Evil foreseen by Convention
has broken down barrier**

The growth of the evil which the Constitutional Convention endeavored so faithfully to forestall has long been watched with apprehension by capable men. Thirty years before the election of 1944, when the Federal payrollers through the land (3,121,153), *with* the vote of the big cities which were supporting the administration at Washington in its quest for a fourth term, were larger in number than the plurality (3,596,278) which the President received, Senator George W. Norris of Nebraska said this:

"When this influence [patronage] is combined and used for the perpetuation in office of the head of our Government, it is a danger to free institutions and strikes at the very root of democracy. Such a danger leads directly toward a monarchy and takes away from the people themselves the right to select their own Chief Magistrate. . . .

"It exists now to a greater extent than it did, because Federal offices have been multiplied manyfold and partisan political machines . . . are now enthroned in power greater than ever in our history."

In 1914, when Senator Norris made that statement, there were 482,721 Federal payrollers living on the tax-

A HISTORY OF LAWLESS GOVERNMENT 277

payers and "doing politics" throughout the country for the administration in power. As previously seen from a report of a committee of the Senate, there were 3,596,278 of them in 1944 within the Executive Department of the President.

Direct election would not give popular control

Even had an amendment to the Constitution made legal the direct vote of the people for a President, as some persons have advocated, the free will of the people would have been frustrated in 1940, 1944, and 1948 by that controlled vote and the vote of like inclination which went with it. The constitutional vote is needed.

Since 1907 Congress has been striving unsuccessfully to keep suppressed the corruption and the peril to Government necessarily latent in this burlesque on constitutional procedure which we call the Presidential campaign. Corrupt Practices Laws have been enacted, amended, and rewritten, but to no effect. A revision in 1925 of the Corrupt Practices Law made it unlawful for any *corporation* "to make a contribution in connection with any election" for the choice of Federal officers, including a President and a Vice President.

A series of futile acts against corruption

In 1939 an Act to Prevent Pernicious Political Activities forbade *persons* to contribute, directly or indirectly, in excess of $5,000 a year in connection with a Federal election. That would allow a person to put up $20,000 during a Presidential term. It also prohibited intimidation of Federal employees, the promise of employment, the use of relief funds, and some other activities respecting such an election. Then it forbade those in the Executive branch "to take any part in political management or political campaign." The present-day extraordinary campaigning activity of the President is seemingly covered by that prohibition, as it should be.

In 1940 the foregoing act was amended by an act retaining in effect the act of 1925 and prohibiting a *political committee* from collecting and spending over $3,000,000 a year in relation to a Federal election. That would permit the gathering of $12,000,000 by a political committee during the term of the President! It also prohibited the purchase of advertising or any commodity in connection with a Federal election.

In 1943 an act relating to the use and operation by the United States of plants, mines, and facilities for the promotion of war amended the act of 1925 by writing "*labor organization*" along with "corporation," which was the first contributor to be checked by Congress. It forbade contributions respecting a Presidential or other Federal election and fixed a penalty of $5,000. Every officer was made liable to a fine of $1,000, or imprisonment for one year, or both. This law did not come until seven years after a reported contribution by a labor union of $60,000 to the support of President Roosevelt in the campaign of 1936. It is stated in Beard's *American Government and Politics* that "labor organizations contributed $770,218 to the Democratic National Committee in 1936."

Thus the corporation, the person, the political committee, and the labor organization have been successively brought under the Corrupt Practices Laws. But with the extension of the laws the collecting and spending of money in Presidential campaigns have grown larger in amounts and more offensive in methods.

The only way to prevent "cabal, intrigue, and corruption" in relation to the election of the President was thought out in the Constitutional Convention with an imperative direction that it be followed.

The President as a gatherer of party funds

The act of 1940 undertook also to cure a sore which appeared in the Democratic campaign of 1936, when the party was in debt $400,000. In addition to Jackson Day Dinners at $100 a plate in Washington, and at lower prices throughout the country, which were addressed by the President by radio, and which yielded $315,000, the "Book of the Democratic Committee" was prepared and autographed by the President—the autographed copies selling for $100 each. They were taken in large numbers by the heads of corporations. Of course, the general manager of a great company had to consider what might happen if he should decline to buy a dozen or two of the books. While the money was gathered to meet the debt of a campaign gone by, and the Corrupt Practices Act relates to an election "to be held," the spirit, if not the letter, of the law was violated by the transactions. The Attorney General ruled that the law was not violated, but Congress expressed its dissent from that ruling by providing in the Act of 1940 that it would be unlawful for any corporation or person "to purchase goods, commodities, *advertising*, or *articles* of any kind or description" where the proceeds would benefit candidates for Federal elective offices (italics added).

From advertisements and sales the book brought in $860,000. As before stated, the Jackson Day Dinners yielded $315,000, making the two devices for avoiding the Corrupt Practices Act a total of $1,175,000.

Almost another million was raised and spent by organizations outside of the political party—the Good Neighbor League, the Progressive National Committee, Labor's Non-Partisan League, Young Democratic Clubs, and many others.

In the campaign of 1940 the Democratic Committee prepared to repeat the use of the book autographed by the President, but the Second Hatch Act, of July 19, 1940, dashed the plan. Already contracts for advertisements in the book had been made up to $340,000.

President Roosevelt by-passed Corrupt Practices Act

In the campaign of 1944, the use of the money-coining book autographed by the President in 1936 having been prevented by an act of Congress, which made the transaction illegal, President Roosevelt proposed the formation of a Thousand-Dollar Club of at least a thousand members. A million or more was raised almost on the instant. It was promised that each person contributing $1,000 would be taken into the councils of the Government and that he would be treated with special favor during the services of inauguration. The dispatches from Washington on January 20, the day of the fourth inauguration of the President, told of the presence of the contributors and of "a full-scale program of Inauguration Day social events" which had been prepared for them.

What activities to occupy the mind and time of the President of the United States! [3]

And what will the authorities in Moral Philosophy say (leaving to one side the question of constitutional observance) of the offer of the administration to take into the councils of the United States nonelected and nonchosen persons in consideration of money! And what should the people say?

As long as there are so many persons and "interests" seeking advantage or pecuniary gain from the party in control of Government, and as long as the party must look to them for funds with which to function, corruption will necessarily underlie the nomination and election of a President by the present unconstitutional method.

In the good days that may be ahead

When the States resume their constitutional function in the choice of a President and a Vice President, then the members of the legislatures chosen at the ballot box by the people will "appoint" electors of a President and a Vice President who will look over the country and vote for the two men standing highest in their opinion or in public

---

[3] From the speech of acceptance of Grover Cleveland in 1884 and one speech thereafter, and the address of acceptance of William McKinley from the front porch of his home in Ohio in 1896 and two or three others from the same standpoint to visiting groups, we have come a longer way than the years indicate to the "sound and fury" of the late Presidential campaigns, with the nominee racing around the country in special trains and calling at every stop to the people to support him. Since the special train was first employed, the radio has come, and both means are availed of by the candidate for presenting to the masses the merits of his party and himself. The spectacle presented is far from edifying.

Choice of the President by the electors of the Constitution will stop that unseemly exhibition, along with the grotesque Nominating Convention and the evils of the campaign fund.

esteem. That will produce nonpartisan and highly competent Executives. We shall have a President of the United States instead of a political party. That is to say, for illustration, a President so chosen would not appoint to the courts of the United States 185 Democrats and only 3 Republicans, most of them neophytes in law; ignoring in his selections seasoned jurists on the Supreme Courts of the 48 States. Nor would he name to the Supreme Court of the United States 9 of his political supporters, because he would not be in debt for the help of a party.[4] Nor would he be interested in caring for persons rejected by the people at the polls, affronting their former constituents by giving to "lame ducks" offices, in some instances for life, with good salaries.

President would not be embarrassed by political bargains

He would not be forced by political considerations "a very difficult letter to write," asking one of the ablest men in the service to resign to make place for one who "deserves almost any service which he believes he can satisfactorily perform: I told him this at the end of the campaign, in which he displayed the utmost devotion to our cause." The President should not become involved in a debt like that, nor should the people be given service measured by such a standard.

In short, we should have in every instance a nonpartisan President.

[4] The Lord High Chancellor of England, whose duty is to select and appoint the judges of the Kingdom, spoke to the American Bar Association in 1947 and mentioned that he had never appointed to the Bench a member of his own political party.

Men of capability would have chance to serve Republic

The electors will be able to consider governors who have won public approval by wise and economical administration. They will weigh in the balance members of Congress who have exhibited in service true American vision of the proper place of this Republic in the family of nations, and who have been guided in all their actions by the provisions of the Constitution.

Those two classes are mentioned because, generally speaking, no one without the training of experience in the field of government or law should be thought of for the Presidency.

How many Presidents of this century would have been kept out of the White House had the constitutional method of choosing been employed! And how much of the disastrous to constitutional Government would have been prevented!

Political parties as at present could be maintained

The party organizations could be maintained in the States as usual. They could send Republican or Democratic believers to Congress as they are doing now. Congress could then resume its constitutional function as General Manager of the United States, which would have administration according to the tenets of the party in control. The President would withdraw from determining policy and new laws and confine his industry to the comparatively few duties assigned to him by the Constitution.

There is just one way to put the President in his constitutional place. That is to elect him by electors "appointed" by each State "in such manner as the legislature thereof may direct," [5] the members of the legislature having just come from the people at the ballot box. They act quickly in voting for a President and a Vice President. It was this which made the members of the Constitutional Convention feel that they had, by shortening the time and quickening the action, removed the subject from the opportunities for the cabal, intrigue, and corruption to which Hamilton referred in *The Federalist* and which have been among the most striking features of the National Nominating Convention and its "campaign."

The tyranny of the Executive which Jefferson said would come "at a remote period" is here. By the power of patronage, chiefly, and money he has overcome the Legislative Department and reduced the Judicial Department below respect. The craven Senate enabled him to set up a Judiciary to his liking. The farcical vote for "electors" of a President is controlled by his appointees on the rapidly enlarging pay rolls of the Executive Department.

Illegal Presidential power responsible for departures from Constitution

No other practice in Government has gone so far from the Constitution, and that transgression has been attended by correspondingly bad results.

Most of the evils in National Government of which peo-

---

[5] The legislators should *themselves* "appoint" from among the competent people of the State the number of electors to which the State is entitled. In view of what has resulted from allowing political parties to name electors to be voted upon by the people, the legislature should return to first principles and allow no intermediary to have anything to do with the great duty. It should courageously perform this function in relation to the choice of a President and a Vice President of the Union of States.

ple complain will disappear when the States take back their Union. The third term and the fourth have told what to the observing and educated American was not in need of telling. "A conclave of anthropophagi" has ousted the Government of the Constitution.

In support of the proposition of this chapter, that the present method of selecting and electing the President and the Vice President is a disgrace to our constitutional system, another quotation from Henry L. Stoddard's *It Costs to Be President* is made.

Roosevelt not choice of his own State in 1932

In the Democratic National Nominating Convention of 1932 Franklin D. Roosevelt could not muster the number of delegates required by the two-thirds rule of the party established by Andrew Jackson to prevent the choice of a man not in the very highest favor. Stoddard wrote:

"Roosevelt realized that he must make a drastic move. He had to have aid.

"There was just one man who could supply enough votes in a bunch to insure success. That man was William Randolph Hearst. He was sponsor for the John Nance Garner boom. He had persuaded the Texas Congressman into the race and had aided him to carry the Texas delegation. He was solely responsible for defeating Roosevelt in the California primaries, and for instructing the Golden Gate delegates, headed by William Gibbs McAdoo, for Garner.

"Roosevelt knew that there was no need to open negotiations with Garner and his lieutenants; the real decision was with Hearst—the others could be talked with later. Farley was given the job of telephoning Hearst at his San Simeon ranch in California. He did it. Straight to Hearst went the Roosevelt argument that 'if you don't take me you will get Smith or Baker.' That was no news to Hearst; he had foreseen that possibility. He preferred Roosevelt to either of the other two.

"Two hours later Paul Block, the well-known publisher, and I sat in his room for a good-night exchange of opinion. He then said that he had been talking over the telephone with 'W. R.' and that a deal had been arranged by which the 69 Texas and California delegates, after complimenting Garner on two or three ballots, would swing to Roosevelt. He added that Garner would go on the ticket as Vice President and McAdoo was to have no opposition in California for the Democratic nomination for U. S. Senator.

An outsider controlled convention nominating Roosevelt

"The news was in confidence, however, for Hearst, of course, had no power to release delegates pledged to any candidate. That was for Garner and McAdoo to do. Hearst, however, undertook to talk with both of them and with Mayor Cermak of Chicago, who controlled the Illinois delegation. He persuaded all three that after a few ballots they should turn to Roosevelt, and they did.

"It all happened that way, as the convention records attest, but it also happened that 190 delegates, including a majority from Roosevelt's home State of New York, stubbornly refused to make the nomination unanimous.

"When Roosevelt airplaned from Albany to Chicago to accept '100 per cent' the tendered leadership and party platform he faced the only National Convention that had ever failed to give its entire vote finally to its nominee—

except the Republican National Convention of 1912, when Taft had his battle with Theodore Roosevelt.

"So turns the wheel of fortune in politics."

But what the Constitutional Convention strove from first to last to exclude from the choice of the President and the Vice President was "politics"—what Hamilton described as cabal, intrigue, and corruption.

Badly reasoned proposal to amend Constitution

A resolution to amend the Constitution is pending in Congress by which, instead of letting *all* the electoral votes of a State go to the candidate carrying the popular vote, the electoral votes would be apportioned between or among the candidates according to the shares of their parties in the popular poll.

In case of failure of choice by that method, the proposal would send the election to Congress in joint session, where the vote would be by members, not by States. That would give the large States control. Equality among the States is the first idea of the Constitution.

And the emphatic design of the Constitution (Twelfth Amendment) is that when the electors appointed by the States fail to choose a President and the election thus goes to the House of Representatives, "the votes shall be taken *by States,* the representation from each State having one vote; a *quorum* for this purpose shall consist of a member or members from *two-thirds of the States,* and a majority of all *the States* shall be necessary to a choice."

Therefore, the new resolution, which passed the Senate on February 1, 1950, by a vote of 64 to 27, is at war with the paramount idea of American constitutional government as repeatedly expressed from the Declaration of

Independence down—the equal position of the States in the Union. Indeed, the only amendment forbidden by Article V is one by which a State, "without its Consent, shall be deprived of its equal Suffrage in the Senate."

In the Farewell Address, Washington cautioned that we resist "the spirit of innovation" upon the principles of the Constitution, "however specious the pretext." What is the pretext for the resolution? That the Presidential election should be determined by an approximation of the direct popular vote for candidates named by the parties.

First step in electing President taken by people

But the idea is quite erroneous that the electoral system of the Constitution denies to the people a voice in the election of the President. In *The Federalist* (No. 68) Hamilton wrote (italics inserted):

"It was *desirable* that *the sense of the people should operate* in the choice of the person to whom so important a trust was to be committed."

On the same point, Jay wrote in No. 64 of *The Federalist:*

"They [the States in the Convention] have directed the President to be chosen by select bodies of electors, *to be deputed by the people* for that express purpose."

That is where begins the choice of the President and the Vice President *by the people at the polls.*

No voting at primaries, or for the head of the ticket, or otherwise, has any constitutional relation to the election.

The manacles which the Constitutional Convention put on the Chief Executive to prevent him from becoming Caesar—manacles which he has slipped—must be restored to place by the lawful election.

Proposed amendment would be futile anyway

But what good would such an amendment accomplish after a man over two thousand miles from the National Nominating Convention had named for the Presidential ticket the two candidates of a party to which he had not consistently belonged? Or, after external and presumably mercenary forces had nominated a Democrat for the Republican ticket? Or, after an aspirant reputed to be a master of organization had snuffed out other candidates in the Nominating Convention and taken the place on the ticket for himself? Or, after a President had nominated himself for a second term and then picked his successor? Or, after another President had nominated himself for the second, third, and fourth terms?

It is not a pro rata distribution of the electoral vote of a State that is called for. Indeed, strictly speaking, there is now no electoral vote. What is called the electoral vote is an amorphous creation rising from the delinquency of the States and the permitted, if not invited, manipulations of party organizations and politicians.

Proposed amendment carries unconstitutional theory of "democracy"

The idea behind the resolution to change the Constitution for the removal of misunderstood factors in the problem dates back at least to 1893, over 56 years, nearly half of the 160 years that our Fundamental Law has been in effect. It is the idea from which the Initiative, the Referendum, and the Recall came, which brought the direct primary and the "presidential preference" primary, and which broke down the House of States—the idea that democratic or popular action should supersede the representative Government by which George Washington and his compatriots put the United States "in the forefront of nations," as the British historian Green expressed it.

It is an alarming fact that for more than half a century the pressure for "more democracy" has not been relaxed in seats of learning, so called, in parts of the Press, in some political groups, and in organizations of the social minded.

The pending proposal to amend the Constitution by introducing the popular vote to a dangerous degree—never before legally involved—in determining the result of the election, would be the beginning of the end of the representative or Republican process.

Nor would the suggestion from several quarters, that Congress (the taxpayers, now so comfortable financially!) put up a campaign fund of $3,000,000 to each of the two parties and thus keep out "contributors" in quest of something, help against the evil which the delinquent States have brought upon the country.

Governmental battle between populism and constitutional republicanism

The paramount question in this land today is whether the representative method of the Constitution will be restored as to the choice of the President and the Vice President, or whether the democratic or popular infiltration of the last half century and more will be extended to that.

Writing ninety years ago (2 *Thirty Years' View*, p. 787) in condemnation of the National Nominating Convention, Senator Thomas Hart Benton of Missouri put the choosing of the President with slavery as one of the two "trials" confronting the Republic. War disposed of slavery. The other "trial" remains before us.

The jurisdiction of the problem and the plain solution are wholly with the States.

In 1874 a committee of the Senate made use in a report of the following language:

"Whatever provisions may be made by statute, or by State constitutions, to choose electors by the people, there is no doubt of the right of the legislatures to resume the power at any time, for it can neither be taken away nor abdicated."

That language was quoted by the Supreme Court of the United States (146 U. S. 1) in an election case in 1892.

People of the States can direct legislatures to appoint electors

It is for the people of each State, who cannot be unaware of the peril of present conditions, to rouse themselves and direct their legislatures to appoint presidential electors in pursuance of the constitutional command and in protection of the Republic.

This vigilance has become the more imperative because correspondents in Washington, who scatter to the country curbstone opinions on the laws and the Constitution, have begun to write frequently of the "inherent powers" of the President and what he may do by the use of them—perhaps in retiring Congress altogether! To accept that notion would be to turn him loose in "a boundless field of power," of the dangers in which Jefferson gave warning, "no longer susceptible of any definition."

The *man* in the White House has heritable rights and

powers, like every other individual, "among which are life, liberty and the pursuit of happiness."

But the Chief Executive in the White House, an altogether different character, is just as much a manufacture as a child's doll—absolutely without any power not specifically conferred by some provision of the Constitution. No power can inhere in this creature apart from those given by the States when they created it to serve—not to master —them.

When State legislatures resume their duty

When the legislatures of the States return to their constitutional duty of appointing as electors the most able and discerning men in their respective commonwealths to vote for a President and a Vice President, the Chief Executive will be a person with adequate understanding of and respect for our governmental theory and practice.

When the first session of the 81st Congress ended in 1949, there were remaining on the calendar a score or more of demands for unconstitutional legislation from the "program" of the President, who is not authorized by the Constitution to have a program and take control of legislation. He is required to "recommend" measures, but Congress may accept the recommendations or not.

The President in disregard of the Constitution

We have learned from Madison, Hamilton, Wilson, and others of the Constitutional Convention; from Jefferson, President Cleveland, and other Presidents, that the limitations in section 8 of Article I against spending by Congress —"to pay the Debts and provide for the common Defence and general Welfare of the United States" only—restrict it

A HISTORY OF LAWLESS GOVERNMENT

to the enumerated instances following in that section, namely:

> To borrow money
> regulate commerce
> establish rules for naturalization
> govern bankruptcies
> coin money
> fix standards of weights and measures
> punish counterfeiting
> establish post offices and post roads
> protect inventors and authors
> constitute courts inferior to the Supreme Court
> punish piracies and offenses against international law
> declare war and make rules therefor
> raise and support armies—for two years only
> provide a navy
> make rules governing all armed forces
> provide for calling out the Militia of the States
> provide for training, arming and disciplining the Militia
> govern the District of Columbia
> govern places in States when permitted to own forts, etc.
>
> And make all laws "necessary and proper" to execute the foregoing.

In all other relations the American makes his way untouched by the National Government. In 1933 that had been the settled doctrine. Legislation since then touching other matters has been unconstitutional.

Departures by the Chief Executive from that chart

From what has been shown, it is plain that in the message of the President to the second session of the 81st Congress, on January 4, 1950, on the state of the Union, these requests for legislation were beyond its constitutional powers to spend money:

> World economic recovery
> Expansion of world trade
> Improvement of living standards in regions of poverty
> Large capital from the United States to undeveloped regions
> Stabilization of agriculture by price supports
> Development by Federal money of national resources, soil, water, etc.
> Promote education by Federal grants of money
> Distribute property fairly
> Aid with capital independent businesses
> Set up Labor Extension Service
> Pursue Federal housing under Housing Act, 1949
> Control rents for another year
> Countrywide development of public electric power
> Develop electric power in St. Lawrence River
> Set up National Science Foundation
> Promote health by Federal grants of money
> Provide unemployment compensation
> Expand hospitals
> Provide medical insurance
> Enact Civil Rights Law
> Expend for growth of domestic economy
> Work for a better life for all (in appendix)

Those subjects that touch "the health, safety, morals, education, and general well-being of the people" fall within the police power of the States, which, we have heretofore seen, the States cannot constitutionally abdicate and Congress cannot constitutionally take over. The others are completely "out of bounds" as to any American government.

It is tragic that the failure of the educator to inculcate

in the youth of the land American constitutional principles, together with the abandonment by the States of their constitutional duty to elect the President, should bring from the White House such a message.

It is equally tragic that a Congress of 531 members should have received without rebuke or protest proposals for such unconstitutional outlays of money, when the spending of the Government in time of peace was 45 billion a year as compared with 31 billion a year during World War II.

President Truman employed more than 5,500 words in urging Congress to take legislative action on 22 matters over which the Constitution gives it no jurisdiction. A character in English fiction set for him an example which he would have done better to imitate. Addressing the voters (as President Truman really was doing), Tittlebat Titmouse promised them that when elected to Parliament he would put through A Bill for Giving Every Body Every Thing.

The philosophy of Titmouse has superseded the constitutional principles of American Government.

XVI

IN CONCLUSION AND IN RETROSPECT

The Constitutional Convention took up a task such as had never before been performed.

It was known by the historians at Philadelphia that alliances of States, or confederations or confederacies, had always bred dissensions and fallen apart. Indeed, it was because their own Confederation had been sinking and was practically gone that they were in convention working for "a more perfect Union."

They knew also that in anything tighter than a confederation the individual States forming it had always lost identity through absorption in the central organization. Thus, the Confederacy of Delos (about 480 B. C.), which was formed by Aristides to consolidate Greek cities and colonies in defense against Persia, and which was to last until the pieces of iron thrown into the sea should float, was before long weakened by secessions. "The confederacy of equal states," says the historian Betten in *Ancient World*, "became an empire, with Athens for its 'tyrant city.'"

Against this loss of identity, in particular, they were determined to guard. The units in the failing Confederation had, by the Declaration of Independence, proclaimed themselves to be "free and independent States."

And in the Articles of Confederation, their first Constitution, they declared that "each State retains its sovereignty and independence." So the individuality of the State in this Union never should have been treated lightly.

The delegates from all of the States represented were of one mind for preserving perpetually the identity and sovereignty of their commonwealths, so far as that could be worked out. They organized a Union (as distinguished from a confederation, which they then were) which would present a front for them to the nations of the world in negotiations and in defense and offense. It would also take over the home concerns which were essentially national, and especially those respecting which there had been lack of harmony among them, as in the case of commerce across State lines.

So, by section 8 of Article I of the Constitution which they drafted, they gave to the Congress of the Union (what that of the Confederation lacked) power to raise money by taxation "to pay the Debts and provide for the common Defence and general Welfare." They gave Congress power to borrow money on the credit of the Union, and the next important grant of power was to regulate commerce among the States and with foreign nations. After those grants came authority for uniform laws for naturalization and bankruptcy, for coinage, weights and measures, counterfeiting, post office, declaring war, raising armies and navies (but for not longer than two years), and for laws making those grants effective.

Then, by section 10, the States surrendered to the Nation the power to make treaties, to coin money, and a few others.

Thus, the lines between the governments of the States

and that of the Union had been very clearly drawn. And thus there had been blended the Confederation and the Nation. But both remained in their respective individualities. By the organization the Confederation would be prevented from falling apart. And the Nation would let the States of the confederation alone.

It was to this system, by which men attempted for the first time successfully to strip themselves of the features of power that tend to tyranny, that Senator Hoar paid this tribute:

"The most sublime thing in the Universe, except its Creator, is a great and free people governing itself by a law higher than its own desire."

That arrangement has, of late years, been failing.

It was to make clear to the reading American the causes of the decline of the constitutional system as set up, and the course which should be taken to stop it, that this book was written.

The three most important conclusions to be derived from this study are these:

1. A Government erected by deep scholarship upon a Fundamental Law must fail without sufficient scholarship in the people who choose its officers to sense instantly and resist courageously every proposal to depart from its principles; and to operate as inoculation against notions, foreign and domestic, for governmental paternalism.

2. The States, which insisted during the writing of the Constitution, and afterward by demanding a Bill of Rights, that their complete independence in all but international and strictly national affairs should be respected forever, must recover the constitutional position which, through the incompetence of their representatives in Con-

gress, they have too much given over to Federal control.

3. As the Judiciary is the keystone of the American arch, only the most experienced and capable legal scholars should be appointed by the President to judicial seats; and it is the high constitutional duty of the Senate to refuse confirmation of appointments of any other kind.

With those three essentials brought into effect, our Republic should serve mankind perpetually.

Remarking that if angels were caring for us there would be no need for the devices which we employ "to control the abuses of government," a writer of *The Federalist* (No. 51) added:

"In framing a government which is to be administered by men, over men, the great difficulty lies in this: you must first enable the government to control the governed; and, in the next place, oblige it to control itself."

That is the surpassing task confronting the American today—to compel his Government to control itself.

Table of Cases

TABLE OF CASES

(From a careful study of this Table a clear conception may be obtained of the contradictions and incongruities which have been brought into constitutional law by decisions of late years)

Page

AGRICULTURAL ADJUSTMENT ACT, 1933

    held unconstitutional as taxing one class for another and invading police field of States. U. S. v. Butler (1936), 297 U. S. 1   23, 133, 200

AMENDING THE CONSTITUTION

    Supreme Court refused to do amending in case arising from Income Tax Law of 1894. Pollock v. Farmers' Loan, etc. (1895), 157 U. S. 429   61

    not to be done by Supreme Court: Chief Justice Hughes in Bituminous Coal Case. Carter v. Carter Coal Co. (1936), 298 U. S. 238   23, 127

    Eleventh Amendment adopted to overrule decision Supreme Court upholding money judgment against State. Chisholm v. Georgia (1793), 2 Dallas 419   250

"ASSUMPTIONS" by Supreme Court

    assumed in case arising under law of New York that Due Process Clause of Fourteenth Amendment makes operative against States First Amendment as to freedom of speech and Press. Gitlow v. New York (1925), 268 U. S. 652   221

    foregoing cited as authority for holding free Press of First Amendment likewise made applicable against States. Near v. Minnesota (1931), 283 U. S. 697   219

                                                             Page

    same proposition assumed in many other decisions. Home Owners Loan Corporation assumed to have been within power of Congress. Graves v. O'Keefe (1939), 306 U. S. 466   109

    assumed, against facts available, that States could not care for needy, justifying entry for police service. Justice Cardozo in Steward Machine v. Davis (1937), 301 U. S. 548   195

BANK

    held United States, without specific grant, could incorporate to aid in transaction of own fiscal business. Chief Justice Marshall in McCulloch v. Maryland (1819), 4 Wheaton 316   102

BILL OF RIGHTS (First 10 Amendments)

    written against Federal power and not made applicable to States by Fourteenth Amendment. Slaughter-House Cases (1872), 16 Wallace 36   227

    foregoing followed. Twining v. New Jersey (1908), 211 U. S. 78   230

BITUMINOUS COAL ACT, 1935

    held unconstitutional as invasion police field of States; amendment of Constitution not for Court. Carter v. Carter Coal Co. (1936), 298 U. S. 238   23, 127

CHILD-LABOR

    law of Congress under Commerce Clause prohibiting movement interstate of product of workers under 18 years, held not regulation commerce. Hammer v. Dagenhart (1918), 247 U. S. 251   86, 186

    law of Congress taxing burdensomely product of workers under 18 years, held police regulation, not for revenue. Bailey v. Drexel, etc. (1922), 259 U. S. 20   87

TABLE OF CASES

Page

CITIZENSHIP, National, State
  Fourteenth Amendment recognized and defined two citizenships. Slaughter-House Cases (1873), 16 Wallace 36   227
  States retain authority over fundamental civil rights, with certain exceptions, for security of which Government established. Slaughter-House cases, before cited   227
  tax by Nevada on persons leaving State held restraint on right National citizenship. Crandall v. Nevada (1880), 6 Wallace 35   226
  California could not abridge National citizenship by law to exclude indigent persons. Edwards v. California (1941), 314 U. S. 160.   214
  practice of law not right of National citizenship and may be denied by State. Bradwell v. Illinois (1872), 16 Wallace 130   230
  National citizenship not involved where Connecticut gave defendant due process of *its* law. Palko v. Connecticut (1937), 302 U. S. 319   232
  tax by State on importers held by Marshall violative of right National citizenship. Brown v. Maryland (1827), 12 Wheaton 419   226
  no right National citizenship violated by requirement of permit to speak on Boston Common. Davis v. Massachusetts (1897), 167 U. S. 43   238
  see also Bill of Rights

COMMERCE CLAUSE
  wrongfully employed by Congress in Child-Labor Act, 1916. Hammer v. Dagenhart (1918), 247 U. S. 251   86, 186
  stretched against all precedents in Packers and Stockyards Act, 1921. Stafford v. Wallace (1922), 258 U. S. 495   97, 101
  Sherman Law adequate in regulating packers and other shippers. U. S. v. Swift (1905), 196 U. S. 375   99

Page

CONSPIRACY

A lawful act, when conceived by many to do damage, is conspiracy as denounced in Criminal Code of U. S. Chief Justice Fuller in Pettibone v. U. S. (1893), 148 U. S. 197 — 32

CONTRACT

right to denied by law of New York fixing prices for milk, and sustained. Nebbia v. New York (1934), 291 U. S. 502 — 171

CORPORATION

United States can create corporation only to aid in discharge of governmental functions. McCulloch v. land (1819), 4 Wheaton 316 — 102

COURTS

when open must be used by Government instead of other means. Ex parte Milligan (1866), 4 Wallace 2 — 35n
adequate in industrial (labor) disputes; strike stopped by injunction and strikers and leader fined. Held, even had Government not seized mines, court could issue injunction pending final decision upon its own jurisdiction. U. S. v. United Mine Workers (1947), 330 U. S. 258 — 36

DELEGATION OF POWER

Congress cannot delegate its legislative power to President, but it may pass administrative power under specified policy. Panama Oil v. Ryan (1934), 293 U. S. 388 — 133, 134

DIVORCE

Full Faith and Credit Clause does not require a State to give effect to a foreign decree in conflict with

TABLE OF CASES 307

Page

its public policy. Andrews v. Andrews (1903), 188
U. S. 14   93
Williams v. North Carolina (1945), 325 U. S. 226   94
judicial power to grant divorce is founded on the domicile, the place where one resides and intends to stay. Williams v. North Carolina, before cited   94

DUE PROCESS OF LAW

defined in quotation from Magna Carta. Twining v. New Jersey (1908), 211 U. S. 78   235
guaranteed against Nation by Fifth Amendment and against States by Fourteenth; "strange misconception" of scope in Fourteenth. Davidson v. New Orleans (1877), 96 U. S. 97   237-8
"this process in the States regulated by the law of the States." Walker v. Sauvinet (1875), 92 U. S. 90   235
Due Process Clause in Fourteenth Amendment "does not draw all the rights in Federal Bill of Rights under its protection," as, for example, against self-incrimination. Adamson v. California (1947), 332 U. S. 46   233
due process of law in Fourteenth Amendment "refers to the law of the land *in each state*," not the law of the United States; due process under National law not required of States. Hurtado v. California (1884), 110 U. S. 516   226

ELECTION OF PRESIDENT

wholly in power of States and cannot be taken away or abdicated. McPherson v. Blacker (1892), 146 U. S. 1   291

EMERGENCY

declaring an emergency to exist does not give Congress expansion of power, or new power. Home Building and L. Ass'n v. Blaisdell (1934), 290 U. S. 398   135

Page

EQUAL PROTECTION
guaranteed against States by Fourteenth Amendment denied by law of Arizona exempting strikers from liability for damage, others not being exempt. Truax v. Corrigan (1921), 257 U. S. 312 — 239
denied by ruling of Texas unfairly draining oil lands of large owners by small owners. Railroad Com. v. Rowan (1940), 310 U. S. 573 — 233
see, further, FOURTEENTH AMENDMENT

ESTATE OR INHERITANCE TAX
tax by Illinois, "graduated," upheld by Supreme Court of United States. Magoun v. Illinois (1898), 170 U. S. 283 — 76
Federal tax of Spanish War upheld, "graduated." Knowlton v. Moore (1900), 178 U. S. 41 — 76

EXEMPTIONS FROM TAXATION
exempting real-estate improvements for certain years held violative of State constitutional provision for "uniform assessment" and against privileges. Koch v. Essex County (1922), 97 New Jersey 61 — 72
denounced as unconstitutional and dangerous by Justice Field in Pollock v. Farmers Loan, etc. (1895), 157 U. S. 499 — 61

FEDERAL SURPLUS COMMODITIES CORPORATION
unconstitutional activity in bounty to voting groups never brought to test in court — 150

FIRST AMENDMENT
against National power, held to have been brought down against States on freedom of Press by Due Process Clause of Fourteenth. Near v. Minnesota (1931), 283 U. S. 697 — 219
theory followed as to freedom of religion where school buildings in Illinois used in religious instruction. McCollum v. Board Education (1948), 333 U. S. 203 — 216

TABLE OF CASES

Page

whether provision for freedom of Press brought down against States passed by, although case dismissed as involving question local law. Patterson v. Colorado (1906), 205 U. S. 454 — 232

freedom of speech held violated by ordinance New Jersey requiring permit for meeting to advocate obstruction to Government. Hague v. C.I.O. (1939), 307 U. S. 496 — 239

ordinances four States prohibiting handbills in streets held violative of free Press. Schneider v. State (1939), 308 U. S. 147 — 240

held violated by tax of Louisiana on newspaper advertising. Grosjean v. American Press (1936), 297 U. S. 233 — 225

assumed to let United States into Georgia for managerial purposes. Herndon v. Lowry, Sheriff (1937), 301 U. S. 242 — 232

Supreme Court Connecticut reversed for sustaining an ordinance requiring permit to solicit in streets for religious or other cause. Cantwell v. Connecticut (1940), 310 U. S. 296 — 240

FOURTEENTH AMENDMENT, 1868

not intended to transfer to Nation protection of all civil rights. Slaughter-House Cases (1872), 16 Wallace 36 (77) — 227

held not to impair police power of States. Barbier v. Connolly (1885), 113 U. S. 27 — 237

held that no general rule that this Amendment brings against States any article of Bill of Rights. Palko v. Connecticut (1937), 302 U. S. 319 — 232

Bill of Rights against Federal power not made applicable to States by this Amendment. Twining v. New Jersey (1908), 211 U. S. 78 — 230

California not required by this Amendment to indict by grand jury as by Fifth Amendment in Bill of Rights. Hurtado v. California (1884), 110 U. S. 516 — 238

	Page
held not to require Utah to employ jury of 12 instead of 8 in criminal cases. Maxwell v. Dow (1900), 176 U. S. 581	239
Due Process Clause of this Amendment "does not draw all the rights in Federal Bill of Rights under its protection," as against self-incrimination. Adamson v. California (1947), 332 U. S. 46	233
does not make Seventh Amendment in Bill of Rights applicable to States. Walker v. Sauvinet (1875), 92 U. S. 90	235
neither this Amendment, "broad and comprehensive as it is, nor any other amendment, was designed to interfere with the power of the States." Barbier v. Connolly (1885), 113 U. S. 27	237
"strange misconception" of meaning and scope of due process in this Amendment: Justice Miller. Davidson v. New Orleans (1877), 96 U. S. 97	237
held by Chief Justice Marshall that Fifth Amendment of Bill of Rights against taking private property for public use without just compensation not brought against States by this Amendment. Barron v. Baltimore (1833), 7 Peters 243	224
due process of law in this Amendment "refers to the law of the land in each State," not the law of the United States; due process under National law not required of State. Hurtado v. California, before cited.	225
"equal protection of the law" required of States by this Amendment denied by ruling of Texas unfairly draining oil lands of larger owners. Railroad Com. v. Rowan, etc. (1940), 310 U. S. 573	233
equal protection denied by law Arizona exempting strikers from liability for damage. Truax v. Corrigan (1921), 257 U. S. 312	239
Due Process Clause of, held to make operative against States freedom of speech and Press of First Amendment. Hague v. C.I.O. (1939), 307 U. S. 496	239

TABLE OF CASES

Page

same holding in many cases overturning police regulations in four States respecting meetings, sales, and handbills in streets. Schneider v. State (1939), 308 U. S. 147   240

whether this Amendment makes Fifth operative against States left open. Dreyer v. Illinois (1902), 187 U. S. 71   232

this Amendment held to make First applicable against States protecting press against tax on advertising. Grosjean v. American Press (1936), 293 U. S. 233   226

Fifth Amendment, protecting against self-incrimination, held not to have been brought down by this Amendment against the States. Twining v. New Jersey (1908), 211 U. S. 78   230

FREEDOM OF PRESS AND RELIGION
See FIRST and FOURTEENTH AMENDMENTS

FULL FAITH AND CREDIT

need not be given by a State to divorce proceedings in another State in conflict with its public policy. Andrews v. Andrews (1903), 188 U. S. 14. Williams v. North Carolina (1945), 325 U. S. 226   93, 94

GENERAL WELFARE CLAUSE

interpreted to give Congress police power in the States. Justice Cardozo in Steward Machine v. Davis (1937), 301 U. S. 548   195

see also SOCIAL SECURITY

held not a warrant for Agricultural Adjustment Act. Justice Roberts in United States v. Butler (1936), 297 U. S. 1   199

GOLD CLAUSE CASES

held that contract of United States in Liberty Bonds to pay in standard gold dollar could not be repudiated; but as gold had been seized, damage not measurable. Perry v. U. S. (1935), 294 U. S. 330   142

GOLD, Seizure of

Supreme Court, by Chief Justice Marshall, held that property cannot be seized without just compensation. Fletcher v. Peck (1810), 6 Cranch 87 (135) — 138

"GRADUATED" or PROGRESSIVE TAX

graduated tax by State on property passing at death upheld on erroneous theory that transmission is privilege, not right. Magoun v. Illinois (1898), 170 U. S. 238 — 76

in Missouri held to be against constitutional provisions for uniformity and equality and "without rhyme or reason." State v. Switzler (1898), 143 Missouri 387 — 69

in Pennsylvania held to be "unjust, arbitrary, and illegal." Cope's Estate (1899), 191 Pennsylvania 1 — 69

Act of Congress, 1898, taxing by graduation *estates* passing at death upheld. Knowlton v. Moore (1900), 178 U. S. 41 — 76

Act of Congress of 1913 taxing *incomes* by graduation upheld. Brushaber v. Union Pacific (1916), 240 U. S. 1 — 76

denounced as unconstitutional and dangerous by Justice Field in Pollock v. Farmers' Loan (1895), 147 U. S. 499 — 61

HOUSING ACT 1937

declaring for "general welfare" by employing Federal funds and credit to assist States, relieve unemployment and safeguard health, sustained. Justice Roberts in City Cleveland v. U. S. (1945), 323 U. S., 329 — 185

INCOME TAX

law of 1894 held unconstitutional because burden not apportioned among States by population as directed. Pollock v. Farmers' Loan, etc. (1895), 157 U. S. 429 — 61

law of 1913 (after Sixteenth Amendment) held consti-

TABLE OF CASES 313

Page

tutional. Brushaber v. Union Pacific (1916), 240
U. S. 1   76

"INHERENT" POWER
  General Government "can claim no powers which are
not granted by the Constitution." Martin v. Hunter's
Lessee (1816), 1 Wheaton 304   21
  idea of inherent power in Federal Government where
States severally cannot deal with a subject has been
rejected by Supreme Court from beginning. Carter
v. Carter Coal Co. (1936), 298 U. S. 238   21
  in foreign relations United States has powers of sovereignty external to the Constitution. Curtiss-Wright
v. U. S. (1936), 299 U. S. 304   20

INJUNCTIONS in Labor Cases
  even though Clayton Act and Norris-LaGuardia Act
practically forbid injunctions against strikers, held,
U. S. Court can stop strike by writ pending final decision of its own jurisdiction. U. S. v. United Mine
Workers (1947), 330 U. S. 258   36
  General Railroad Strike in 1894 ended at suit of Attorney General of United States. In re Debs (1895),
158 U. S. 564   35

INTERPRETATION or CONSTRUCTION
  where language of Constitution is clear, no place for
explanation, addition, or subtraction. U. S. v. Missouri Pacific (1929), 278 U. S. 269   68n
  Chief Justice Marshall quoted on how to apply a constitutional provision. Ogden v. Saunders (1827), 12
Wheaton 213   200
  spirit of Constitution to be respected no less than letter, but spirit is collected from words. Marshall in
Sturges v. Crowninshield (1819), 4 Wheaton 122   265
  Justice Bradley quoted on "mystifying" meaning of
clear provision of Constitution. Ex parte Siebold
(1879), 100 U. S. 393   217

TABLE OF CASES

Page

INTERSTATE COMMERCE

United States may, by injunction, clear it of obstruction by strikes. In re Debs (1895), 158 U. S. 564   35
To same effect, U. S. v. United Mine Workers (1947) 330 U. S. 258   36

JUDICIAL "LEGISLATION"

Chief Justice Marshall on adhering to the text of the instrument, without extending or subtracting. Ogden v. Saunders (1827), 12 Wheaton 213   200
Due Process Clause of Fourteenth Amendment expanded to embrace "freedom of Press" in First. Near v. Minnesota (1931), 285 U. S. 697   219
expanded again to contain freedom of religion in First. McCollum v. Board Education (1948), 333 U. S. 303   216
expanded in score of cases to subvert States in exercise of police power in licensing meetings and the selling and distributing of literature in streets.
    Schneider v. State (1939), 308 U. S. 147   240
    Hague v. C.I.O. (1939), 307 U. S. 496   239
    Cantwell v. Connecticut (1940), 310 U. S. 296   240
Supreme Court refused to amend Constitution to effectuate Income Tax Law of 1894. Pollock v. Farmers' Loan, etc., (1895), 157 U. S. 429   61
amending not to be done by Supreme Court: Chief Justice Hughes in Bituminous Coal Case. Carter v. Carter Coal Co. (1936), 298 U. S. 238   23, 127
against three earlier decisions holding title to tidewater lands to be in the States, Supreme Court, without overruling, held "paramount rights" to be in United States. Justice Black in United States v. California (1947), 332 U. S. 19   243

LABOR IN THE COURTS

law of Utah limiting hours in mines and smelters upheld. Holden v. Hardy (1898), 169 U. S. 366   27

TABLE OF CASES

Page

law of Oregon limiting length of day for women upheld. Muller v. Oregon (1908), 208 U. S. 412   27

law of Illinois limiting age of youthful worker upheld by both State and Federal courts. Sturges v. Beauchamp (1913), 231 U. S. 320   27

amendment Constitution Nebraska and statute North Carolina providing that no person be denied opportunity to obtain or retain employment because not member labor organization, and forbidding employer to agree to exclude non-union workers, *held* valid, notwithstanding National Labor Relations Act of Congress. Lincoln Union v. Northwestern Co. (1949), 335 U. S. 525   171n

law of Congress limiting hours railway trainmen in interstate commerce upheld. Wilson v. New (1917), 243 U. S. 332   27

law of State of Washington prescribing minimum wages for women upheld. West Coast Hotel v. Parrish (1937), 300 U. S. 379   28

law of Congress of 1926 for collective bargaining by interstate workers given full effect by U. S. District Court, by U. S. Circuit Court of Appeals, and by Supreme Court of United States. Texas and N. O. RR. v. Brotherhood, etc. (1930), 281 U. S. 548   28

law of Kansas creating Industrial Court to hear and decide controversies in employment, held invalid. Wolff, etc. v. Court Industrial Relations (1923), 262 U. S. 522   170

for strike in 1946 United Mine Workers fined $700,000 and leader $10,000; as mines had been seized by Government, held, acts of Congress limiting issue injunctions not applicable. Workers, not leader, spread strike. United States v. United Mine Workers (1947), 330 U. S. 258   36

a partial list of the decisions of the Supreme Court of the United States, and of the lower courts, favorable to labor, cited   27, 28

MATERNITY LAW, 1921

unconstitutionality of, under General Welfare Clause, side-stepped by Supreme Court. Massachusetts v. Mellon (1923), 262 U. S. 447 — 92

NATION and STATE

their origin, relation, and functions stated clearly by Chief Justice Marshall. Barron v. Baltimore (1833), 7 Peters 243 — 224

why state powers not enumerated in Constitution. Marshall in Sturges v. Crowninshield (1819), 4 Wheaton 122 — 231

NATIONAL INDUSTRIAL RECOVERY ACT, 1933

held unconstitutional as invasion police field of States. Schecter v. U. S. (1935), 295 U. S. 495 — 23

NATIONAL LABOR RELATIONS ACT, 1935

upheld as "emergency" measure to prevent obstacles to and "burdening" of interstate commerce by strikes. N. L. R. Board v. Jones & Laughlin (1937), 301 U. S. 134 — 163

OLEOMARGARINE

invasion of States by Congress to restrict manufacture and sale and burden with tax and regulations upheld. McCray v. U. S. (1904), 195 U. S. 27 — 175

Act of Pennsylvania prohibiting manufacture altogether, upheld. Powell v. Pennsylvania (1888), 127 U. S. 678 — 175-6

POLICE POWER

over health, safety, morals, education, and general welfare of people States cannot surrender, nor can Congress take over. House v. Mays (1911), 219 U. S. 282 — 86, 182

TABLE OF CASES 317

Page

State can exert it to control price of milk against contract. Nebbia v. New York (1934), 291 U. S. 502   171

Housing Act of Congress of 1937 to assist States and relieve unemployment held within power of Congress. Justice Roberts in City Cleveland v. U. S. (1946), 323 U. S. 329   60

Fair Labor Standards Act held to justify exertion of police power by Nation in States, contrary to but not overruling House v. Mays, cited above. Justice Stone in U. S. v. Darby (1941), 312 U. S. 100, overruling Hammer v. Dagenhart, cited under COMMERCE CLAUSE

RECALL OF JUDICIAL DECISIONS

provision for in Constitution and laws of Colorado held violative of terms of admission to Union and of Federal Constitution. People v. Western Union (1921), 70 Colorado 90   4

RECONSTRUCTION FINANCE CORPORATION, 1932

Congress not authorized by Constitution to create it; but, as engine of bounty, validity never tested in court.   108

SHERMAN ANTI-TRUST LAW

See COMMERCE CLAUSE

SOCIALISM

changing Republican form of government, in North Dakota, upheld. Green v. Frazier, Governor (1920), 253 U. S., 233   5

SOCIAL SECURITY

Act of 1935, in an "emergency," for giving "everything to everybody," upheld. Steward Machine Co. v. Davis, Collector (1937), 301 U. S. 548   200

Page

not within General Welfare Clause. United States v.
Butler (1936), 297 U. S. 1   200

STATES, Powers of

proceed, wrote Chief Justice Marshall, not from the
people of America, but from the people of the States,
except as abridged by the Constitution. Sturges v.
Crowninshield (1819), 4 Wheaton 122   231

within their power, notwithstanding Full Faith and
Credit Clause, to prevent decrees of divorce to "birds
of passage." Andrews v. Andrews (1903), 188 U. S.
14; Williams v. North Carolina (1945), 325 U. S. 226

93, 94

resistance of States to the unlawful seizure of their oil-
bearing tidelands by the United States was ineffectual. United States v. California (1947), 332 U. S. 19
(38)   243

they extend as police, to the absolute exclusion of the
Federal Government, over the health, safety, morals,
education, and general well-being of the people.
House v. Mays (1911), 219 U. S., 282   86, 182, 282

Amendment Constitution Nebraska and statute North
Carolina providing that no person be denied opportunity to obtain or retain employment because not
member labor organization, and forbidding employer to agree to exclude non-union workers, *held*
valid, notwithstanding National Labor Relations
Act of Congress. Lincoln Union v. Northwestern Co.
(1949), 335 U. S. 525   171n

STRIKES

may be prevented by injunction from obstructing commerce and the mails. In re Debs (1895), 158 U. S.
564   35

National Labor Relations Act declared "emergency" to
prevent obstruction of commerce by strikes. N.L.R.
Board v. Jones & Laughlin (1937), 301 U. S. 1   163

TABLE OF CASES

Page

    strike in coal mines ended by decree of Federal Court. United States v. United Mine Workers (1947), 330 U. S. 258   36

    lawful act of quitting service, when conceived by many to do damage, is conspiracy as denounced in Criminal Code of U. S. Chief Justice Fuller in Pettibone v. United States (1893), 148 U. S. 197   32

    seizure of railroads and other property unlawful, courts being open. Justice Davis in Ex parte Milligan (1864), 4 Wallace 2   35n

TAXATION BY CONGRESS

    held by Chief Justice Marshall that power does not lie for purposes within province of States. Gibbons v. Ogden (1824), 9 Wheaton 1   182

    Taxing Clause wrongfully employed in placing destructive levy on product of workers under 18 years. Bailey v. Drexel, etc. (1922), 259 U. S. 20   87

    see also EXEMPTION FROM TAXATION; "GRADUATED" or PROGRESSIVE TAX; INCOME TAX

TENNESSEE VALLEY AUTHORITY

    without authority in Constitution, Congress created for manufacture and sale electric power, chiefly; but upheld. Chief Justice Hughes in Ashwander v. T.V.A. (1936), 297 U. S., 288   119, 121

TIDE-WATER OIL LANDS

    absolute title to soil under navigable boundary waters came to States by Revolution. Chief Justice Taney in Martin v. Waddell (1842), 16 Peters 367   245

    a like holding by the Supreme Court by Justice McKinley in Pollard's Lessee (1845), 3 Howard 212   246

    upon admission of California into Union absolute property in soils under tide-waters vested in State. Justice Field in Wear v. Harbor Commissioners (1873), 18 Wallace 57   246

United States has no constitutional capacity to exercise jurisdiction over such lands, 3 Howard 212   247

United States, not California, has "paramount rights" over soil and oil resources. Justice Black in U. S. v. California (1947), 332 U. S. 19   243

UNITED STATES IN CONQUEST

oil-bearing tidelands belonging to States by settled law from the beginning seized by Federal Government. Illegal action sustained. United States v. California (1947), 332 U. S. 19   243

Index

INDEX

AGRICULTURAL
  ADJUSTMENT ACT, 1933
used to devalue gold dollar, although held unconstitutional, 133

AMENDMENT TO CONSTITUTION
a proposal give Congress control young workers rejected, 88
badly reasoned proposal to amend respecting election president, 287
for Ultimate Court, the People, not the Judiciary, 61
Income Tax proposal quoted: "graduation" not mentioned, 60
interpretative suggested curing governmental wanderings, 250, 251
Seventeenth proposed by Congress changed House of States, 11
Sixteenth proposed common tax with one rate, 60
Supreme Court should not amend Constitution, 23, 126, 127
Washington cautioned against innovations by amendment, 11

AMERICAN BAR
  ASSOCIATION
appointed committee opposing recall successfully, 4
and other associations inactive while dissenting justices stood ground, 241
concerted effort Bar Associations needed for better judges, 241
found Constitution required in only 8 of 25 universities, 26

ANTI-TRUST LAWS
Sherman Law and supplements adequate against monopolies, 99
two parties charge each other with failure to enforce, 98n

ATTORNEY GENERAL
wrote book defending attempt at court-packing, 25

BANKS
neither bank nor corporation mentioned in the Constitution, 102, 103n
creation National upheld by Marshall to aid governmental functions, 103n
how one bank grew to thousands, 107
living largely on tax-exempt Public Debt, 73
failed to defend their field against Socialism, 105

BAR ASSOCIATIONS
failed to object sufficiently to unconstitutional proposals, 47, 241

323

should compel appointment seasoned jurists Federal courts, 242
tongue-tied while four dissenting justices stood ground, 241

BILL OF RIGHTS
interpretation 160 years rejects idea States affected by, 234
of what it consists, 231
held no general rule applying provisions against States, 232
not one article of lies against the States, 225
States prepared Bill of Rights against Federal Government, 184, 210

BREWER, JUSTICE DAVID J.
dissented as to all inequalities in Taxation, 77

BROWDER, EARL
his statement explaining Communism, 174
said Communism promoted by strikes, 172, 175

BRYCE, JAMES
praised principle of agency in Constitution as greatest conception, 133
quoted on "Encompassing power of numbers," 263
said Congress dashes against walls of the Constitution, 88
tribute to members Constitutional Convention quoted, 11
wondered why President's office has not big men, 254

BUREAUS
General Eisenhower quoted on extraordinary growth dangerous bureaus, 113
Hoover Committee said "billions" could be saved, xi, 104
1800 in Executive Department under President, xi
propagandizing power has become dangerous, 127
salaries for Soil Conservation alone 24 million a year, 206
Secretary Morgenthau for sending to Far East foodstuffs in storage, 158
table showing unbelievable accumulation in storage, 159
wires crossed: importing foodstuffs, in storage at home, 158

CHASE, CHIEF JUSTICE SALMON P.,
explained meaning due process of law, 235
said we have "an indestructible Union, composed of indestructible States," 201

CHILD LABOR AGITATION
Department Labor reported 1920 no objectionable child labor, 84
less child labor when National Labor Relations Act passed, 85
two laws failing, Congress proposed amendment, 88
proposals immediately rejected in legislatures 20 states, 88
unconstitutional tax on salary Federal Judges followed labor decisions, 89
acts to suppress under Commerce Clause invalid, 83, 87
act taxing produce workers held not for revenue, 87
Governor Roosevelt denounced misuse of Commerce Clause, 86
President Roosevelt urged adoption proposed amendment, 88

INDEX 325

CITIZENSHIP, NATIONAL AND STATE
Fourteenth Amendment shows citizenship in State and Nation, 212
both citizenships for Negroes conferred by Fourteenth Amendment, 212
National held violated by Nevada law taxing interstate travelers, 226
National held violated by law of Maryland taxing importer, 226
Slaughter-house Cases involved State citizenship: no Federal question, 227
Justice Washington quoted on State citizenship, 227
before Civil War no local claim for Federal protection, 228
claims under State citizenship outside Federal Government, 228
some privileges National citizenship mentioned, 228
court rejected theory Fourteenth Amendment designed to handicap States, 229
in Slaughter-house Cases court rejected National control States, 229

CLEVELAND, PRESIDENT GROVER
advocated strict construction of the Constitution, 13
defended against Senate "dignity and vigor" of Executive, 43
vetoed bill for "Federal Aid" to drought area, 194
on "partitions" between National and State Governments, 194

COMMERCE CLAUSE
favorite cloak Congress for years invade States, 252
Governor Roosevelt denounced "stretching" of, 86, 97
quoted and explained, 97
"stretched" to justify Packers and Stockyards Act, 1921, 96
importance of commerce dating from Magna Carta, 1215, 164
Edmund Burke on importance American commerce, 165
design of Constitutional Convention to make commerce free, 165

COMMUNISM
abolition private property one objective, 57
aims at political control by proletariat, 57
amazing that party legally recognized, 58, 176
can be met only by superior doctrine, not arms, xiii, xiv
defined according to Karl Marx, 57n
promoted by strikes, Browder said, 172, 175
weapon of, "graduated" income taxes, 57
Karl Marx quoted and Manifesto 1948 cited, 56
quotations from writings of Karl Marx, 57
first "American way of life" in Plymouth Colony, 58
Lenin quoted on method in Russia, 58
Governor Bradford on failure Communism at Plymouth, 59
American spirit called "wealth" by Hamilton, 59

CONGRESS
legal scholar of Convention explains limitations on powers of, 190
abandoned to President authority to write laws, 183

acts must be in "pursuance" of Constitution, 20
attacks on Judiciary of the Constitution, 14
boundaries to Congressional power stated by Madison, 186, 187
by Norris-LaGuardia Law oppressed employer, 46
Constitutional Convention denied it power over Judiciary, 41
created unconstitutional Reconstruction Finance Corporation, 110
declared "emergency" for seizure gold property, 135
enacted invalid Maternity Law for children and women, 91
favored findings Interstate Commerce Commission unduly, 44
guilty of perpetrating first American *coup d'état*, 135
without authority from Sixteenth Amendment to "graduate" taxes, 63
preferred *coup d'état* to constitutional procedure, 76
Hamilton said powers limited to enumerated subjects, 255
influenced too much by social theories, beyond powers, 62
its "graduated" income taxes not authorized by Amendment, 60
men of old-time stature are missing, 90
misuses Commerce and General Welfare Clauses, 252
National Labor Relations Act disguised by Commerce Clause, 161
persistent disregard of Tenth Amendment, 163
possesses no judicial power, as such, 41, 44

powers limited to enumeration, sec. 8, Article I, 186, 187
repudiated gold contract in bonds of the United States, 136
"Rubber Stamp" title was earned by it, 183
Social Security Act not warranted by Constitution, 195
should have repealed income- and estate-tax laws, 76
Tennessee Valley Authority cloak for establishing Fascism, 112
former minister to Denmark quoted on deterioration of Congress, 257

CONSTITUTION, THE
adopted by Canada, Australia, Argentina, Brazil, and others, xiii
defines "Supreme Law of the Land," 19
first system successfully to control man in power, xiii
gives no authority for Social Security Act, 195
guarantees Republican form of government to States, 7
most important of original objections to, 185
National Labor Relations Act misuse of Commerce Clause, 161
President Cleveland advocated strict construction, 13
provides just method for soil conservation, 205
States will compel thorough teaching of eventually, 50
study of indispensable to survival of Republic, 10, 255

CONSTITUTIONAL CONVENTION
task accomplished never at-

INDEX

tempted in world before, 296
tribute by Senator Hoar to unprecedented achievement, 298
contended that large territory requires Republican system, 4
denied authority to Congress over Judiciary, 41
feared such legislation as Social Security Act, 185
for government by representatives instead of crowd, 272
Hamilton quoted on its ideas for choosing President, 272
planned for statesmen in two chief offices, 275
proclaimed sanctity of public debt, 139
set up representative system in all departments, 7
several members refused to sign instrument prepared, 185
sought to prevent "cabal, intrigue, and corruption," 264
theory respecting House of States given, 11, 12
tribute of Bryce, members belonging "to history of world", 11
members of explained fully operation of courts, 17

COOLEY, JUDGE THOMAS M.
quoted against police power in Congress, 184
advised courts to read and apply law by its history, 218, 219
said exemptions from taxation not legal, 72
tax should be "in proportion to the interest secured", 64

COOLIDGE, PRESIDENT CALVIN
said taxes not needed in economy are "legalized larceny", 56

CORRUPT PRACTICES ACTS
Congress forbade Roosevelt's method of gathering funds, 279
Laws of forty years have proved futile, 277, 278
not necessary before National Nominating Convention, 260
reveal discreditable and tragic situation, 280, 281

COUP D'ETAT, THE
Emergency Banking Relief Bill for seizing people's gold, 135
seizure field of relief by Social Security Act, 69, 70, 75

DEBT OF GOVERNMENT
vast repudiation by devaluation of dollar, 136, 137
"profits" to Government from repudiation, 137
Chief Justice Marshall quoted on honor in debt, 138
Hamilton said government cannot change its contract, 139
Constitutional Convention declared for payment of debts, 139
"sacking" of people done with insolence, 140

DELEGATION OF POWER
in violation of law, Congress authorized President to devalue dollar, 133, 134
Congress must declare method and policy for *administrative* cases, 135
administrative and *legislative* functions distinguished, 135

DEMOCRACY
adopted after panic and several crop failures, 5

Initiative, Referendum, and Recall explained, 3
Introduced in 1893 from Switzerland, 3
not suited to large areas and populations, 4, 13
spread of un-American idea still persisting, 8
why Constitutional Convention rejected told in "The Federalist", 8
insistence upon "more democracy" for half century alarming, 53, 290
battle is between the Republican and the Populist forms, 290

DEPARTMENT OF JUSTICE
Demonstrated industrial disputes are for courts, 35, 36

DILLON, JUDGE JOHN F.
lectured on Constitution at Yale half century ago, 130
quoted whether Judiciary could resist popular demands, 130
denounced decision in Oleomargarine Case, 176

DIVORCE
States delinquent in not regulating, 93
principle of regulating set by Massachusetts in 1903, 93
North Carolina law regulating held valid, 94
decree void where no real domicile, 94

DUE PROCESS OF LAW
Justice Brandeis on "procedural regularity", 235
in Fourteenth Amendment relates to law of States only, 226
in States regulated by law of States, 235
Magna Carta quoted on, 235
application of illustrated, 236
Justice Miller quoted on misapplication to Fourteenth Amendment, 237
explained by Justice Moody in Twining case, 235
in Fifth Amendment restraint on National law, 235

EISENHOWER, DWIGHT D.
on "a creeping paralysis of thought" bringing dictatorship, 112

EMERGENCY
assumed to justify National Labor Relations Act, 163
Bank Act 1933 for seizure gold of American, 135
"Does not create power"—Supreme Court, 135
receives no recognition in any provision Constitution, 135
using to seize power began with devaluation of dollar, 135
Chief Justice Hughes quoted respecting, 134
made excuses by Congress for invading States, 162
NLRA upheld, overriding decisions for half century, 163

ESTATE OR INHERITANCE TAX
"Recrudescence of Feudalism" says English authority, 79
Spanish War tax and "graduated" income effective, 76
Causes break-up or sale of sound properties, 79n
See PROPERTY

EXECUTIVE DEPARTMENT OF PRESIDENT
contains 1,800 different administrative units: Hoover Committee, xii

INDEX

"billions—not millions" unnecessarily spent, xii
on payrolls, 3,400,000 in 1945, 262
propagandizing aggressive and dangerous, 88, 117
protected "in all its dignity and vigor" by Cleveland, 43
third and fourth terms made possible by payrollers, 262

EXEMPTIONS FROM TAXATION UNCONSTITUTIONAL
held by Supreme Courts of several States Unconstitutional, 72
law in New Jersey exempting new buildings held void, 72
Judge Cooley quoted in condemnation exemption from tax, 72
President and other officials in Washington enjoying exemptions, 73
colossal properties illegally exempted from taxation, 74
enormity of prejudice to overburdened taxpayers, 74
wrong should be righted by representatives of guilty States in Congress, 75
at violence to all constitutions, 72
Justice Brewer dissented in all exemption cases, 77
Justice Field predicted (1895) present disastrous result, 73
banks, trusts, universities enjoying exemptions, 75

FAIR LABOR STANDARDS ACT, 1938
held to warrant police control in States, 185

FASCISM
defined by showing 22 corporations of Italian system, 38n
long time coming; now well "dug in", 39n
forbidden because not authorized by Constitution, 39
by Tennessee Valley Authority Fascism introduced in government, 112
did General Eisenhower see Socialism and Fascism coming? 112
thrust upon Tennessee Valley by "planners", 132
many Fascist corporations manufacturing electric power, 111
Tennessee Valley Authority planned before election 1932, 132
origin of term, a Roman recollection, 38n
corporation of Fascists to take over private business, 106

FEDERAL AID
poured out illegally in floods to States and individuals, 108
bill in early Congress aiding fishermen: Madison defeated, 188
President Cleveland vetoed bill giving seed grain to farmers, 194
press dispatch told that King of Hoboes favors, 197n

FEDERAL EMERGENCY RELIEF ACT, 1933
first American *coup d'état*, revolutionizing Government, 76
instead, repeal tax incomes and estates indicated, 75

FEDERAL SURPLUS COMMODITIES CORPORATION, 1933
authorized by U. S. issue bonds 4 billion, 750 million, 155

charter for "perpetual existence", 149
dumped 14 carloads spoiled eggs in 1944, 153
"ever-normal granary" fed wheat to pigs, 154
for relief farm emergency by expanding markets, 151
one of many corporations borrowing and spending, 157
sold at heavy loss 26 carloads eggs for hog feed, 153
subsidies in 1949 over 500 million, 157
to process, store, handle surplus agricultural commodities, 151
to act "without restriction or limit", 149
War Food Administration lost $150,000 on eggs, 153, 154
incorporated in Delaware by two cabinet members and another, 150
tip-top corporation of Fascism, 151
incorporated for all time with world-wide powers, 151, 152
no activity of FSCC authorized by Constitution, 153
vast waste of grains and foodstuffs, 153, 154
capitalized for $100,000; stock owned by U. S., 155
subsidies to favored classes 15.5 billions in 17 years, 155
President Jackson quoted on leaving business to business men, 156
table showing some astonishing losses of taxpayers' money, 157
Former Secretary Morgenthau proposed sending stores to Near East, 158
he revealed an unbelievable amount and value in storage, 159

FEDERALIST, THE
by John Jay, Alexander Hamilton, and James Madison, 186
denies power for Social Security or other police action, 188
most brilliant work on philosophy of government, 186
says Senate would bar invasion States by Nation, 54, 162

FIELD, JUSTICE STEPHEN J.
denounced as unconstitutional exemption from taxation, 73
said Fourteenth Amendment does not touch State police, 237

FIRST AMENDMENT (RELIGION, PRESS, SPEECH, PETITION)
correct interpretation given, 228
non-Federal questions occupying Supreme Court, 229
not rewritten or absorbed by Fourteenth Amendment, 287
erroneous theory of Court on freedom of Press, 220
decision based on irrelevant cases, 221
legislation of Minnesota was sound, 223
four justices dissent, quoting Chief Justice Marshall, 223
Supreme Court avoided applying to Press, 232
history underlying this amendment related, 218
in School Case Illinois did not violate, 218
decision in Illinois School Case affected 2,000 communities, 219

INDEX

held effective against States through "liberty" in Fourteenth, 220
Supreme Court Minnesota upholding law against libels reversed, 220

FOURTEENTH AMENDMENT, 1868
"liberty" in does not connote religion or Press, 213
analysis of and citation decisions, 214
written without thought of religion or press, 214
Supreme Court employs "latitudinarian construction", 213
Due Process in relates to processes under State, not National, law, 226
rights of State citizenship not protected by, 227
held not confer right National citizenship generally, 227
held to authorize United States to manage Georgia, 232
regulation oil production by Texas held denial Due Process, 233
Justice Field quoted that it does not affect police power, 237
Justice Miller quoted on misapplication Due Process, 237
review of decisions sustaining invasion of States, 238
cases holding State laws not controlled by Slaughterhouse, 227
decisions under in disagreement, 239
does not control police power of States, 229
erroneous application in Illinois school case, 218
First Amendment not rewritten by it, 232

Judicial assumptions cannot alter application First Amendment, 221
many police regulations of States overturned, 184, 240
misconstrued in Minnesota Press case, 219
used by courts for dealing with non-Federal questions, 229

GENERAL WELFARE CLAUSE
Hamilton said Congress limited to enumerated powers, 189
Supreme Court ignored history and precedent, 195
Wilson and Baldwin, of Constitutional Convention, explained, 189
adoption Constitution resisted: this Clause said to be unlimited, 186
Madison explained clearly limitations of power under, 186, 187
Jefferson's brilliant elucidation of General Welfare, 191
early interpretation of should be respected, 192
acts of New Deal listed which Jefferson would condemn, 193
Senator Benton of Missouri condemned "latitudinarian construction", 193
President Cleveland vetoed bill for aiding farmers, 194
Social Security Act erroneously sustained under General Welfare Clause, 195
held not to support Agricultural Adjustment Act, 200
this Clause and Commerce Clause cloaks for Congressional marauding, 252

GOLD DOLLAR "CLIPPED," 1934
authority to President in Agricultural Act, held unconstitutional, 133
bondholders thoroughly "frisked" by Government, 142
by "directive" President cut 25.8 grains to 15-5/21, 135
Congress abdicated to President power over coinage, 134
Congress declared "emergency" required seizure of gold, 135
Congress recognized damage done by repudiation, 143
Constitutional Convention proclaimed debt would be paid, 139
Hamilton on promises of a borrowing government, 138
Madison on morality in relation to public debt, 139
Marshall, Chief Justice, on seizing property individual, 138
President given by Constitution no authority over coinage, 134
"profits" gained by United States and States, 137
Secretary Treasury boasted on radio of "profit" made, 145
Senator boasted of wealth to be "transferred" from holders, 144
all gold and gold certificates seized from Americans, 135
Congress repudiated gold contract in its bonds, 136
vastness of debt repudiated, 136, 137
Supreme Court held contract inviolable; but no remedy, 141, 142
four dissenting justices found aid to farmer the purpose, 143
usefulness of Gold Clause stated by dissenting justices, 145
dissenting justices said "legal and moral chaos appalling", 149

GOVERNMENT, PRINCIPLES OF
are not outmoded; *first to chain man in power*, xii
Constitution written to limit powers, 20
conflicting decisions of "inherent powers" cited, 20, 21
purpose of Constitution to exclude "inherent powers," 21
most "problems" in United States caused by Government, 60
"new thought" is bringing forward "inherent power," 20, 291
no power that is not granted by Constitution exists, 21
scientific, or based on classified knowledge, 254

GOVERNORS OF STATES
complained in convention that President ignored them, 177n
had failed to stand for sovereignty of commonwealths, 178
yet their hands are out for "federal aid," 178

GRADUATED TAXES UNCONSTITUTIONAL
equality of treatment removed by Income Tax Amendment, 61
fallacious belief in property expressed by Supreme Court, 76
instrument of Communism for confiscation, 56

INDEX 333

not called for in Sixteenth Amendment, 60
President Roosevelt advocated confiscation incomes by, 65
in 1908 Socialists demanded "graduated" income tax
income tax not graduated is desirable, 54
first act Congress employed graduation: not in amendment, 54
States drained of needed revenue by graduated tax, 55
graduation not applied to any other property, 64
cases cited showing graduation wrongfully adopted by Congress, 67n
condemned by Supreme Courts of several States, 69
very slight in Civil War laws, 70
graduated income tax adjudged war measure by Congress, 71
fallacy of Supreme Court in sustaining, 76
dissent by Justice Brewer to all graduations, 77
State Supreme Courts understood subject clearly, 77
decisions Supreme Court upholding on incomes and estates unsound, 80
lawless government resulting from, 80, 81

HAMILTON, ALEXANDER
said constitutional election would insure able Presidents, 275
stated limits on power of President, 255
believed "abuse of power taxation" guarded against, 61
Congress must "pursue" lines of Constitution, 20
explains Constitutional Convention's ideas on choosing President, 272
had great hope in House of States, 11, 12
Judicial powers expounded, 17
quoted on making government "control itself," 299
quoted respecting Gold-Clause repudiation, 138
said Judiciary, without initiative, needs protection, 49
thought States would resist National encroachment, 54, 162
quoted against unlimited national power, 189

HOAR, SENATOR GEORGE F.
beautiful tribute to spirit of our Constitution, 298
corrupt cities drag States to corruption, 91
heard Webster tell Supreme Court he had voted against each, 12
quoted on need of statesmen jurists on the Bench, 229n
said old-time members of Congress told White House what, 256

ILLITERATE WRITERS
attack Judiciary of the Constitution, 16

INCOME-TAX AMENDMENT
Sixteenth Amendment did not propose "graduation," 60
gave Nation most corrupting form of power, 54, 55
money from took Congress beyond its constitutional field, 62
President Taft asked for plain income tax in 1909, not graduated, 50, 60

panic 1907 made "scrip" necessary for money, 50
in 1908 Socialists demanded "graduated" income tax, 50
"progressive" income tax advocated by Karl Marx, 53, 57
brought unintelligent relinquishment by States of their power, 54
income tax not "graduated" is desirable, 54
first act Congress employed "graduation": not in Amendment, 54
States drained by "graduated" tax of needed revenues, 55
intended only to meet decision on tax 1894, 61
gave Congress no new power to tax, 61
money in excess caused lawless government, 62
people showed no enthusiasm for, 63
men and money retired to enjoy tax exemptions, 68
cases cited showing "graduation" wrongfully adopted by Congress, 67n
States should repeal and resume control of their treasury, 75

INITIATIVE, REFERENDUM, AND RECALL
ideas borrowed by North Dakota from Switzerland, 3
recall judicial decisions rejected by Colorado, 4
Kansas limited recall to appointed officials, 4
initiative never extensively used and now seldom heard of, 4
introduced after bank panic and crop failures, 5
where language of Constitution clear, no place for explanation, 68n
imported from Switzerland in 1893, 3
spread of the evil idea of "Democracy," 8
idea behind, threatening constitutional Presidency in 1950, 289

INJUNCTIONS
American's right to crippled by Norris-LaGuardia Law, 46
Blackstone quoted on right to and how obtained, 47, 49
labor organizations often benefit by writ of injunction, 27, 28
long line decisions deny charge courts disfavor labor, 27, 171n
long-standing Rule Supreme Court gives all full protection, 49

INTERPRETING CONSTITUTION
Senator Benton of Missouri denounced "latitudinarian construction," 193

INTERSTATE COMMERCE COMMISSION
findings partially immunized by invalid Act Congress, 44
needlessly wiped out property railroad stockholders, 45, 46
threats in Congress of impeachment, 46
President never appointed big men of commerce or industry, 45

JACKSON, PRESIDENT ANDREW
quoted on government keeping out of business, 156

JEFFERSON, THOMAS
predicted formidable power in the President, 255, 257

INDEX 335

said Tenth Amendment real body of the Constitution, 192
wrote brilliant exposition General Welfare Clause, 191
feared "perpetual re-eligibility of the President," 257

JUDICIAL "LEGISLATION"
expansion or diminution Constitution our greatest peril, 207
Supreme Court struggles to put First Amendment in Fourteenth, 207
search for the unperceivable, 208
"Liberty" in Fourteenth Amendment not "religion" from First, 213
people, not courts, must blend the two Amendments, 215
misconstruction of Fourteenth Amendment has overloaded Supreme Court, 215
State Republics invaded by National through judicial interpretation, 215
using school buildings for religious instruction held unconstitutional, 215
Supreme Court Illinois held such use lawful, 216
decision overruling Supreme Court Illinois absolutely untenable, 216
analysis of decision and constitutional provision, 217
history of Fourteenth Amendment ignored in decision, 218
religious persecution underlying First Amendment shown, 218
decision in Illinois school case affected 2,000 communities, 219
held First effective against States through "liberty" in Fourteenth, 220

appointees to Federal courts should be seasoned jurists, 242
Chief Justice Marshall showed how to avoid danger, 209
disagreements among justices of Supreme Court, 209
distinction between National and State citizenship, 212
each State a Republic, supreme locally, 6, 7
First Amendment not rewritten or absorbed by Fourteenth, 214, 215, 216
Fourteenth Amendment quoted and explained, 212, 214
for Ultimate Power to change Bill of Rights, 210
frequent assertions become accepted law, 109, 219, 221
interpretative amendments suggested, 249
most dangerous to Constitution because insidious, 207
no amendment ever proposed to change application First Amendment, 215
Slaughter-house cases, New Orleans, leading authority, 227
State sovereignty not reduced by Fourteenth Amendment, 237
States upset by interference local affairs, 239
the question that has embarrassed the Justices, 234
Twining case followed Slaughter-house decision, 230
Justice Bradley on "mystifying" constitutional language, 217
Congress without authority to aid schools in States, 217
Cooley on history of words in law to be interpreted, 218, 219

fallacy in Supreme Court decision shown, 218
history of religion found in First Amendment, 218
Illinois case examined and law stated, 215, 216
Republic of Illinois competent to manage its affairs, 219
Supreme Court Illinois decided no violation Constitution, 216
theory decision rejected by 140 years practical application, 219
what Supreme Court should have said in Illinois case, 217
wide effect of erroneous decision of Supreme Court, 219

JUDICIARY OF THE CONSTITUTION
Constitutional Convention intended statesmen foreseeing consequences of errors, 92
Constitutional Convention denied Congress authority regulate courts, 41
Congress has no judicial power to confer, 44
Federal courts should be replenished from State courts, 242
"The Federalist" said judiciary weakest Department and needs defense, 242
indefensible appointments by President and Senate shown, 241n
accepted dictation from Congress; acts reviewed, 183
acted in defense of the Constitution in former days, 83
adequate in labor case when Government in corner, 169
attacked by President when war impending, 14, 38
attacks on by Congress, 39, 40, 43
attacks on by labor leaders, 19
attempt at court-packing in 1937, 23
Attorney General wrote book against, 25
bar should compel appointment experienced judges, 242
Congress taxed salaries judges since 1919: violating Constitution, 89
Congress taxed unconstitutionally salaries Federal judges, 89
equity power for injunction given by Constitution, 47
failed to resist attacks by Congress, 41, 43, 47
favorable decisions for labor, 27
industrial disputes justiciable, for courts, 171
injunctive power inherent, 47
"Keystone of American Arch," said Von Holst, 18, 242
power extends to litigation by States, 42
powers clearly set out by Hamilton, 17
recall of decisions of, by voters advocated, 4
salaries taxed after Child Labor decision, 89
will it maintain constitutional limitations? Judge Dillon, 130

JURY, THE
the Court of Last Resort for liberty—"the Country," 37

LABOR AND COURTS
decisions of half century for labor cited, 27, 28
"labor's gain" under President Roosevelt built on closed shop, 30
workers have right to quit but not conspire for damage, 32

INDEX

strikes during war gave "aid and comfort" to enemy, 33
strikes destructive of private enterprise, 33
courts can prevent destruction of property, 34
Debs Strike 1894 ended by injunction Federal Court, 35
seizure railroads and other property illegal with courts open, 35n
ability courts to protect public shown in Communist cases, 36, 37
importance of "the country" to Americans in court, 37
Norris-LaGuardia Act denial of justice, 46
Blackstone quoted on principle governing issue of injunctions, 47, 49
ancient rule Supreme Court covered all requirements of justice, 49
United States forced to get injunction against strikers, 169
paramount interest public makes labor controversies for courts, 31, 170
Industrial Court of Kansas held unconstitutional, 170
labor controversy has ceased to be personal to parties, 171
industrial controversy handled at Washington with eye on elections, 172
Washington friendly to sit down strikes, 173
workers asked for injunction, bringing great illustrative case, 28
"collective bargaining" long before "New Deal," 29
favored by many judicial decisions, 27

National Labor Relations Act oppressive to industry, 175
organized attacks on Judiciary of the Constitution by labor, 19
questions solved by court when Government in corner, 36

LAW SCHOOLS
only 8 of 25 universities required study Constitution, 26

MADISON, JAMES
believed States would resist National aggression, 101
denied General Welfare Clause authority over States, 186, 187
on morality and the National Debt, 139
quoted on line dividing National and State powers 182, 186, 187
set forth advantages Republican form of Government, 7
stated limited powers of the new Government, 7
assembled protests of States into Bill of Rights, 187, 188
fought and defeated "Federal aid" in first Congress, 188

MARSHALL,
CHIEF JUSTICE JOHN
creation National Bank upheld by Marshall to aid Government, 103n
quoted on honor in debt of Government, 138
said Congress cannot tax for purposes within States, 182
quoted on adhering to text of Constitution, 209, 265
quoted by dissenting justices in Minnesota Press Case, 224
held tax of Maryland on im-

porter violation National citizenship, 226
quoted on power of people in States, 231
quoted on relation of Nation and State, 224
quoted on seizure gold by United States, 138

MARX, KARL
advocated abolition of estates passing at death, 56
"graduated" income taxes for confiscating property, 56
stated theories and purposes of Communism, 56

MATERNITY ACT, 1931
authority over women sought by unmarried, 91
cost 11 million and accomplished nothing, 92
police field of States invaded by Congress, 91
Supreme Court avoided passing on Constitutionality of, 92

McREYNOLDS, JUSTICE JAMES C.
exposed fraudulent pretenses Tennessee Valley case, 123
"moral and legal chaos appalling," in Gold Clause cases, 149

MINNESOTA PRESS CASE
Act Minnesota stopping libelous publications valid, 220
"assumption" of predicate too often employed, 221
"authorities" relied on by Supreme Court examined, 221
case in Illinois preceded by case in Minnesota, 219
decision against 70 years application First Amendment, 223
each decision cited by Court invasion of State, 221
fallacy in reasoning Supreme Court, 224, 225
first definite trespass on State authority, 220
local government Minnesota overturned, 220
Chief Justice Marshall on relation State and Nation, 224
statement by dissenting justices, 223
Supreme Court held State violated First Amendment, 220

MONEY
Constitution quoted respecting power given to Congress, 22
dangerous power in hands of Government, 22, 81
Congress can spend only for specified purposes, 22
Constitution gives President no authority over, 134
opinion financial writers on content gold dollar, 141
Congress should have returned value for gold seized, 147

MUSSOLINI
Fascism by Italian structure now in United States, 39
set up 22 corporations for management of government, 39n

NATIONAL DEBT
Madison on morality connected with, 139
"profits" on gained by Government stated, 137, 145
United States repudiated part of its obligations, 136
vast increase in time of peace, 136

NATIONAL EDUCATION ASSOCIATION
favored "Federal aid" to schools; and centralism, xi

INDEX

NATIONAL LABOR RELATIONS ACT, 1935
passed under cloak of Commerce Clause, 161
made a Nation of Union of States, 161
Hamilton could not see that representatives would diminish States, 162
"emergency" excuse for invading police field of States, 162
after Act strikes tripled in number, 167, 168
table showing number strikes by years, 167n
government of Wisconsin on lawlessness of strikers, 168
Department of Justice inactive respecting strikes, 169
four Justices Supreme Court dissented, 163
Government driven to corner by strikers, 169
Governor New York protested use Commerce Clause such cases, 164
Supreme Court, supporting, overrode long line decisions, 163
title denies law for regulation under Commerce Clause, 163

NATIONAL NOMINATING CONVENTION
long platforms promising everybody everything then unknown, 260
an author describes a saddening spectacle, 285
appalling consequences of Convention 1932, 284
Charles Sumner quoted against its methods, 261
dominated (1920) by senators and other officials, 270
evil instrumentality from delinquency of States, 267
first 11 elections without Convention or Platform, 259
instrumentality of "cabal, intrigue, and corruption," 286
non-delegate 2000 miles distant nominated F. D. Roosevelt, 286
no Corrupt Practices Acts before Nominating Convention, 260
Senator Benton, Missouri, denounced it in 1859, 261
States can abolish unconstitutional peril, 291
through "cabal" Roosevelt nominated in 1932, 286

NEW DEAL
all of its remedies were ancient failures, 53
unconstitutional in all its features, 53
put in effect platform National Socialist Party 1908, 52
a historic subterfuge for statecraft, 53

NORRIS-LaGUARDIA ACT, 1932
denied in practice employer's legal rights, 46
industry, winner of war, near friendless in Government, 47n

OLEOMARGARINE
act of Congress restricting and overtaxing upheld, 175
law of Pennsylvania forbidding manufacture absolutely sustained, 176
decision in Pennsylvania case condemned by Judge Dillon, 176
act Congress repealed after 64

339

years (1950) legislative folly, 176

PACKER AND STOCKYARDS ACT, 1921
entirely needless; Illinois was in control of situation, 97
Governor Roosevelt condemned such use Commerce Clause, 97
legislation superfluous and illegal; Sherman law adequate, 98
decision sustaining submerged long line of cases, 100
became precedent for National Labor Relations Act, 101
Madison believed States would resist such encroachment, 101

PAYROLLERS, EXECUTIVE
astonishing and steady increase of: 1800 bureaus, 113
numerous enough to turn Presidential Election, 113
trampled on customary law against third term, 259, 262

POLICE POWER IN STATES
Marshall held Congress cannot tax for State purposes, 182
power inheres in States and cannot be surrendered, 182
Judge Cooley quoted on inhering in States, 184
illegal Housing Act Congress aiding States upheld, 185
last word in Bill of Rights protecting police power, 185
Congress exercises under Fair Labor Standards Act, 185
not affected by Fourteenth Amendment: Justice Field, 237

POWERS OF GOVERNMENT
union of "very definition of despotism," xii

division of powers failed in Rome, xii
those granted to Congress by the Constitution enumerated, 293
"inherent" powers now coming to the fore, 20, 21, 29

PRESIDENT, THE
method of Convention would insure choice of big men, 275
appointments by governed by political considerations, 36
Constitutional election will clean out stables, 284, 285
peril in patronage shown by Senator Norris long ago, 276
President F. D. Roosevelt devised Thousand Dollar Clubs, 280
given no authority by Constitution over money, 134
Madison quoted on his limited field of authority, 255, 195n
Jefferson predicted formidable power of President, 255, 257
Third term, fourth, and fifth owing to payrollers, 262
the "perpetual re-eligibility of" was frightening to Jefferson, 257
Press, by conferences, enabled President to reach dictatorship, 256
Senator Hoar quoted on time when President was shown the way, 256
political chief, nominating himself and his successors, 258
quotation from his secretary showing handling of nomination, 258n
payrollers in President's Department and families control election, 259, 262
popular election would be de-

INDEX

structive of Republic, 259, 261
first eleven elections without farcical Nominating Convention, 259
Congress forbade one of his fund-raising schemes, 279
President Roosevelt by-passed Corrupt Practices Acts, 280
illegal power brings disregard of Constitutional restraint, 284
asked Congress for 22 enactments beyond Federal power, 293, 294
extraordinary call for unconstitutional acts provoked no criticism, 294, 295
Constitutional Convention intended and directed States elect President, 264, 265

PRESIDENTIAL ELECTION, THE
a careful plan against popular vote frustrated by States, 263
author quoted on senators controlling National Convention, 270
bargains by President should be unnecessary, 282
controlled by 3 million employees Executive Department, 113, 259
Corrupt Practices Acts consequence Nominating Convention, 260
Charles Sumner denounced (1872) Nominating Convention, 261
choice of executives greatest achievement at Philadelphia, 289, 290
clause for appointing electors quoted, 265
Constitutional Convention for Representatives, not crowd, 272
Congress forbade President's money-gathering method, 279
Convention 1932 and before what Philadelphia feared, 264
election 1948 proved popular vote real danger, 261, 262
evil consequences election 1932, 258
Roosevelt did not have full New York delegation, 1932, 286
Governors accused White House of ignoring them, 177n
great learning underlay at Philadelphia electoral plan, 264, 272
half electorate did not vote in 1948, 263
Hamilton quoted fully on idea Constitutional Convention, 272
"interests" providing funds will remain interested, 281
in the promising future, 263, 264
issue is between Populism and constitutional Republic, 277
Jefferson on tyranny of the executive, 255
managed vote of corrupt cities sought, 259
members Thousand Dollar Clubs feted, inauguration 1945, 280
men of highest capacity could be selected constitutionally, 275
office-holders excluded from participation in election, 269
present political party system can be maintained, 283
"Populism" danger in Presidential elections, 277
slavery and Presidential elec-

tion two "trials" Republic, 290, 291
unsound ideas commentators on constitutional method, 287
when Legislatures again *themselves* appoint electors, 252
certificate education in Constitution should be requisite to voting, 90
Senator Hoar quoted on conditions in States, 91
restoration of Australian ballot is imperative, 91
industrial disputes handled in view of, 172
first eleven without farcical Nominating Conventions, 259
no Corrupt Practices Laws necessary then, 260
States should resume control and follow Constitutional direction, 260
Presidential so farcical nearly half electors do not vote, 263
Bryce quoted on "the fatalism of the multitude," 263
corrupt election greatest fear of Constitutional Convention, 264
States put duty on themselves to elect President, 265
Marshall quoted on following letter of Constitution, 265
legislatures of States have abandoned election to politicians, 266
short ballot made bad situation worse, 268
methods of confusion in different States, 267
Federal office-holders forbidden to manage elections, 269
four senators dominated convention 1920; one became President, 270

States shown quite competent to nominate President, 271
Constitutional Convention feared "cabal, intrigue, and corruption," 274
statesmen, not politicians, sought by Constitutional Convention, 275
in 1914 Senator Norris predicted disaster from patronage, 276
in present conditions "popular" election would not be popular, 277
Corrupt Practices Laws for 40 years ineffectual, 277, 278
President Roosevelt by-passed Corrupt Practices laws, 280
candidates' conduct today compared with Cleveland's and McKinley's, 281n
Constitutional method would remove Chief Executive from politics, 282
men of highest capacity would occupy Presidential Office, 283
illegal Presidential power causes disregard of Constitution, 284
State legislatures should *themselves* appoint Presidential electors, 284n
badly reasoned proposal to amend Constitution, 287
people at home intended to make choice, 288
Hamilton and Jay quoted on this point, 288
proposed amendment would be futile and "democratic," 289
Presidential election and slavery two great trials: Senator Benton, 290, 291
removal of remaining peril lies with States, 269, 291

INDEX

PRESS, THE
guilelessly contributed to President's rise to dictatorship, 256

PRIVATE INDUSTRY
assailed by Fascist corporations in many places, 125, 152
berated as for lese majesty when defending itself, 117
propaganda TVA and other Fascist set-ups fierce, 127, 128
selling out, fearing competition from taxpayers' money, 119

PROPERTY
history of man's right to acquire and transmit, 77
English Charter 1101 quoted showing right of inheritance, 78
English writer says estate tax recrudescence of Feudalism, 79
causes destruction of business at death in United States, 79n
erroneous idea Supreme Court on man's right to, 80
Hallam and Blackstone on man's inherent right to, 79
President F. D. Roosevelt would take by taxation, 56
private to be abolished by Communism, 57
scourge of unconstitutional taxation exhibited, 74, 81
stupendous volume illegally exempted from taxation, 74
Supreme Court's error root of tyrannical taxation, 80

RECALL JUDICIAL DECISIONS
American Bar Association took issue to country, 4
Colorado only State to adopt; held unconstitutional, 4
Theodore Roosevelt advocated; later repented, 4
to be by voters unlearned in law, 5

RECONSTRUCTION FINANCE CORPORATION, 1931
as not necessary to functioning Government, invalid, 110
at large with developments in Alaska, 152n
abolition advised by Hoover Committee in 1949, 104
flood of Federal moneys lent beyond national field, 104
resists proposal Hoover Committee for abolition, 104
string of non-Governmental corporations followed it, 108
patterned after Wilson's War Finance Corporation, 102
not warranted by any clause of Constitution, 102
only in aid governmental operations can corporation be created, 102, 103n
expended money illegally serving banks, railroads, etc., 103
now 30 Federal agencies lending money of taxpayers, 104
departed from purpose of domestic help; loans become world-wide, 104
in 1949 reported loans at all-time high, 105
5400 borrowers "touched" taxpayers for 416,000,000—1949, 105
former head RFC said it would make bad loans, 106

REPUBLICAN FORM OF GOVERNMENT
Nation and States all given representative governments, 7

Madison quoted on restriction to Republican form, 7
fully and ably discussed in Constitutional Convention, 7
belief that it would control effects of factions, 8
frustrated by direct election of senators, 9

ROOSEVELT, FRANKLIN D.
third and fourth terms given by his payrollers, 262
totally lacking in knowledge of taxation, 55
proposed by tax to keep down incomes, 65
his argument for Fascist corporation, 117
Governor condemned misuse Commerce Clause for acts like NLRA, 163, 164
as governor against Federal interference in business activities, 86, 166
in fourth election by-passed Corrupt Practices Act, 280
devised Thousand Dollar Clubs to meet campaign funds, 280
not choice of his own state in 1932, 285
nomination of described in Stoddard's book, 285
nomination whole ticket "fixed" by long distance to California, 285
nominating convention refused unanimous vote, 286
advocated bills misusing Commerce Clause, 86
attack on Federal courts not first, 14, 38
confiscation incomes by taxation urged on Congress, 56
his National Labor Relations Act misuse Commerce Clause, 163, 164
sent "must" bills to Congress, in manner of George III, 183

ROOSEVELT, THEODORE
displeased by decisions; advocated recall by people; repented, 4

RUBBER STAMP CONGRESS
abdicated money power to President, 183
accepted "must" bills from President, 183
enacted National Labor Relations Law, 161
passed Social Security Act, 179
passed Emergency Banking Act to seize the American's gold, 135

SCHOOLS
Congress without constitutional authority to give money to, 217
have neglected courses in Constitutional history, xi
lack of learning in Constitution dangerous, 10, 255
lack of scholarship caused Congressional attack on judiciary, 14
law schools blamable for lack of Constitutional education, 26
only 8 of 25 universities require Constitutional study, 26, 211
Missouri law requires teaching Constitution in schools and universities, 50
have failed to make America foresee coming evil, 81, 82
laws of 40 states requiring Constitutional education dead letters, 89
erroneous belief prevalent that Washington should take over, 97
President's call for 22 unconsti-

INDEX

tutional acts provoked no criticism, 294, 295
only way to challenge Communism and other sophisms, 12
peril of uneducated public opinion, 50, 294

SENATE, THE
capable men excluded by expenses of election, 10
illustrious examples of holders of long term, 10
"The Federalist" quoted on value House of States, 11
"The Federalist" quoted on Senate checking House, 12
broken by Seventeenth Amendment, 1913, 9, 11
campaign for seat now too costly, 10
constitutional election was by legislature, 9
theory Constitutional Convention stated, 11, 12
Webster on duty respecting President's appointments, 12

SHERMAN ANTI-TRUST LAW, 1891
Supplemented by Clayton Act and Federal Trade Commission, 98n
sufficiency of had been proved in many cases, 99
both parties for in campaign year: Senator Borah, 98n

SOCIAL SECURITY ACT, 1935
Constitutional Convention feared such legislation, 185
Cooley quoted on police power of the States, 184
did President Cleveland foresee such legislation?, 194

Hamilton said Congress limited to specifications, 189
Jefferson expounded General Welfare Clause brilliantly, 191
most complete abandonment constitutional doctrine, 179
Nation has no constitutional interest in the subject, 199
no State would have ratified under other view, 192
States must provide care for those needing it, 199
Taxing and Spending Clause of Constitution quoted, 186
act based on error, law and fact, 75
comment President Roosevelt upon signing, 181
many Presidents vetoed "Social Security" measures, 182
subjects covered by act for police power states, 182
Madison quoted on separation National and State powers, 182, 188
Congress cannot tax for State purposes: Marshall, 181
upheld in disregard history and learning on welfare, 195
Supreme Court erred on ability states to aid, 197
made permanent by court on "cyclical" depression, 198
decision upholding let Congress take "boundless field of power," 201

SOCIALISM
defined by demands National Socialist Platform, 1908, 38, 52n
"New Deal" put Socialist platform in effect, 52
no authority for in the Constitution, 39

Supreme Court of the United States sustained it in North Dakota, 5
dependence on government brings unfortunate conditions, 6

SOIL CONSERVATION
AAA cloak of Congress to subsidize farmers, 202
grants by Congress in 1947 were 2.2 billion, 203
those subsidies supported prices of grain to $3, 203
conservation important, but not to Washington, 204
conservation deceiving term like National Labor Relations Act, 204
Constitution affords plain method for conservation, 205
bureaucrats administrating cost 24 million per year, 206

STATES, THE
Hamilton believed States would defend against Congress, 54
conference of governors complained of disregard by Washington, 177n
States blamable through members in Congress for conditions, 178
yet governors still want "Federal aid," 178, 179
representatives of in Congress must take back Union, 180
did not intend to restrain themselves by Bill of Rights, 210
no restraint on by any article in Bill of Rights, 225
Marshall quoted on power of people in, 231
held no general rule applying Bill of Rights to, 232
self-incrimination provision Fifth Amendment not applicable to States, 233
toppled in groups by misapplication Fourteenth Amendment, 240
blamable for National Nominating Convention, 267
each a Republic independent in local affairs, 7, 224
education in Constitution should be made imperative by, 50
given benefit of National Judiciary, 42
House of States broken by popular election senators, 9
invaded by Stockyards Act, 97
legislatures elected senators to their House, 9
Madison said would rise against National encroachment, 101
must adhere to Republican form of government, 7
should abolish "straight ticket" in elections, 91
States alone must help the helpless, 211
when, only, Nation can enter States, 214
would not have accepted Constitution with Social Security, 192, 193
abdication of constitutional powers and duties by, 183

STRIKES
Communism active in American strikes, 174
Earl Browder quoted to that effect, 174, 175
public rights paramount where strike probable, 31
strikes during war gave "aid and comfort" to enemy, 33
strikes destructive to private enterprise, 33

INDEX

Debs Strike 1894 ended by injunction Federal Court, 35
President stopped strike 1946 by getting injunction, 36
United States forced to get injunction against strikers, 169
after National Labor Relations Act strikes trebled in number, 167, 168
table showing number strikes by years, 168
government of Wisconsin on lawlessness of strikers, 168
Department of Justice inactive respecting strikes, 169
courts have shown capacity to handle disputes right, 34, 36, 37
no right in law to concerted strike in large employment, 171
public interest makes controversies justiciable, for court, 31
sit-down strike not disfavored in Washington, 173

SUBSIDIES
appeared in first Congress: Madison opposed and defeated, 188
between 100 and 150 million in eggs by WFA not wanted, 153, 154
"ever normal granary": fed wheat to pigs, 152
FSCC dumped in 1944 14 carloads spoiled eggs, 152
purchased 10,500 carloads eggs to support price, 153
sold at heavy loss 26 carloads eggs for hog feed, 153
total reported for 17 years, $14,571,060,000, 155
Washington dumped millions bushels rotten potatoes, 154

almost immeasurable losses in support of agriculture, 157
rapid spread of unconstitutional evil shown, 197

SUPREME COURT, THE
attempt by President Franklin D. Roosevelt to pack, 23, 14, 38
long continued attempt by Congress to intimidate, 14
Congress piqued by holdings acts violated Constitution, 15
decision by majority historical and Constitutional, 15
men in schools join in attack on judiciary, 15
samples of books against judiciary by supposed scholars, 16
Hamilton quoted in "The Federalist" on function courts, 17
judicial system of Constitution praised by foreign scholars, 18
organized labor demands curb on courts, 18
Canada and Australia adopted American judicial system, 18n
American Federation Labor favors amendment curbing Supreme Court, 19
Constitution, not court, "invalidates" act Congress, 19
does not "veto" act Congress when citizen brings suit, 22
acts of "New Deal" held unconstitutional cited, 23
President Roosevelt kept plan to pack from people, 24
mathematics of court packing plan exhibited, 24
Senate rejected President's attempt court packing, 25
President Roosevelt had once ob-

jected to increasing number judges, 25

book by Attorney General supported court packing, 25

attempt to pack not sudden outburst of alienism, 38

great statesmanship is exhibited in Slaughter-house decision, 230

Slaughter-house decision sensed peril appearing in Minnesota and Illinois, 230

Slaughter-house cases followed over third of century later, 230

"assumed" frequently Fourteenth Amendment absorbs First, 221

Canada, Australia and other countries copied Court, 17

changed from Republican majority of one to 8 Democrats, 242

declined to pass on validity Maternity Act, 92

erroneous decision in Illinois school case, 216

fallacious idea on man's right to property, 76

held Income Tax Act 1894 invalid, 61

held tax on salaries judges prohibited by Constitution, 200

ignoring history, sustained Social Security Act, 200

importance of far-seeing judges: Senator Hoar, 229n

its Equity Rule protects all alike in injunction cases, 49

Jehovah's Witnesses given illegal latitude, 240

labor favored by many judicial decisions, 27

misapplied Fourteenth Amendment in Minnesota Press case, 219

overrode cases in upholding National Labor Relations Act, 163

should be replenished from Supreme Courts of States, 242

refused in 1895 to amend Constitution, 61

said "emergency" does not confer power, 135

Senator Webster voted against every Justice hearing him, 12

took narrow view of wide record Tennessee Valley Authority, 119, 121

told by Cooley consider history of a provision Constitution, 218, 219

warned against "mystifying" constitutional provision, 217

SUPREME LAW OF THE LAND

specified in the Constitution, 19

words of provision quoted, 19

TAXATION

President Coolidge quoted; needless taxation "legalized larceny," 56

President Cleveland denounced avoidable taxation, 56

President Roosevelt's "tax processes" from Communist Manifesto 1848, 56

principle eminent domain applies: Government must give value for tax taken, 64

Judge Cooley quoted tax must be proportionate to "interest secured," 64

must be for revenue, not punishment, or regulation: Justice Story, 66

Edmund Burke said Americans anticipated grievance, 81

grant of power by Constitution quoted, 186, 187

INDEX

President vetoed tax reduction bill demanded at election, 206
spenders "scourge, rather than govern, the state," 206n
"abuse of this power" Hamilton thought prevented, 61
incomes and estates only property taxed by graduation, 63, 64
President F. D. Roosevelt deficient in knowledge of, 55

TENNESSEE VALLEY AUTHORITY, 1933
electrical power corporation created with pretense regulating floods, 110
admitted by government no grant for manufacturing power, 110, 122
selling electrical power in great volume now, 111
people misled by easy getting, 111
other unconstitutional power projects followed TVA, 111
projectors purposed to introduce corporation of Fascism, 112
took over Muscle Shoals Dam of World War I, 113, 114
National Defense Act, 1916, revealed purpose manufacture power, 115
Intention behind TVA kept secret in campaign 1932, 115
multiform activity and losses to taxpayers, 116
private investors being driven out, 119
President Roosevelt's argument for Fascism, 117
President's "yardstick" becomes a bludgeon, 120
figures show power, not flood control, purpose, 121
United States District Court held Congress without such power, 121
reversed by Supreme Court, 121
matter in court record prophesied "electrification of America," 123
private corporations would be put out of business, 123
later President Roosevelt confirmed dissent Justice McReynolds, 124
Congress rejected application for steam plant, 124
power projects now cover 44 of 48 states, 124n
flood control fraudulent pretense of Fascism, 125
question should have been left to Ultimate Court, 126
Supreme Court should not amend Constitution, 126, 127
TVA powerful and dangerous propagandist, 127, 128
taxpayers provide money; big business takes the power, 128n
mathematics proves private capital cannot stand such competition, 129
can court maintain Constitution against such legislation: Judge Dillion, 130
project destroyed 500,000 acres productive land, 130
yearly production foodstuffs over 14 million gone forever, 131
Fascism thrust upon Tennessee Valley, 132
power project carried to Alaska 152n
"a deliberate step into forbidden field"; Justice McReynolds, 123
act creating of great length and difficult detail, 115
agricultural and industrial de-

velopment by Congress illegal, 114
all valleys before developed by dwellers therein, 111
apparent success will proves fundamental failure, 111
Congress becoming weary of costs, 117
Constitution authorizes only control of interstate river, 114
disadvantage suffered by private investors, 116, 119
displaced 13,433 families, 131
engaged in many non-governmental activities, 115
escapes taxes and pays no interest, 116
fallacy in reasoning Supreme Court, 129
Fascist corporation planned before 1932 election, 115
Fascist corporations overspreading the map, 152
Federal Power Act 1935 further development Fascism, 125
investors objecting denounced as "anti-social," 117
losses in 1946 8 million; from beginning 100 million, 116
McReynolds, Justice, saw private investors "put out," 120
private competitors pay taxes and interest, 116, 119
private investors selling out in fear, 119
prophetic lawyer foresaw such decisions, 130
revelation extraordinary growth power plants, on taxpayer, 125, 152n
Supreme Court took narrow view of wide record, 122
was Gen. Eisenhower's "creeping paralysis" aimed at this? 112

TENTH AMENDMENT
last word Bill of Rights protecting police power States, 185
Chief Justice Chase on importance of States in Republic, 201
disregard of leads to "boundless field of power," 65
Jefferson said body of the Constitution, 192
Maternity Act 1921 in disregard of, 91
National Labor Relations Act forbidden by, 161
persistence of Congress in violation of, 161
President Cleveland on observing boundaries, 13
Commerce Clause and General Welfare cloaks for violation of, 97
cases in pursuance of overruled, 85
quoted on California Tide-Lands Case, 248
Social Security Act contrary to, 182
Soil Conservation Act in disregard of limitation, 201
strongest objections to Constitution brought this Amendment, 185
Stockyards Act, 1921 in contravention of, 96

TIDE-WATER OIL LANDS
property of States seized by United States, 243
seizure upheld in decision of Supreme Court, 243
California had held possession 100 years, 244
Chief Justice Taney held title in States, 1842, 245
so decided again in 1845, 246

INDEX

so decided by Justice Field respecting California, 1873, 246
those cases disregarded but not overruled, 1947, 243, 246
Senator from State started movement against States, 249
two Presidents encouraged illegal seizure, 249
action United States comparable to partition of Poland, 250
States have power to overrule unwarranted decision, 252

ULTIMATE POWER, THE PEOPLE
Article V shows way change or abolish Constitution, 37, 126, 127
first Income Tax Case referred to Ultimate Power, 126
Justice Brandeis on "procedural regularity," 235

UNPRECEDENTED TASK OF CONSTITUTIONAL CONVENTION
to maintain general sovereignty of States in a Republic, 296
confederations had always disintegrated; nations had become imperial 296-297
task was to unite and maintain individuality of each, 297
States surrendered few inherent powers and carefully guarded remainder, 297
first successful attempt of a people to restrain themselves, 298
Senator Hoar quoted on this extraordinary restraint, 298
three lessons taught to posterity by Constitutional Convention, 298, 299
Hamilton said difficulty to make government control itself, 299
that is surpassing task of the American today, 299

VOTING
States should abolish the "straight ticket," 91, 180
should be limited to constitutional scholars, 90, 180
States should bring back strict Australian ballot, 91
eligible voters remain away from polls; above half, 263

WASHINGTON, GEORGE
cautioned against amendments by tinkers, 11

WEBSTER, DANIEL
said our government is last hope of world, xiii, 272
as Senator voted against confirmation of Justices of Supreme Court, 12

WILSON, JAMES
legal scholar of Constitutional Convention explains limitations on Congress, 190
pointed out in Convention two citizenships: National and State, 212

SEP 27
DATE DUE
OCT 30

DARTMOUTH COLLEGE
3 3311 01466 0312